Dangerous Enclosures

By

Del Hardiman

In Memory of Mom, Cordie Mae Wooten Hardiman who sacrificed so much for my sisters and me.

"Your life should be full of stories. Sometimes they're funny, and sometimes they're outrageous. Sometimes you can't comprehend them, and sometimes they're painful...But the more you get hit, the more fun it's going to be."

Nick Nolte,

Actor, in Men's Journal

rd.com 07/08/2018

Like a pin prick, my senses are jostled by the past, a time of youth, adventure and risk taking. Most kept in solitude, best not revealed. From the beginning, I tended to cross the line while others looked the other way. As a youngster, pilot, and soldier, I found my naivety adventurous, not by design but having been presented abstruse opportunities. From island hopping the Pacific, to South America, to Europe, Middle East, Vietnam, Moscow, throughout the U.S. to flying for NASA, I found adventure, romance and on a few occasions, almost more than I could handle. I was a survivor.

TABLE OF CONTENTS

viii

PART I

CHAPTER 1
BERLIN 1972 - 1976 – THE BEGINNING

This morning, I am flying a single engine DeHavilland Beaver, powered by a 450 HP Pratt and Whitney radial engine, designated the U6-A by Uncle Sam. It's 1973, and I depart Tempelhof Air Force Base, Berlin, some 110 miles behind the Iron Curtain. Purpose of this flight is to observe and photograph Soviet and East German military installations within a 20-mile radius of the city, equating to 1257 square miles. Prior to departure, I meet SFC St. John, an Intel specialist who, once we get into the aircraft, will make grease pencil markings on my laminated map with current Soviet/East German installations identified he wants to look at. The old Beaver, a non-hostile aircraft is unofficially designated a 'Training' aircraft. I sit alone in the front left seat of our four-seat aircraft, SFC St. John sits alone in a right rear passenger seat adjacent to the window with two Nikon 35 mm cameras nearby. My knowledge of the territory must be infallible; I need to always know my location to avoid an international incident. It was said we did not fly if the Secretary of State, Henry Kissinger, was out of the country. I was checked out and cleared for these missions by CW2 Dave Hunt. I will be tracked by the Berlin Air Route Traffic Control Center (BARTCC) radar that will notify me when I am close to the edge of the 20-mile ring. My response to them will be "Position verified." We depart Tempelhof after clearance on runway 09 east bound, which takes us over a large cemetery between cavernous gray apartment buildings at the end of the runway. Within minutes we are in East German airspace as I make a right turn to the southwest carefully avoiding the nearby East German Schoenfeld airport. The sky is clear, with unlimited visibility, and my flight will be up to two hours. In time, we leave the confines of the city to open flat terrain. One by one we look at designated areas. Suddenly in the distance I observed a huge Soviet Mi-24 (Hind) helicopter which had rarely been seen by the West. He is departing a Soviet airfield, and I would love to see him up close! With the 120 knots airspeed I could muster, he sees me and slowly moves away, too fast. After our mission we return to Tempelhof but before exiting the Beaver, SFC St. John clears the grease pencil marks on my map and we call it 'mission complete'.

My experience flying the 20-mile ring, as we called it, began on my initiation flight with Dave Hunt in the fall of 1972. This was soon after my arrival on a four-year tour. We had poor visibility that morning and I had no idea what was going on or where we were. Suddenly, Dave jerked the Beaver into a hard left turn as I observed a Soviet MIG 21 jet zoom past! We rolled out to the prior course and the same thing happened; Dave made another hard left turn as yet another MIG 21 zoomed past! We were off the end of a Soviet Airfield, and they were departing. I thought to myself, what have I got myself into!

In time, I became proficient in all aspects of the 20-mile ring flying many missions over the years. On two occasions, I observed in a field some eight or ten Soviet radar-guided ZSU-23-4 self-propelled anti-aircraft vehicles in training. I got really low, with my left wingtip pointed at their site. They picked me up, each with four 23 mm guns following me round and round as I circled tightly left overhead. I think we both enjoyed the exercise. Real life training in which I was the target!

ZSU-23-4 (photo Art Image ZSU-23-4.jpg)

On another occasion, I flew inside the traffic pattern of a mid-sized Soviet Ilyushin IL-28 twin engine tactical bomber, taking photos as we went. I was permitted over the airfield at 2000 feet or higher, which I was. I am sure this would have been frowned on, but I did it anyway.

Inside Soviet traffic pattern north of Berlin, tracking a Soviet Ilyushin Il-28 light bomber.
(Photo SFC St. John)

SFC St. John and I deduced if we removed the cabin door on his side, he would have a clean photo shot. It was cold weather at the time; we were both wearing cold weather suits. St. John placed his cameras between his seat tracks alternating them as he shot his photos. Mission completed, we returned to Tempelhof but to our astonishment, one of his Nikons was missing! It must have fallen out during one of my tight maneuvers. Soon a complaint was filed by the Soviets. Not only did they have the Nikon which had fallen into a military compound, but they developed and showed the film St John shot! We were grounded for a while after the incident. We were told (unverified) that the State Department denied it was our camera. Eventually things got back to normal.

With the Soviet Hind helicopter in mind, I thought of the day I might have another opportunity to play tag with him. To replace the aging U6-A, we acquired two USAF O-2's, the civilian equivalent of the Cessna Sky master; it had twin engines, one in front and one behind the fuselage. With new ARMY green paint, they were the only 0-2's in the Army. As fortune would have it, one day, I happened to be back at the location where I had previously encountered the Mi-24 (Hind). I spotted one airborne but this time, I was in the 0-2! I pulled up on his left side and he nosed the Hind over to move away but I stayed with him at 140 knots! The Soviet pilot never looked over at me as had been the case on other encounters with Soviet helicopters. For some reason, Soviet pilots always just looked straight ahead. Again, I am sure this would have been frowned upon, but I did it!

U6A, One of two I flew reconnoitering Berlin 20-mile ring

ARMY O-2 I flew side by side with Soviet Mi-24 (Hind) helicopter

Soviet type Mi-24 Hind attack helicopter similar to the one I encountered (Photo Microsoft Bing)

More to follow on Berlin…

CHAPTER 2
VIETNAM MID-TOUR, AVIATION SUPPORT TO QUAN LOI SPECIAL FORCES OPERATIONS -1971

5th Special Forces (SF) Camp, Command and Control South (CCS) Quan Loi, Vietnam, fall of 1971. The camp was not far from the Cambodian border in III Corps. This would be a traumatic day only we did not know it at the time. Four ARMY Aviators from the 74th Reconnaissance Airplane Company, Rick Harris, Jim Pickle, CPT Mike Baile and I had 'volunteered for missions supporting the SF Camp crudely built in a former French Rubber Plantation. Rarely were we all at Quan Loi at the same time. Our ARMY Crew chief was SGT Donald Canole. We had a blacktop runway previously used by U.S. forces but are now seeing limited operations primarily of our 0-1 Bird Dogs, USAF 0-2s, (call sign Pretzel), and three Vietnamese H-34 Sikorsky helicopters. Those helicopter pilots in their mid-30's were exceptional, and they had been at it for years. Their call sign was "King Bee". We had three that worked with the Special Forces when we did insertions into Cambodia with Vietnamese Special Forces. Unfortunately, we lost two of the three one evening when they were caught in a storm and crashed, killing all aboard. Occasionally we were supported by ARMY Cobra gunship helicopters call signs 'Playboys' and 'Raiders.' The Air Force had a permanent cadre of two aircraft mechanics (Tech Sergeant Don Cheney and Airman Danny Bilger), a weather sergeant and an operations sergeant to support the 0-2s on station on a daily basis whereas the 0-2 pilots rarely spent the night. We ARMY Aviators flew various missions to include Search and Surveillance, insertion missions in which we reconnoitered areas for insertion of Vietnamese Special Forces Recon Commandos (Loi Ho) discreetly into Cambodia by the King Bees. With teams on site, we stood off at a distance in the Bird Dog to provide communications with the teams and help them confirm their location in the often-triple canopy jungle. These missions could be hours in duration and continue for five or six days. Another mission was the 'High/Low in which one of us would rendezvous with a 0-2 at a predetermined location around 2000 feet over Cambodia. When cleared by the 0-2 crew, we would descend to the treetop level, receiving guidance from the above. We always had a back seater with a motorized Nikon camera to possibly capture enemy operations. These were dangerous missions, and it was not uncommon to receive ground fire and hopefully live for another day.

F-4 down – Recovering deceased Pilot.

On this day, we were notified by Special Forces Operations that an F-4 aircraft was down close by. Rick and I quickly departed in separate 0-1s in search of the crash. Rick had Sergeant Canole, our crew chief, with him, and I had Special Forces Sergeant First Class (SFC) Tony Aquinoc with me. We soon observed the smoldering crash site. Circling above we picked up an emergency call from one of the F-4 crewmembers. He was using his hand-held PRC 25 emergency radio and was asking for help. We located his parachute near the burning aircraft and requested King Bee support to pick him up. In time, a King Bee was on site to retrieve the downed pilot. He seemed to be very calm. With some difficulty, the captain was able to climb up on the hovering King Bee's right landing wheel tire to get onboard whereupon he was taken to the small remote airfield Loc Ninh. We were waiting to interrogate him about the other missing pilot when he arrived. Upon exiting the King Bee, he gave Rick a big hug. He was taken to a large tent with open flaps by the runway where he lay down on a table. His back was hurting from the ejection. He was given a cigarette but by then, the adrenaline was wearing off and he had difficulty with his shaking hand putting the cigarette in his mouth. It was then we discovered he was a Weapons System Operator (WSO), not the pilot. He said the pilot told him they were in trouble, and they might have to eject but not yet. He ejected anyway just prior to the crash. His parachute made two swings before he touched down. Awfully close to not making it. Where was the pilot? Had he made it out or was he in the now simmering wreckage? Tony and I climbed aboard the King Bee and headed to the crash site. We were put down next to the wreckage in a tight spot with just enough room for the hovering King Bee. Tony and I surveilled the scene and eventually made out the pilot's body or what remained. Suddenly a body bag was dropped at our feet by the King Bee hovering above us. Tony and I made it to the body to retrieve what we could which was only the torso. We placed the remains in the body bag and returned it to Quan Loi. One of the Pretzel pilots carried the remains to Saigon to be turned over to the morgue. A day or two later that pilot found out the deceased pilot had been one of his instructors while in training back in the States. Years later my friend (Chris Nauer) doing research on this crash, showed that this aircraft, RF-4C, tail number 66-0439, of the 432nd Tactical Reconnaissance Wing, Udorn, Royal Thai Air Force base, 14th TRS, was on record of being shot down by AAA (Anti-Aircraft Artillery), Pilot KIA and WSO rescued.

Operational Missions and close call incidents

Time at the Quan Loi camp changed my life in a number of ways, in fact, Rick and I and to a lesser extent Jim Pickle developed a Devil - May - Care attitude which you will read. CPT Baile was a 'Straight Arrow", always towing the company line. We were soldiers and Airmen first. In my case a tour in the North Carolina Air National Guard before going to ARMY Flight school at Fort Rucker, Alabama. Basic training two times, first U.S. Air Force, then U.S. ARMY; lots of schooling in preparation for war, formations, saluting, and leadership skills. Before my time at Quan Loi, I had been in the 54th Aviation Company at Long Thanh Vietnam where I met my future wife Nga, now Paula. I will describe those adventures later but for now, Quan Loi in support of SF Command and Control South (CCS). To quote Rick: "Right before you and I got to Quan Loi, President Nixon said he was withdrawing all Special Forces units from Vietnam. All that happened is they pulled off their SF patches and put on USARV (US ARMY Vietnam) patches. However, that is the time when the teams we covered were more and more Vietnamese with Montagnard's and Chinese Nungs (minority fierce fighters of Chinese ancestry who supported the SF throughout the war)". We were somewhat isolated from the 74th Company Headquarters (HQ) in Phu Loi. Our assigned platoon, 3rd platoon, was in Cu Chi, CPT Harris the platoon commander left Rick, Jim, and me to our own volition while others in the platoon had duties such as flying cover for convoys in the greater III Corps region. So, there we were, free to come and go without much question as long as the mission came first. I took great advantage of the situation. While at Quan Loi, being exposed to dangers in some frequency one developed that Devil-May-Care attitude afore mentioned. The SF did not mind, in fact we learned from them, the 'professionals.' Case in point, we needed a jeep to transport our gear from the flight line back to the camp, a long walk. Our crew chief at the time Sergeant Redding flew down to Company HQ with me to 'Procure' a jeep. Redding confiscated a jeep from the motor pool and headed north alone, tanned shirtless California body, blond hair blowing, driving our new ride up Hwy 13 at breakneck speed while I flew cover back to the compound. CPT Baile refused to ride in a 'stolen' jeep. One day, he mentioned the stolen jeep to the SF Commander, MAJ Frank Carbone. MAJ Carbone told CPT Baile to look around at the vehicles in the compound. He pointed out a jeep sitting on blocks and said: "See that jeep, that's the only authorized vehicle in the compound; all the others are stolen."

Rick Harris' Close Call

Rick had a number of close calls. On one occasion, well…. I will let Rick tell the story:

"As far as how many hits I took, I don't really know. The most I ever took was 13 or 14 on one of my first Hi-Lo missions. I was flying with Gunny Moran (US Marine Corps), and USAF CPT Ed Hooker was the high O-2. I came to a heavily forested area, and it seemed like the whole world opened up on us. I have been in Cobras when they fired their minigun, and that is what it sounded like. Mini guns going off all around me…. constant automatic gunfire. I could hear the bullets hitting the aircraft, and Gunny was yelling and pointing to my left wing. I was carrying Wp's (White Phosphorus rockets) and evidently bullets had hit the rocket motor portion of one of the rockets, it was spitting and flaming under the left wing. I salvoed the rocket pods and an explosion went off next to the aircraft. There were some shrapnel holes in the wing and an assortment of holes everywhere on the aircraft. The flaps were shot out and part of the exhaust stack was blown away. We made it back to Quan Loi to be greeted by Major Bacon (74th Commander) and the First Sergeant, who were cruising around and visiting the platoons. Major Bacon put me in for my first DFC (Distinguished Flying Cross).

There were quite a few more occasions when I got hit with one or two rounds. Another memorable time was when I flew the Kratie mission (Kratie,

Cambodia). We all knew how dangerous that area was. The part that I remember most was when I started taking fire, I was flying up a small stream and came upon the Mekong (river). I turned left and flew as close to the water as I could. I looked to my left and there was maybe a 20 foot embankment where I saw many people firing down at me. I looked to my right and there was the shadow of the aircraft in the water, with bullets impacting on the water all around it. One of those bullets took off the ADF sensing antenna coupling in the back of the fuselage, and I heard it bouncing around the aircraft and ended up hitting me in the leg. No blood, just a small bruise. I still have that mangled coupling today."

I had a similar experience as Rick. Flying low level along the Mekong river shoreline of Cambodia, I looked to my left and saw bullets hitting the water to my left. Made an abrupt left turn and flew away without getting hit.

74th Reconnaissance Airplane Company, Quan Loi, 1971, Rick Harris behind 0-1 propeller prepares for mission, Our good friends, TSGT Cheney (L) and Airman Danny Bilger (R) volunteering to load rockets. Two of our Vietnamese mission coordinators with ground teams standing by. 5,000-gal fuel blivit in right rear. (photo courtesy Rick Harris)

Del Hardiman

Time with the SF, Rick and I developed some crazy habits; being young and with no one monitoring our comings and goings, we began to take on things like the two of us 'Dog Fighting each other with our Bird Dogs. Rick commented in our correspondence: "I remember many dogfights with you!! I am surprised we both lived through those.!! One dogfight I remember, I was behind you going up a small river, both of us on the deck. You put a wheel in the water and sprayed my windshield where I could hardly see!"

On another occasion, we had an idea of installing two 0-2 rocket pods, one under each wing of my 0-1 Bird Dog. Each pod held 7 folding fin rockets which was quite a load for the wings. Just to make sure it would work, I took the bird out and did some loops with the heavy 14 rockets on board. No problem, the girl held! Rick's comments about that day: "I remember you doing that loop with 14 rockets right off of the end of the runway.... pulling out not more than 50 feet. That was impressive!! I also remember you firing all 14 rockets into the garbage dump next to Quan Loi. You must have pissed off the local Viet Cong because I think it was the next night we were attacked by sappers."

My Bird Dog with 0-2 rocket pods mounted (photo, Rick Harris)

Hit by Viet Cong Sappers

Yes, we were hit by sappers (Viet Cong infiltrators) who made it into the compound at night setting off explosives throughout. My first indication was a blinding light followed by a nearby explosion. I thought these were incoming mortars. Rick and I were sharing the same room, our bunks covered with mosquito nets. Rick yelled at me to "Get out!" as he grabbed his helmet and gear heading out the door into the darkness. For whatever reason, I took time to collect myself and joined the others in our perimeter foxholes. Eventually, we had an Air Force C-47 circling overhead dropping flares until daylight. Next morning, we observed the well-orchestrated carnage left by the sappers, who were long gone. Several buildings were damaged, vehicles were disabled by explosives, and quite a few unexploded ordnances.

Close Call

Viet Cong Undetonated explosive

Careful collection of the handmade non detonated explosives wrapped in banana tree leaves was done by the SF Sergeant Sampson, small in stature but a hell of a soldier; he brought me back to my room to show me an unexploded ordnance not more than six feet from where I slept. Fate was looking out for me! The explosives were put in a pile and detonated. Sampson's specialties were supply and ordnance as I recall.

Un detonated explosives recovered the next morning after the sapper attack. One meant for me.

(photo courtesy of Rick Harris)

Rick Harris, morning after Sapper attack

(photo courtesy of Rick Harris)

Me, holding Viet Cong Sapper homemade backpack for carrying explosives.

(photo courtesy of Rick Harris)

Damage inflicted by Viet Cong Sappers (photo courtesy of Rick Harris)

Detonating Viet Cong explosives (photo courtesy of Rick Harris)

Next day after the Sapper attack. Don Canole far left Rick Harris front left with camera, I'm center between two Air Force pilots, Jim Pickle far right, second row, To Jim's right, CPT Mike Baile. The six Air Force pilots, CPT Baile and Jim Pickle were not there during the attack, but ground personnel were. Top rear, adjusting watch, USAF TSGT Don Cheney, front right USAF Airman Danny Bilger. (photo courtesy of Rick Harris)

Del Hardiman

Close Call

Flying into tree over Cambodia 1971

On one occasion, I was scouting an area over Cambodia when I suddenly noticed two 'Bad Guys' down to my right in a long, slim motorized wooden boat in a stream hiding under the foliage. I kept my heading as if I had not seen them. Continuing straight ahead until out of site, I dropped down on the deck circling to my left and went back to the stream to find them. With my attention distracted on the search, I looked up and suddenly there was a tall tree right in front of me! I could not avoid the tree and impacted it almost immediately! The aircraft sustained some damage but was flyable. Now the 'hunter' almost became the 'hunted'! I dropped my search and headed back to camp. When we checked my aircraft, there was a good-sized tree limb in the right tail horizontal stabilizer. It had crushed the stabilizer back nearly to the elevator. Also, the engine air intake was covered with leaves with more small tree branches wrapped about the right landing gear.

Hi/Lo missions

I had a special technique for beginning my Hi/Lo missions. After receiving briefings for the mission, I would rondeaux at a predetermined location to join up with my USAF 0-2 cover. When cleared down, I pulled the Bird Dog into an extremely nose high position while adding full power, at time of breaking into a stall I would pull the stick hard back to the right rear while at same time pushing hard left rudder. This put the aircraft in a tight left graveyard spiral. I figured it appeared to the 'Bad Guys' I was crashing and thus received little ground fire on my way down. On more than one occasion, my back seat observer threw up. They were on the long end of the fulcrum so to speak. At times I would hear a comment from the 0-2 crew something like "Holy Shit!".

One day after completing a mission I was directed by my 0-2 crew to an old French fort which was built in a concrete oval, the walls built wide to contain quarters. From above, it would appear as an elongated doughnut. This was not part of the mission, but we had discussed the fort earlier as a possible holding site for POWs. When I was directed, it was understood by both of us where I was headed. Flying mere feet above the ground at high speed over open terrain, the fort came into view. I was below the wall but popped up over and back down literally for seconds within the confines of

22

the possible prison before popping up over the far wall. I noticed someone off my left sitting on a step suddenly looking up to observe this strange phenomenon as I zoomed past. My rear seater had his motorized Nikon taking pictures. We were not able to make any determinations, but I got a bullet hole in my left wing for my effort.

On another occasion, after a mission, we were near the city of Kampong Cham located on the Mekong River. I was already back at altitude when I got a hair brain idea. I looked down at the dusty runway and decided I would land (we were prohibited from landing in Cambodia) just for the hell of it. On this day, I had two USAF 0-2s covering me. I let them know what I was about to do. I made the landing on what appeared to be an abandoned airfield. While rolling out, I noticed a short guard standing off the right side of the runway. He had his back to me and had not noticed me approaching him quietly taxing fast. He was poorly clad with a cloth camouflaged hat. Suddenly he turned around to reveal an AK-47 held near his chest. I caught him by surprise, so I was surprised when he gave me a salute, palm out with his right hand. I noticed he had a damaged right eye as I returned his salute passing by just a few feet away! Off to the right was an open structure about 100 X 100 feet square built with tall poles having a stretched cloth canvass type top for shade, dirt floor. I thought this must be the airfield terminal. I noticed a few peasant looking civilians standing underneath. At the end of the runway, I turned around and took off in the opposite direction from whence I had come. Someone in the 0-2s circling overhead said, "You got a pair of balls!" That is the evolution of what we young guys evolved into after months of these missions.

Inserting Vietnamese Long Range Patrol Teams

Another primary mission was to guide the King Bee helicopters into remote sites to quickly drop off Vietnamese Long Range patrol teams (LRPTs). Before doing so, I/we would reconnoiter at least three sites to keep the 'Bad Guys' guessing. By looking at three sites, they would not be sure which location we would use. The LRPTs were sometimes flown into our camp at Quan Loi in a black C-46 cargo aircraft. They were kept isolated until their mission. They dressed in what I was told North Vietnamese uniforms. Whichever of us had the mission, we would direct the low flying

King Bees to the site and start counting 5,4, 3, 2, "Bingo," at which time the helicopters, fulling trusting us, would flare and land to unload the teams. Seconds later the King Bees were airborne, and our job would be to stay on target some distance away as the team headed out on their mission. We had a Vietnamese observer in the back seat in communication with the team. Communication was kept to an absolute minimum for security. When the team on the ground spoke, their radio operator whispered to avoid being noticed. Their missions lasted up to five or six days and during the day we were there for hours to cover them. At times, the team got lost and needed our assistance to help them locate their position. On several occasions, they used mirrors to flash us by which my back seater would give them their location. I remember the time one of our teams on the ground was being pursued. I did not understand what was being said but I could tell the radio operator on the ground could barely speak, out of breath. I asked my Vietnamese rear seater, Bucky as he was known, what the operator was saying. He told me the operator said he could not run anymore. What did you tell him? I asked. Bucky looked at me with a big grin and said, "I told him he better run!"

Close Call

Navigating and lost at night over Cambodia

   One night over Cambodia, I was running communication relay for a Loi Ho team well after dark in my single engine Bird Dog. Never experienced such darkness. No stars, only the dark abyss below; so dark, had it not been for the dim cockpit lights, doubt I could see my hands. My concern was finding my way back to the camp. I was in contact with CCS (Special Forces camp), but the camp did not have a navigational aid in that rubber plantation. I only knew roughly which direction I needed to go. We were taught in flight school a rudimentary type of navigation (FM Homing) probably never to be used in practice. As luck would have it, I used this technique and was able to home in on the CCS transmissions and find my way back. When I got the camp in sight, the CCS Sergeant Major, German by birth, had his jeep on the end of the unlit runway, lights shining down the runway. I lined up on his jeep lights and did a loop off the end of the runway, my landing light making a Star Wars lightsaber arc in the night sky. At the bottom of the loop, I passed over his jeep and touched down just beyond it. That was one of the most relieved feelings I have ever had!

On one occasion, I had an Air Force 0-2 (not one of ours) fire on the team I was covering! I was highly pissed and headed for the 0-2 while screaming on the Guard frequency, which 'all' aircraft monitored to get the Hell out and cease fire! I called out the 0-2 tail number for the world to hear! I headed for the 0-2 but could not get close before he slunkered away. This area was designated a 'NO FIRE' area to protect our teams. Obviously the 0-2 had not checked No Fire zones. No one on the team was injured.

The 'Pink' snake

One day, I taxied out from our refueling bladder to depart on a mission. The former French rubber plantation, where the Special Forces compound was located aligned on the right side of the runway and a Vietnam military compound on the left. I wore my helmet with pulldown face shield, Velcro shield covering my chest referred to as chicken plate, a cut open flak vest under my feet, a holstered .38 Smith and Wesson revolver and a CAR-15 Carbine rifle next to me on my left. My vest included my 'blood chit' a waterproof map of Vietnam/Cambodia, compass, and emergency radio. My seat, also Velcro, offered some protection from small arms fire. As I aligned with the runway, something in front caught my eye on the black top runway. It was a large PINK snake maybe seven feet long! Snakes terrify me! I taxied up to it as it was crossing right to left across the runway. My instinct was to shoot it from my left open window but attempts with my .38 failed, missing with each shot using my left hand. Then I proceeded to run over it. As I approached, it coiled and bit my left tire, which made me flinch as if it had bitten me! The snake made it off the runway into the red powered dirt to my left. Some confused guys who had been watching me shoot into the runway had not seen the snake. When they saw it, they dispensed it with a few shots. I taxied back and shut down to have a look. The snake was covered with powdered dirt which made it appear pink. Somewhat shaken by the harmless snake I continued my mission.

Elephant in tall grass

I was over Cambodia one day with a rear seat observer holding his Nikon camera. We saw an elephant in a field of tall elephant grass. The elephant

25

carried a large basket on its back in which his dutiful master rode. Following behind was someone walking. As the elephant pushed forward, it left a distinct trail in the tall grass as seen from above. We decided a close-up photo would be something special. I zoomed down at high speed but spooked the elephant in doing so! It headed straight ahead for a nearby forest like a demon was chasing it, the poor guy on top was holding on for dear life; the basket looked as if it might spill any moment. When the elephant disappeared into the woods, you could follow it by the flexing tree tops it was knocking around. Felt bad about that one. Still have the photos.

Calling in fake B-52 bombing strike

Captain Troy, one of our 0-2 pilots and I hatched a plan to call in a "fake" B-52 strike over the city of Kratie. Kratie, along the Mekong River in Cambodia, was long suspected as being a North Vietnam headquarters and most likely monitored our frequencies, especially the Guard frequency, which all military aircraft did. CPT Troy, an Air Force Academy grad wrote up the typical warning which I would regurgitate over the Guard frequency as I neared the city. B-52 strike warnings were transmitted shortly before strikes by sending repeatedly the message: "Arc Light"! "Arc Light"! Followed by the coordinates of the strike location. On this day, I came up on Guard frequency reading our message loud and clear: "Arc Light," "Arc Light" along with the coordinates for the city of Kratie! I was south of the city observing at the time. Did not notice any unusual activity, but if it worked, there were some bad guys thinking their time was up!

Playing pranks

More events followed which, in retrospect were not the smartest I can look back on. Case in point, one day Rick and Sergeant Canole were in a military pickup truck heading south down Highway 13 after recently departing Quan Loi. Rick was driving; Don Canole was riding shot gun. Cannot remember how I knew it was them, but I did from above in the Bird Dog. I slowed up and maneuvered over the top of them. Remember Don looking up out his right window as I gently placed my left tire on the truck top, riding along with them for a distance!

On another occasion, Rick and I departed Quan Loi in our respective Bird Dogs heading south down Highway 13. It was late afternoon, and we were going back to Cu Chi. We were wing tip to wing tip side by side no more than a few feet above the deserted blacktop road, I had the left side, Rick the right. Suddenly I noticed some lights ahead flashing off and on from a jeep on my side of the road coming toward me. I thought this will be fun, so I flashed my landing lights off and on back at the jeep. I knew I could easily pop up over the jeep with no harm but those in the jeep did not know that! As we merged closer, the jeep veered off the road into a ditch and I observed someone who had exited the jeep on the passenger side angrily waving his fist at me as I passed by. The next morning, I got a call from Rick who by then was back at headquarters in Phu Loi. Rick said, "We're in trouble. That guy you ran off the road was a Lieutenant Colonel (LTC), the province advisor to the Vietnamese! "They know it was us since we were the only two Bird Dogs in that area at that time." I thought about it for a minute, then came up with a story. Just so happens there was a Vietnamese Artillery base nearby and had been known to fire without putting out an advisory. I told Rick to tell our Commander we were flying low to protect us from 'possible' artillery fire. It worked. A few days later, when I was back at Phu Loi, our Commander got me off to the side and told me to watch after Rick. He said Rick was young and I, a few years older, might be a good influence. "Will do Sir," I said.

CHAPTER 3
Cu Chi

I have spoken often of Cu Chi. Perhaps you have heard of the 'Tunnels of Cu Chi,' a book has been written about them. We were not aware at the time but below were miles of multi-layered tunnels that began in the late 1940s. These tunnels were occupied by Viet Cong (Communist) guerrillas and had villages, hospitals, armament production and entertainment. It is said that the Viet Cong built thousands of miles of tunnels in Vietnam from which to carry out raids and protect them from B-52 air strikes. Ref-1 Today the Tunnels of Cu Chi are a historical site of which tours are given.

The 3rd Platoon, 74th Aviation Company Rick, Jim and I were assigned to was located at Cu Chi formerly occupied by the 25th Infantry Division later replaced by the Army of Vietnam (ARVN) 25th Infantry Division. At one time, it was a large headquarters but by the time we were there (1971), the airfield was aligned with empty revetments in which helicopters and aircraft once parked. Our Bird Dog platoon used revetments on the southeast end of the field. Enlisted support had quarters near this site, Warrant Officers and CPT Harris, our platoon commander, along with Naval Intelligence occupied one of the quarters in a compound also occupied by Military Assistance Command Vietnam (MACV) advisors. There was a nice dining facility there as well. The living quarters were air conditioned! I am told ours was the previous doctor's quarters of the 12th Evac Hospital which departed Cu Chi earlier in the year. Each of us had small rooms which usually contained a locker, bunk, and our stereo. We had women referred to as 'Hooch Maids' come daily to wash our clothes and shine our boots. When I came and went, it was nice to find clean clothes and freshly shined boots to switch out. Occasionally I would meet and be greeted by the other pilots in a common area of the quarters where they hung out. Other than an overnight stay, I did not have much interaction with the others.

Setting off CS grenade

One night, Jim Pickle knocked on my door. Jim, always with a quiet demeanor stood there with a CS (teargas) grenade. "What's going on?" I asked. Jim told me of a recent incident in which the others had wanted him to join them and when he did not, they lit some rags (as I recall) and put them at the bottom of his door. He could not get out of his small room because they had put a screwdriver in the hasp, which locked his door. Jim told me he could barely breathe from the smoke. He was going to set off the grenade to get "Even" with the others and came to warn me ahead of time. Rick was not there at the time. I thought about it and then came up with an idea. I told Jim he would be in trouble if he set off the grenade, but we could make it impossible for anyone to know who set it off. Our quarters had central air so I told Jim we could fire off the grenade, and put it on the outside air intake which would suck the gas into the entire structure. We did this in the wee hours of the morning. Within minutes, coughing, confused men came staggering out of the building along with CPT Harris, innocent of the caper. Jim and I stood there pretending to cough and gag with the others. What a plan! Unexpectedly, the gas was sucked up by the intakes of other living quarters. This was not part of the plan! In no time, people were bailing out of their quarters! The MACV Command Sergeant Major found the burned grenade on the air intake and made a proclamation to get fingerprints off the grenade to find out who the culprit was. I had a sinking feeling as I stood near the Sergeant Major holding that burned grenade. As it turned out, there were no fingerprints to get. Whew! Jim and I kept that as our secret, not even talking about it to each other, as I recall. Years later, I noticed an individual at the Atlanta Hartsfield airport rental car turn-in parking lot. I recognized that walk. It was Rick Harris, now a civilian. I called out to Rick, who gleefully greeted me! Rick invited me and fellow Army Pilot Bill Schaefer over to his apartment for grilled steaks. We had many war stories to share. It was then that I told Rick about the CS grenade and that Jim and I had been the ones who set it off back in Cu Chi those many years ago. Rick was aghast! He could not believe it was us! Of note: Rick and Jim were both later Captains for USAIR retiring from that airline.

Stealing another jeep

One more daring deed while at Cu Chi. The jeep our flight line used was in great disrepair. The front wheels were not aligned, in fact each wheel spread outward which made it go through the front tires quickly and difficult to control. It was not unlike WWII cartoonist Bill Mauldin's Stars and Stripes depiction of 'Old Sarg' looking away with eyes covered as he prepares to shoot his jeep. Do not recall how Jim Pickle, the quiet one, joined me to 'procure' a jeep for the flight line personnel but he did. Inside the extensive compound, a few miles from our quarters, was a Vietnamese restaurant which catered to both Vietnamese soldiers and GI's. Outside in the gravel parking lot on any given night could be found a quantity of jeeps. Jeeps had an anti-theft device consisting of a heavy chain with which to lock around the steering wheel using a padlock. High tech! One dark rainy night Jim and I drove the old jeep to the restaurant and parked near other jeeps. We sat there contemplating our move when suddenly a jeep drove up with two Vietnamese soldiers in it. They exited their jeep in the darkness and canvassed some of the other jeeps, tugging on the steering wheel chains as they went. How about that, they were looking for a jeep to steal! Not finding an unlocked jeep, and not observing us, they ventured into the restaurant which had sounds of music and laughter from within. Would you believe they did not lock their jeep! What a deal, our new jeep was sitting there for the picking. I quickly got into the Vietnamese jeep and roared out of the parking lot, Jim in hot pursuit with our old jeep. We hurried to the flight line a few miles away with plans to hide the jeep. The compound was locked down, so we had no place to go but the empty revetments. Next morning, at the flight line preparing for a flight, we observed numerous Vietnamese vehicles driving around looking for that jeep! In time, they found their jeep giving us the dirty eye as they slowly drove past. They knew we 'Americans' were guilty. Turns out that was the ARVN 25th Infantry Division Commander's jeep, holy cow! I knew it was special since it had a single windshield whereas jeeps, I was familiar with had two windshields joined at the center. She was a beauty, high gloss paint. Bet someone got an ass chewing for losing that jeep. Jim and I let the flight line personnel in on what we had done. Our old jeep never looked so good; all we got for our troubles was another war story to tell in our old age.

Lloyd Rainey

As my tour in Quan Loi came to an end in December 1971, my replacement was CW2 Lloyd Rainey. I did not know him long, he had a nice personality and was easy to like. He too was assigned to the 3rd platoon at Cu Chi. As I recall, he had a previous tour in Vietnam as a UH-1 helicopter pilot. At Quan Loi I showed him around to bring his attention to a metal walk-in container referred to as a Conex in which we kept some equipment. One of the things I impressed on Lloyd was to be sure and take the flack vest and chicken plate from the Conex, place the flak vest on the floor under his legs and secure the chicken plate across his chest. A little cumbersome but added protection from small arms fire. I was merely passing on advice I had been given when I started these missions. I am sure Lloyd was appraised of the missions by Rick and others. December 12th, I was at Cu Chi when word came that Lloyd had been shot down by small arms fire on his first mission, later to learn that both he and our dear Marine Gunny Sergeant, MSG Bernard Joseph Moran Jr assigned to the ***Military Assistance Command Vietnam – Studies and Observations Group*** (MACV-SOG) were killed. This was a shock to all of us. I flew back to Quan Loi the next day and looked in the Conex. The flak vest and chicken plate were still there, not taken by Lloyd. I have often wondered if having them might have made a difference. A memorial tribute to Lloyd was held at Company Headquarters. Lloyd, from Alaska was married with no children, Gunny Moran, born and raised in Philadelphia, PA was married with two young teenage daughters. Gunny had been through many close calls with us always a professional Marine. He loved showing photos of his daughters.

Departing Vietnam

I departed Vietnam in early February 1972 along with my wife and new son Michael who would grow up to be an attorney, sworn in by Supreme Court Justice Roberts to practice before the Supreme Court. Rick departed

Del Hardiman

Quan Loi in late February. Not long after, the Quan Loi operation was shut down. According to Rick, that area got very hot....and then the Battle of An Loc started in March. All the CCS guys were evacuated in early April and the base was overrun as they were being helicoptered out. An Loc was a short jeep drive from Quan Loi. I had flown missions to/from An Loc while in the 54th Aviation Company in Support of U.S. Rangers. During the historic battle of AN LOC, lasting three months, 14 North Vietnamese Army (NVA) Divisions of some 125,000 troops and approximately 1,200 tanks and other armored vehicles, participated in the offensive laying siege to An Loc having some 7500 South Vietnamese defenders along with a few American Advisors. Without air support for defense and supply, An Loc would have been overran. Ref-2 Much has been said of the heroism of the U.S. Air Force support. June 30th, 1998; through DNA testing the Vietnam War Unknown Soldier was identified. He was Air Force 1st Lt. Michael Joseph Blassie, who was shot down near An Loc in 1972. Ref-3

Side note:

Unbeknownst to those of us in the Vietnam War during my time of 19 months, negotiations of some three years had been ongoing between the U.S. and North Vietnam with interested partners being the Chinese and Soviet Russia. This ultimately resulted in the Vietnamization of Vietnam. Behind the scenes was intensity placed on the Nixon Administration to end the War and get American POW's home. The month prior to my entry to the Vietnam War, U.S. and South Vietnamese troops attacked Communist sanctuaries in Cambodia. This led to anti-war protests in the U.S., resulting in four protesters being shot at Kent State University by National Guard troops. Ref-4 I observed remnants of the Cambodian incursion by hulls of destroyed tanks on the side of Highway 13 (QL-13) in Cambodia. As mentioned, mere days after our departure (February 1972), North Vietnam troops attacked the relative safe areas I had ventured to many times, An Loc and Quan Loi, the area I had operated from for six months. The Special Forces unit I had worked with withdrew from Quan Loi, just in time.

-More to follow on Vietnam-

CHAPTER 4
Air National Guard

I had always intended to become a pilot with Piedmont Airlines, but circumstances intervened. To keep my flying skills, I took brief jobs at my hometown airport, at the same time attending my local junior college, while working the night shift at Hunt Manufacturing Company, running three machines mass producing parts for Boston Pencil sharpeners. In time, I spent my 21st birthday employed at Brockenbrough Airport near Charlotte, N.C. hopping passengers on weekends and doing some charter flights. Having completed Air Force Basic Training at Lackland AFB, San Antonio, Texas followed by a five-month aircraft mechanic school at Shepperd AFB, Texas, I was a "Weekend Warrior," as some call it with the Air Guard. I asked for and was accepted for a full-time position with the Guard in Charlotte as an aircraft mechanic. Also wedged in at this time, I used my Sea Plane rating to hop passengers on weekends at Lake Norman; also picked up my multi-engine rating and Flight Instructor certificate. As you can see, I was busy earning a living while at the same time keenly focused on my chances to make it to the airlines, my dream for years. I knew I had to make something happen soon before time passed me by. Eventually, Piedmont had some new classes coming so I made a visit to Airline headquarters in Winston Salem. My application was on file, and I had previously been interviewed several times by Captain Tadlock, chief pilot. I had been recommended by several Piedmont Captains and it was just a matter of time before I would get my chance. Unfortunately, on my visit to Piedmont, hiring was now being done by an HR person, not a pilot. He was still moving into his new office when I met him. He told me the bad news, if I didn't have at least 2000 hours of jet time and a four-year degree, he would not hire me. Airlines were being saturated with Air Force, Navy and Marine pilots, veterans of Vietnam getting out of service and going to the airlines. I was devastated! I had neither of the requirements needed.

My job at the Air Guard in Charlotte as a mechanic was memorable. I was accepted by the team and had many friends. We were like a family; those I worked with had been there for years and knew each other well to include their families. They were former Air Force and now content to keep these jobs as a career until retirement. I was the youngest. Also, I was supporting my dear Mother back in Statesville. Rather than commute daily from Statesville, I bunked during the week, alone in a large barracks next to the hangars where I worked.

Mechanic in NC Air National Guard 1967. C-124 in background. (Photo by Roy Howard)

One of my best friends, Roy Howard, fun to work with, was the only mechanic who rigged engine controls on the C-124. Engine and propeller controls had to synchronize, using cables, with both pilots and flight engineer levers.(photo courtesy Roy Howard)

FLIGHT ENGINEER

In 1967, I was selected to attend Flight Engineer ground school in Minneapolis, MN followed by simulator training with our Guard instructors and pilots at Dobbins, AFB, GA. We trained to handle emergencies as a crew.

While in Flight Engineer Ground School, I was assigned to Minnesota Air Guard, my first flight pay was on the KC-97.

At Easter break from Flight Engineer School, I caught a ride in the Air National Guard Bureau B-26, which came in to pick some of us up, then to Andrews AFB, Maryland. The bomb bay was converted to a small passenger compartment. I would like to say my first flight to Andrews was in a B-26 and my last was in a Gulfstream jet! The tail number 03461, coincidentally, corresponded with tail number of U8F I flew in Berlin. Years later I saw my U8F (03461) parked on a ramp in Iowa.

For the first time, I felt I truly belonged, supporting my country, and contributing to a worthy cause. The Charlotte Air National Guard, 145th Airlift Wing (145 AW) at the time consisted of 8 C-124 Globemaster II's which I helped maintain as a mechanic for my daytime job. Forget for a moment the large jet cargo aircraft of today and embellish the C-124 as it was in its heyday. The Globemaster II served faithfully for 25 years before being replaced by C-141's, C-5's and the C-17 Globemaster III's.

First Flight to Vietnam in a C-124

0500 Sunday morning, summer 1967, driving to Charlotte for a long journey in the C-124 to Vietnam. This will be my first of two trips to Vietnam in 'Old Shakey', as she was fondly referred to. On my arrival at my Air National Guard facilities, I meet others, nine in total who will be crewmembers as I, each professional with separate tasks. We have three pilots on this trip who carefully mapped the planned courses of the five-leg journey. Our Navigator will track our flight when we are no longer within range of navigation sources. As Flight Engineer, I, along with two other Engineers had carefully inspected the aircraft, the day prior, checking systems and due to this being an overseas flight, dipping a long measuring stick into each fuel tank from atop the wings to ensure quantity agreed with fuel gages. Engineers are responsible for plotting a **Takeoff and landing data card** (TOLD) which projects power settings adjusted to current weather. Pilots will be furnished with copies of the TOLD card. Our two Load Masters are responsible for ensuring loads are properly arranged for weight and balance. This first leg across the country from N.C. to Travis AFB, CA will be empty. We picked up our cargo at Travis.

External power provides electrical assistance for ground operations until power is provided by the engines. From the large cabin, a slanted metal ladder with two cable hand holds provide access up to the cockpit. In the cockpit will be two pilots, a navigator at his table and an engineer sitting at the right-side facing engineer's panel. There is also a bunk in the rear along with a shelf of technical manuals for reference.

The **Before Starting Engines Checklist** is coordinated through the intercom system. When ready to start the four large radial engines, an engineer, acting as an observer, stands out in front of the aircraft with a long intercom cord to count the 17-foot diameter blades out loud for the engineer inside, who could not see the engines. Blade count is "five, ten, fifteen blades," at which time the Flight Engineer hits the ignition switch. This is repeated three more times at which time the observer climbs on board through a hatch with ladder in the nose of the aircraft.

When cleared to taxi, the observer positions himself up through an open hatch above the cockpit as an observer using intercom to keep the aircraft with a 174-foot wingspan clear of obstacles. This is a thrill, so high up, always reminded me of being on a whale's back looking at the huge fuselage behind. After taxiing to the runup area, the Flight Engineer begins the **Before Takeoff checklist** to check the health of each engine.

When cleared for takeoff, the Flight Engineer, scanning gages, sets **MAX Power** as calculated, when engine temps are ok, he calls out **"GO"** over the intercom. The pilot releases the brakes, and our 10 hour, 2,125 miles first leg to Travis, AFB, CA begins.

With positive climb speed established, **METO POWER** is called for by the pilots, followed by **CLIMB POWER**; on level off, **CRUISE POWER** is set. During this time the observer engineer departs the cockpit to make observations. One check is to open 'P' Compartment door in the cabin floor, go down to make visual checks. From this rather large compartment, he has access through wing tunnels out to all engines which are compartmentalized with space to stand and perform limited inflight maintenance on engine accessory case from behind. An example would be shearing the shaft of an overheating generator. Using headsets in communication with the Flight engineer, having previously shut down the engine, the other engineer could stick a large screwdriver through a small opening in the generator shaft. The Flight Engineer would turn the starter which would shear the shaft; afterwards, restart the engine and have that engine back online.

The C-124 is sometimes referred to as the 'Flying Cloud.' With no sound proofing, the four radial engines at full power, each producing up to 3600 Horsepower, project an extremely loud noise. At cruise, power and blade RPM are reduced. It is tolerable.

The cabin will be our home for days. Engineers alternate usually two-hour shifts on the Engineer panel, then downstairs to the cabin. As a young, relatively inexperienced engineer, I am permitted to sit at the panel in flight but for takeoff and landings, those duties are handled by my two contemporaries each with thousands of hours of Engineer panel time. I was permitted full operation of Engineer controls during training flights to gain experience.

We arrive at Travis in the late afternoon, park, refuel, load cargo for Vietnam, then crew rest. Next day, same routine with exception of thousands of pounds of cargo. Our next stop will take us over the Pacific, alone, destination Hickam AFB, Hawaii, a 10.5-hour flight. During the flight, which is usually 8000 to 10000 feet, one could engage in conversation, or in my case, enjoy the vast ocean below, searching for an elusive ship but rarely seeing any.

While enroute, I'd like to tell you more about this great aircraft. She was a post WWII product, handed down to the Air Guard by the Air Force. In total, the C-124 was in inventory approximately 25 years. By today's standards of solid-state electronics, she was burdened with heavy operational systems. The large set of technical manuals in the cockpit would easily fit on a CD today. Airspeed was restricted to 200 kts (230 MPH) due to fatigue of outer wing panels. Maximum altitude was restricted to 10,000 feet since we were unpressurized. There was no air conditioning but ample heating. Each wing was heated by a 720,000 BTU heater, the cockpit had a 200,000 BTU heater and the cabin was heated by 720,000 BTUs.

Cargo could be loaded either by opening the large clam shell front doors by lowering hydraulic loading ramps for Tanks, bull dozers, trucks and personnel. Cargo could also be loaded by an elevator platform, capable of holding 9000 lbs., lowered by cables, through a bomb bay type door to the ramp; loaded repeatedly until all cargo aboard, then ramp raised to become part of the cargo floor. Balancing the cargo freight was calculated by using painted markings along the lower cargo walls indicating inches from nose of aircraft. It was important to have loads evenly balanced, not too much weight forward and not too much aft. Loadmasters did these calculations, but Engineers were qualified as well. Passengers commonly sat on side-facing troop seats. Often used for airborne training, the Globemaster II could carry up to 200 fully equipped airborne troops who could deploy from two exit doors, one on each side of rear cargo area. Also, with double decking it could carry up to 123 litter patients with attendants. We only carried cargo.

Each pilot up front, sitting side by side had four engine throttles respectively on center console. They used these only for taxiing and landing. The Flight Engineer controlled power settings all other times. If something strange was happening, the pilot would usually look back and ask, "What do you think Engineer?" It has been said, the Engineer controlled the aircraft and that the Globemaster II was the last truly Flight Engineer aircraft.

The Flight Engineer monitored 60+ instruments on the Engineer panel, including 19 levers consisting of throttles, prop levers, mixture controls, carburetor controls, and emergency engine shutoff levers with fire extinguishers. An electrically powered fuel control panel with an assortment of 24 switches to include boost pumps managed fuel from the 12 wing tanks, 6 per side. Fuel could be transferred from one wing to another in an emergency. The fuel control panel was not unlike a Rubik's cube. If you accidentally interrupted the fuel momentarily to an engine, you might get a prop overspeed which was an emergency. There was a saying, "Either you have 'had' an overspeed using the fuel control or you 'will,'" luckily, I never did. The Engineer had an oscilloscope mounted near the top of the Engineer's panel with which to check the firing of 224 spark plugs. A check, using a hand selector was conducted hourly; this was important in order to identify potential issues. Each R4360-63A engine had 28 cylinders, two spark plugs per cylinder.

C-124 Flight Engineer Panel like I operated. (photo source unknown).

The Navigator used a sextant for celestial navigation when out of range of navigation stations, which could be hours and hours over the oceans, particularly the Pacific.

After our second long leg, we arrive at Hickam AFB, deplane, Post Flight inspection and refuel 'Old Shakey' for tomorrows' flight to Wake Island, 2300 miles, 11.5 hours away.

I am reminded of another trip to Hickam in which we were part of a large contingency of C-124s acting as backup for a massive C-141 operation. Quarters were in such demand that each crewmember was allowed just eight hours of bunk time. I recall going into transient quarters for rest; the bunk I was assigned was occupied. The Airman was awakened and told his eight hours was up. Clean sheets were placed on the bunk, and I slipped under covers for my eight-hour nap.

Our third leg to Wake is hot, during runup until just before takeoff the two emergency exit doors remain open for ventilation, this is routine. Arriving at the small Atoll we are greeted with a beautiful cloudless sky. Not much here but the runway, support personnel, some transient barracks, a chow hall and a bowling alley.

Also, there is a rundown looking club with a sign "Drifter's Reef". Inside is a bar along with rustic accouterments—great memories of this place.

Drifter's Reef on Wake Island in the 60's (photo credits unknown)

Wake was an important refueling stop, historic from WWII fighting with Japan. The Japanese kept captured prisoners here. I enjoy swimming in the crystal-clear waters since the chloropicrin levels are safe at the time. Beautiful fish come right up to me! At this time, a recent typhoon had leveled the Atoll of all trees. I venture into some Japanese pillboxes and find names inscribed on the walls. I find a soldier's name and the date he passed through on his way to Vietnam. Next to it, the soldier has returned a year later with the inscription, "Going Home."

The flight from Wake to Clark AFB, Philippines, is our longest, 13.5 hours. Same routine, post flight inspection, refueling. We are told NOT to drink the water, so we drank either San Miguel beer or Coca Cola. Hot tropical climate.

We depart the next day for Anderson AFB, Guam, a 1,550-mile leg. After landing, as we taxi by the Flight Operations building, "Smitty," an active-duty instructor loadmaster, points to the beautiful palm trees surrounding the building. "See those trees", I planted those 20 years ago".

Our remaining leg, 2,450 miles, is to Cam Ranh Bay, Vietnam, a large AFB on the east coast. We are to limit our time as much as possible for safety reasons. We offload, refuel, and pick up cargo going back to the States. Standing on perforated metal planking near the aircraft, it dawned on me I had not touched Vietnamese soil, so I ran over into the dusty soil and stomped my feet just to say, yes, I've been to Vietnam. Little did I know at the time, I would return someday for a 19 month stay. One sad item we carried on our return was the remains of a U.S. serviceman in a Styrofoam chest packed in ice. Our return home is the reverse of the flight over. Each stop, the chest is signed for and taken for repacking in ice. We hand over the remains at Hickam Field on our stop in Hawaii.

Some interesting side notes on these flights.

On my second trip, returning home, we lost an engine on takeoff departing Wake Island for Hickam Field, Hawaii. There were no spare R4360 engines, so our entire crew hopped a ride on another Globemaster to Hickam, leaving our aircraft behind. From Hickam, we caught a hop on a C-141 to Travis AFB, California.

Tricked by Navigator

During celestial navigation, there was usually only one pilot in the cockpit to make position reports, and the Navigator kept track of our position. On a particular night, drumming along over the dark Pacific, as a young rookie engineer, I sat monitoring engine readings; a young loadmaster came up to the dimly lit cockpit by the ladder from the cargo compartment, closed the hatch and sat down on it. We both sat in silence listening to the drone of the engines, each observing the Navigator behind me with a pencil in his teeth taking readings from his sextant mounted above him in the cockpit ceiling. We noticed some concern on the Navigator's face, pencil in his teeth hurriedly rechecking his readings. Suddenly, the Navigator bit the pencil in two with his teeth, then proclaimed frantically, "We are lost'! Scared the bejesus out of the two of us! Finally, the Navigator smiled and said, "Gotcha didn't I!" We later learned this was an old trick he routinely pulled on rookies such as us.

Panama City, Panama

C-124 flight from Charlotte, N.C. to Panama: With a day layover at Howard AFB, Panama near the Canal Zone in 1968, there were rumors of unrest in the capital city; we were advised to stay on base and not go downtown but in the early hours of darkness, three of us elected to hire a taxi to see the city anyway. On our arrival, we noticed the city was dark, mostly only car lights, you could feel the tension. Not wanting to linger, we had our driver return us to the base.

The following day, after our arrival back in Charlotte and my return home, I turned on the TV to see news of rioting from where I had been a mere 24 hours prior. Not a wise choice to visit the city that night.

CLOSE CALL while a Flight Engineer

Near Miss over Gainesville, Florida.

On a C-124 return flight from Howard AFB, Panama, near Gainesville, Florida, north bound, middle afternoon, while seated at the Engineer's panel, I happened to look to my left toward the two pilots in the front seat when I noticed our Commander, LTC Elliott in the left seat jerk his head back and at the same instant, our cockpit window filled with the belly of an airliner! I could see grease streaks on its belly as it zoomed past. In a nanosecond it was gone. We were mere feet from a midair collision! Apparently, the airliner saw us and made a diversionary maneuver barely missing us. In those days radar was not tracking as it does today; there was no altimeter monitoring by the ground controllers, so we thought the airliner was descending through our altitude, not caught by the controllers. LTC Elliott reported the 'Near Miss', and we continued home. Later, LTC Elliot filled out an Operational Hazard Report (OHR). That was as close as it gets!

2nd CLOSE CALL while a Flight Engineer

Nearly blown off C-124 wing at the Azores

Two days before Christmas 1967 as a young 22-year-old Flight Engineer; we were on an overnight refuel stop at Lajes Field, Azores in the Atlantic about 900 miles west of Lisbon Portugal. We had come from Germany the day before. On this leg of the flight from Lajes to McGuire Air Force Base, New Jersey, I was designated to be a spotter from the cabin area as we taxied out to make our runup checks prior to takeoff. With headset, I was in communication with Don Creason, chief Engineer, who was in the cockpit operating engine controls. Looking out over the wings, I noticed a small access panel to the rear of the left outboard engine (#1) was not latched down, so I called Don upstairs to let him know. He replied, "Ok, I'll tell you when you can go 'out' there." When we were in position to do our "Before Takeoff" checks and the engines were idling, Don gave me the go ahead to 'Go Out.' As stated previously, on warm days, we kept both cabin emergency exits removed and set aside to let cooling air into the cabin/cargo compartment until takeoff. One could step out the open exit onto the wing which I did. I walked on the wing behind the loud turning engines to the #1 outboard engine and secured the access panel. Just then, the engines began revving up; I was about to be blown off the wing! Immediately, I lay prone on the wing with nothing to hang on to. Inches above was a torrent of high wind from the propellers. As Don was going through his engine checks in the cockpit, I was the recipient out on the wing! Very slowly, fingernails on rivets, I shimmed back to the cabin in between Don's power reductions. When I made it to the outer cabin, I noticed the cabin emergency exit was installed and closed! No one knew I was out there! Lying flat, I raised my fist and banged on the window exit numerous times, eventually a loadmaster saw me and opened the exit door. Never forget him opening the door. He nonchalantly opened the door to let me in then went on with his duties as if it was quite common for someone to be on the wing during runup checks! I was shaking, thinking of how close I had come to being blown off the wing and possibly killed, injured at least. On the long journey from Lajes Field to McGuire Air Force Base, New Jersey, I said nothing to Don about what I had endured but once we arrived and shut down, I asked him why he brought the power up with me on the wing. He turned pale and said, "You were on the wing"! I replied, "Yes." He conveyed to me that he had intended I go out through the wing tunnel, but I understood he meant 'on' the wing since the access panel could not be reached from within the wing. Being young with little experience can sometimes be deadly. I was fortunate to live for another day.

The Wing area I was almost blown off while engine checks were being made! Person on wing not identified. (photo source unknown)

Flying through a thunderstorm in the Globemaster

On another return trip from Panama, closer to home in South Carolina. Our radar was inoperative and bad stuff was about to happen. It was dark out, and all passengers sat with seat belts, in fact everyone had seat belts on but me, the observer. We went right into a storm; I heard the pilot through my headset calling the Engineer for 'Descent Power' (reducing power). Even with 'Descent Power,' the crew reported that we were climbing 4,000 feet per minute. I noticed rain on the cargo door window streaking up at a 45-degree angle. Suddenly when we fell out the other side of the storm updraft, I went airborne stuck to the double cabin ceiling for a couple of seconds. As I went up, I remember the loadmaster and I kept eye contact with each other on my trip up and down. I came crashing down, breaking the seat I landed on, my headset around my neck like a horseshoe. It was an exhilarating ride and I laughed it off. Did not seem to be injured.

Dinner with Soviet MIG pilots in Madrid, Spain.

On a layover at Torrejon, AFB, Madrid, Spain, many of the crew ventured downtown to a swanky restaurant. Somehow, it was revealed there were two Soviet MIG pilots there as well. They were invited to join us, the enemy, so to speak, but tonight, we were comrades enjoying each other's company, though we had a language barrier to contend with.

Longest Flight – near fuel limits

My longest flight 15 hours, 15 min. Lajes Field, Azores, to Dover AFB, DE. Our first stop was to have been Goose Bay Labrador, but since we were making good time, the commander elected to 'Fireball' (bypass) Goose Bay and head on to Dover AFB, Delaware. When we got within range of Dover, the weather was below minimums to land. We did not have enough fuel to divert to an alternate. Remember Approach Control doing us a favor. They came up on frequency and reported "Special Observation, Ceiling 200 feet, half mile visibility"; that made us 'Legal' to do our approach. It was tense for a while on the approach, finally through the fog, we caught a glimpse of the runway and made a safe landing. Glad to be on terra firma once again!

One of our NC Air National Guard C-124's on landing (photo credit unknown)

Leaving the Air Guard

Through a phone conversation with the brother-in-law of my co-worker Tom Pilon, I discovered the ARMY had a Warrant Officer program in which one could be trained as an ARMY pilot with no degree requirement. He, Tom's brother-in-law, had just graduated from flight school, at Fort Rucker, home of ARMY Aviation training; while speaking to him on the phone, he was so excited, I knew at that moment, that another option awaited me.

I visited the local ARMY recruiter in Charlotte, SGT Smiley, who looked at me incredulously when I told him I planned to leave the Guard and would like to sign up for the Warrant Officer program. This was at a time when young men were clawing to get into the Guard to avoid going to Vietnam. He

51

told me if I did not make it through the flight program, I would be required to stay on active duty for two years as either a cook or Military Policeman. I took the gamble. My teammates were in disbelief when I told them I would be going into the ARMY! Some tried to talk me out of it since I had a deferment being in the Guard and would not be going to War. One, a Flight Engineer instructor, "Pinky" Springs told me my butt would be sore. I asked him why, and he said from kicking yourself in the ass for leaving this comfortable position to go into the ARMY. I made my rank easily, graduating at the top of my class in Flight Engineer School. Now a Staff Sergeant, promotable to Tech Sergeant, it was sad to say good-bye to my wonderful fellow co-workers, Gary Kidd, my supervisor, Bill Randle, Roy Howard, Jim Murdock, RB Summerville, Don Kirby, Tommy Lee and many more. My Flight Engineer teammates, most instructors included MSG Lowery, Jim Young, the two Lathan twins, Terry and Jerry, their cousin Gary, Don Creason, Pinky Springs, Dobie Dixon, Wilburn Livengood and Homer Whitington.

CHAPTER 5
Army Basic Training, then to Flight School

March 4, 1969, a year after the infamous Tet Offensive in Vietnam, I was at the airline terminal at Charlotte Municipal Airport waiting for my departure for ARMY Basic Training at Fort Polk, (Camp Swampy) Louisiana. I looked across the runway, observing in the distance my glorious C-124s, thinking my friends were there at work, a place I had been a week before. Would I make it, or would I have a two-year commitment as a Military Policeman or a cook? Time will tell.

This would be my second time of grueling Basic Training, the first being in the Air Force. Spent a lot of time in mud and physical training this time! Now, I was a Soldier in top physical condition.

Del Hardiman

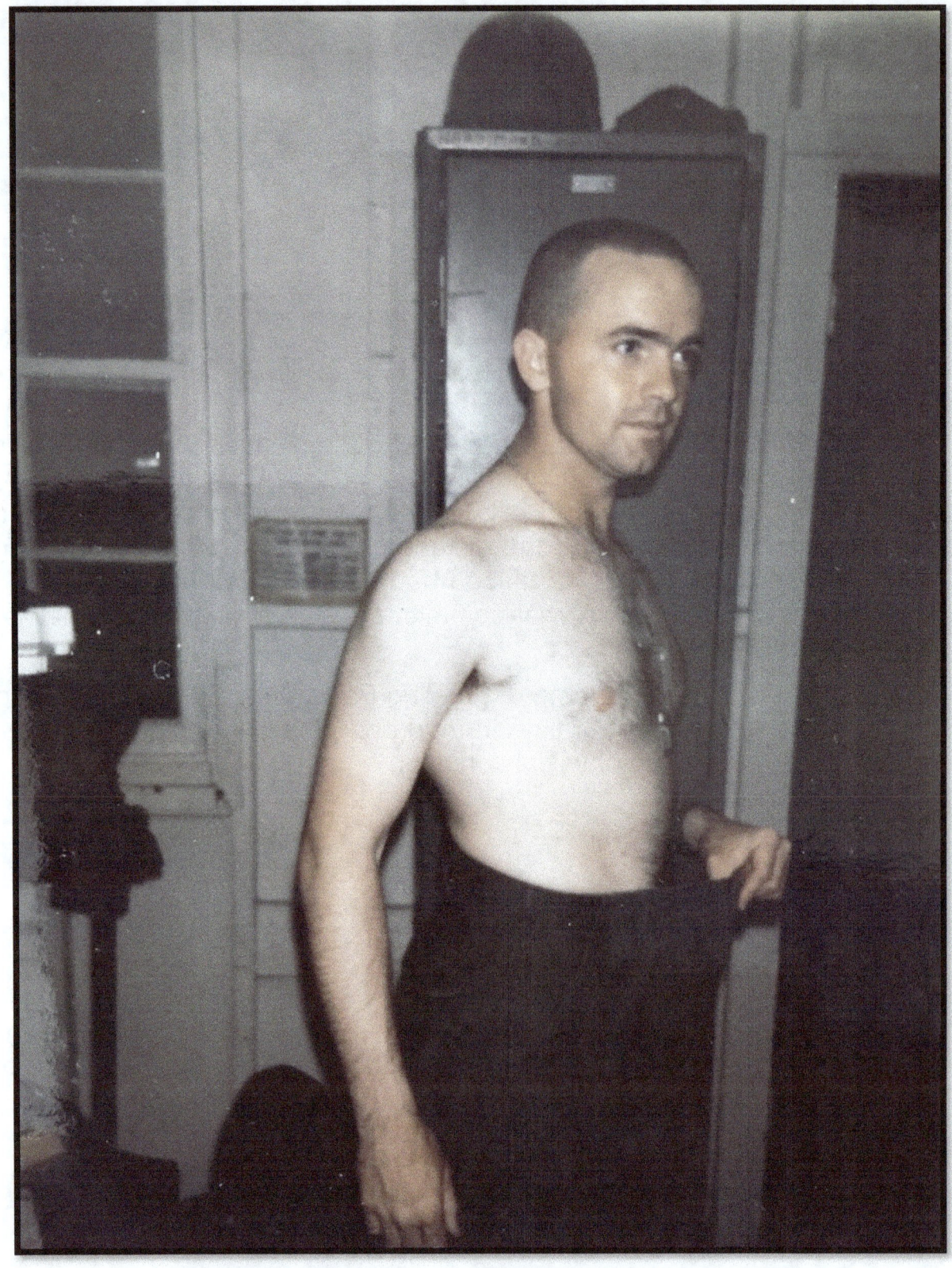

ARMY Basic training, Fort Polk, LA (Camp Swampy)

54

Receiving High Firer trophy

On completion of ARMY Basic I was awarded the 'High Firer' trophy for being the top company marksman with the M-14 rifle, earned by walking a predetermined trail where silhouettes were unexpectedly popping up from a few feet close by, more in the distance and two 300 meters away as I recall. I got both of those which were so distant they were hard to pick out. My independent observer let out a gasp! When I completed the range, I had five unused rounds remaining. Our Company Commander, CPT Palmer made the presentation in front of the company. I was so proud of the unanticipated recognition...but wait! Just as I was getting on the bus to depart for Fort Walters, TX, CPT Palmer came to me and asked for the trophy. I reluctantly retrieved it from my duffel bag. Seems that my good friend to this day, Wayne Guffy had outfired me by one round! Wayne has the trophy with no name tag, and I have the name tag with no trophy. One of my biggest regrets, not using those unspent rounds; fate has a way of messing with you.

CHAPTER 6

Fort Wolters, Tx for Initial Flight Training – Almost

From Basic, I reported to Fort Walters, TX, 50 miles west of Fort Worth. Here I was to begin 'Pre-phase' classes, a course of becoming an officer, then initial Rotary Wing (helicopter) training in small trainers, followed by advanced flight training at Fort Rucker, Alabama. But as you will see, once again, fate intervened.

I naturally assumed I would be going to a Rotary Wing (RW) Class. In fact, I was assigned to Rotary Wing Class 69-49 but before we left our holding area waiting for class to start, I discovered there was a small group of 10 to 12 candidates in the 200+ class that would later arrive to be attached as Fixed Wing (FW) candidates but only in the 10th Warrant Officer Candidate (WOC) Company. As it so happened, I was going to the 10th WOC! Inquisitively I asked to see the 'Holding' Company Commander, a Captain, to inquire about going to Fixed Wing, he replied, telling me there was a Special Forces E-7 in our group who had a general officer pulling for him and he could not get FW so I would not stand a chance. I saluted and departed. On my way out, the Executive Officer (XO), a second Lieutenant, sitting at his desk, stopped me and said: "So you want to go FW huh? "Yes Sir," I replied. Well, here's what you do. When you march with the company up to the 10th ask to see Mr. Baker (Warrant Officer W-2 and above are addressed as Mister), and tell him you want FW.

CW2 Baker was a short guy back from a tour in Vietnam as a RW pilot and the current Tactical (TAC) Officer for the FW class. We marched up the hill to the 10th (there were a total of ten WOC companies). I marched, along with two others, beside the large formation calling cadence for 200+

individuals. When we arrived that hot summer day, one could sense an unease since we had been forewarned about hazing from upper classmen. We stood in formation with duffel bags by our side while the Intermediate Candidates identified with orange tabs on their epaulettes worked their way through the ranks harassing us. A number of candidates dropped out right away. When one of the orange tabs came to me, I asked to see Mr. Baker. Why, he asked. I told him I wanted to go FW. In due time, Mr. Baker stood before me, looked up and said you want to go FW? "Sir, yes Sir, I would like to go FW". He asked me about my qualifications, and I told him. 1700 hours total time, Certified Flight Instructor, Commercial, Instrument, multi-engine, and Sea Plane ratings. He said, fall out over at the supply room which he pointed to. "Don't leave that spot, I don't know you. If you leave, I will not know how to find you." I did as told. As it happened, near the supply room was where the dropouts were being held. The orange tabs thought I was one of those. One asked me, What's the matter candidate, can't you take it? I replied in the proper form that I was going FW to which he replied. "Can you afford to lose $40,000? I asked him what he meant. He said it costs $80,000 to train an RW pilot and only $40,00 to train a FW, can you afford to lose $40,000? Always thought that to be an amusing statement. In time, Mr. Baker caught up with me amongst the pandemonium, pointed to a specific barracks and said take your stuff and wait for me there. I now realize I owe so much to Mr. Baker, he gave me a chance which would be beneficial throughout my ARMY career.

I entered the barracks, pointed out by Mr. Baker. As soon as I opened the door, a cool rush of air encompassed me. I observed empty double bunks on either side of the center aisle. To my astonishment, the aisle had been painted to resemble a runway, numbers and all! I went over to a lower bunk on my left next to a window where I observed my fellow candidates in the heat, doing pushups, emptying their duffle bags, a place I had been moments before! Here comes that Fate thing again! I sat in silence for hours, not moving as I watched from my air-conditioned perch. Mr. Baker never came. Later I heard the rear door open, and a head appeared around the corner. It was the current Fixed Wing Class returning. They occupied the upstairs. I was told to get my things and join them. These twelve candidates had a myriad of Aviation backgrounds. One I recall was a glider pilot, who had flown along the Rocky Mountains to record wind data.

Open bay barracks with empty bunks similar to what I waited in as mentioned above.

This group took me under their wing, so to speak, when possible; they avoided rules, in retrospect, near felonious! While with them, I was assigned to the supply room to await my small class's arrival. We fell out each morning before daylight with the whole company to a lighted baseball field for physical training (PT). After only a few jumping jacks, our leader called our small group to attention, and then we doubled timed (ran) from the field leaving the company behind. Once out of site around the corner, we stopped and relaxed, those who smoked, smoked. In time, we formed up and double timed back to the field just as PT was concluding, no one the wiser. Not supervised, we got by with many things.

One morning during PT, a strange thing happened. A small TH-55 trainer helicopter came out of nowhere, hovered over to Homeplate at the ball field where we were doing our exercises. From Home plate the helicopter methodically ran the bases back to Homeplate. The pilot, wearing a white helmet, saluted us, then was off and gone. Found out later it was Mr. Baker!

Hughes TH-55 Osage, like the one Mr. Baker ran the bases at our PT ball field.
Photo source unknown

In a few weeks, my group arrived, and Mr. Baker put me in charge of my small FW class designated Class 70-1. Initially strangers, we came to be close knit. Our class spent four weeks, beginning May 12, 1969, in Pre-phase, then on to Ft. Stewart, GA for Basic FW training in T-41s followed by final training at Ft. Rucker, AL where we had two phases with the 0-1 Bird Dog and one in twin engine T-42s in which we did instrument training and cross-country flights. At Ft Stewart I soloed with minimum required hours and was permitted out alone in the T-41 a single engine Cessna 172 with larger engine and constant speed propeller canvassing the Georgia countryside while my classmates were in training.

Del Hardiman

T-41 Trainer at Fort Stewart, GA

Fixed Wing Class 70-1 at Fort Stewart, GA. Front row, L/R, Dave Slatinsky, Bill Braswell, Tim McDonald, Eldon Forsee, Alex Mello, Del Hardiman (class leader). Back row L/R Rick Harris, Jack Brunson (KIA, Vietnam flying an OV-1 Mohawk, remains found in Laos 2004), Lynn Decker, George Coleman, Jack Carroll, Joseph Wright. To my left rear far right is Frank Blaine.

In Flight School, we were all promoted to E-5. In the 0-1, at Fort Rucker, we were taught military training, tactics, and maneuvers, operating from leased farm fields and night takeoff and landings on purposely built parallel

short blacktop runways dimly lit with oil burning smudge pots .You land on one runway, taxi over to the other to fly another pattern to repeat another landing. I asked my backseat instructor if he minded, if I made my night landings without landing lights. He paused for a moment, then cautiously said: "Go ahead."

By this time our class was joined with commissioned officers. One of my classmates and friend was Captain Algernon Guess, one of the Davidson College ROTC students taught by Miller Aviation back home in Statesville. We hadn't seen each other for five years. One night, when our training was completed, Algernon, riding with me in the back seat, asked if I would do a loop while in a string of Bird Dogs headed back to Cairns Field, Ft. Rucker, I accommodated him with joy! In all, we spent 11 months in training.

Interestingly, as a youngster of 15, there was an ARMY Reserve Captain, Ken Conger, who brought the first 0-1(at that time called L-19) I had ever seen to my hometown airport where I worked. He would leave it a month at a time to come out and put flight time on it. I liked to sit in the cockpit and dream of flying it, with no idea I would someday be in that cockpit in Vietnam getting shot at.

Losing a close friend

Before graduating from Flight School, I learned my good friend Robert (Bob) McComb was killed at Fort Rucker in a UH-1 training accident just prior to the George Washington Birthday weekend. Bob and I shared two level bunks at Fort Polk in Basic training. We were on the same trip by bus to Fort Wolters, Texas where I left the Rotary Wing Class and went Fixed Wing. Bob and I renewed acquaintances while at Fort Rucker later. I was informed Bob had completed his final check ride before graduation and was a passenger on a training flight taking pictures as a student and instructor were conducting training. They crashed, killing all on board. Bob was from Virginia, an only child; he spoke of his mother often. Still miss him.

On graduation, April 4, 1970, we were awarded our 'Wings' and promoted to Warrant Officer One (WO1). My sister Brenda came to my graduation and pinned on my wings which was special. Each of us departed for training in advanced aircraft. Joseph Wright, Rick Harris and I went to Fritzsche ARMY airfield, Ft. Ord, CA, near Monterey for a four-week transition in the U-1A Otter prior to Vietnam.

CHAPTER 7
Otter Transition School on way to Vietnam

Fort Ord, California. My first thought when I saw the olive drab green DeHavilland Otters on the flight line was how huge they were. Would I be able to fly that beast? She (Otter) was far from being an advanced aircraft, it was an old radial engine tailwheel workhorse from the past. To get in the cockpit you had to step high on the landing gear tire, then two steps more on the landing gear strut to gain access to the cockpit. It had a motorized tail wheel due to the large vertical tail, in a strong wind you could not maneuver it on the ground with brakes alone. The horizontal stabilizer (tail) was so high, I could almost stand upright under it. There was capacity for ten passengers, a crew chief and two pilots. Entrance for passengers was a removable metal ladder at the rear left side of the cabin. In time, I would learn to love and depend on her in Vietnam but for now I was reminded: "Needs of the ARMY come first"! Joseph Wright, Rick Harris, and I graduated from Otter transition May 17, 1970.

George Artis

A week before graduation from flight school at Fort Rucker, I needed to make a weekend visit home. Flying in my dress green uniform was cheaper but there was a problem, my uniform pants already had black officer's stripes sewn to each leg. As was often my case, I broke the rules. I had a friend drive my blue VW bug up to our barracks back door where I slipped in, wearing my WO1 uniform. With discretion, who would know? On the flight from Dothan, Alabama, to Charlotte, N.C. I was seated next to a friendly black W-2 Warrant Officer, about ten years my senior, also in his dress greens. He assumed I had just graduated from flight school, congratulated me, and was asking questions of my experiences, questions which I did my best to mislead him. If he knew what I was doing (impersonating an officer), there would be hell to pay. His name was George Artis who had a prior tour in Vietnam as a UH-1 helicopter pilot, we became friends.

When I reported to Fort Ord for Otter transition, hard to believe but George was in my class! He had connections, so he arranged for me after our training to get my flight to Vietnam originating from Charlotte instead of flying back to California after home leave. When I reported to the 54th Otter Company at Long Thanh Vietnam, guess what, George was there! He was around 5 feet eight, always smiling, mustached, pipe smoking, a Chivas Regal scotch at night individual. We were roommates for a short time; he and I both were assigned to maintenance. he was a great mentor and great to be with.

George told of an experience in Vietnam on his previous tour. In a UH-1, picking up combat troops, he received fire from a Viet Cong sniper in a tree directly in front of him, hitting his aircraft several times, One of the troops, as I recall, might have been a Captain, shot and killed the sniper in the tree. He quickly hustled over, picked up the dead sniper's rifle, brought it back to George's left cockpit window, handed the rifle to George and yelled, "I believe this is yours". George brought the rifle home.

Later, my wife Paula and I visited George and his wife Mattie in Hampton, VA. They were proud parents of four adult sons.

CHAPTER 8
Vietnam Tour in the Beginning

George Artis at his desk 1970, Long Thanh, Vietnam (photo, Del Hardiman)

I, along with a full complement of soldiers of all stripes, boarded a DC-8 from California to Vietnam. I knew none of them. On our descent to Bien Hoa AFB, east of Saigon, I looked out the window to observe what appeared to be bomb craters in some areas of the tropical landscape. Once on the ground we were taken by bus to Long Binh Reporting Depot to await pick up from our units. We were told to remain in the lower area to keep clear of possible snipers.

I was picked up next morning, riding in the back of a dusty ARMY ¾ ton military pickup truck, 40 minutes' drive from Long Thanh where I would report to the 54th Otter Company for what I thought to be a 12-month tour. The ride in the open bed truck offered my first view of Vietnam; with few vehicles on the road it seemed quiet with exception of the truck. There was an occasional Vietnamese walking by the roadside with white conical straw hats, black silk looking clothing, never making eye contact. They appeared small to me.

Upon my arrival at the 54th, the Executive Officer, CPT Steve McCan interviewed me. When he learned of my maintenance experience, he stopped me and said, "Report to CPT Chase Smeeks in maintenance tomorrow morning". I was extremely disappointed. My intent had been to be in Standards as an Instructor. Maintenance was not at all what I wanted.

Long Thanh North airfield, 27 miles north-east of Saigon (now Ho Chi Minh City) had a 5000- foot asphalt runway; with the following units assigned: 54th Aviation Company, 210th Combat Aviation Battalion HQ, Command Aircraft Company (CAC), 56th Transportation Company (maintenance Recovery), 2nd Signal BN Aviation Detachment, 73rd Surveillance Airplane Company (SAC), 146th Aviation Company Radio Research (RR) and an ARMY-Lockheed YO-3A Unit with engine powered Schweizer Gliders attached to the 73rd for night surveillance. The airfield was surrounded by a protective perimeter, guarded at night.

Our company was on a dirt road, the 73rd OV-1 Mohawk company was on the other side of the road. We had a headquarters building, club, flight operations, wooden two-story living quarters, a bunker in event of mortar attacks and latrine with a five-hole wooden bench in which body waste dropped into cutout metal barrels that were pulled from behind and burned with gas each morning by a Vietnamese papasan. Enlisted quarters and chow hall were nearby. The flight line was a 10-minute walk away.

Early next morning after chow, on my first duty day, I was directed to the flight line where large radial engines were noisily firing up and Otters departing for the day's missions. Aircraft not flying were tied down in separate revetments protected on three sides. I met CPT Smeeks in our small maintenance hangar with offices in the rear.

Shortly after, I was temporarily assigned a room on the lower level of the officer quarters with another Warrant Officer (Harold Wier) and soon after with Warrant Officer Carsten Hauge, who became a lifelong friend who I recently met again after 52 years at a Long Thanh airfield reunion in Santa Rosa, CA. Each room had a two-foot screen opening near the top of three walls. My first evening bunked with Harold, I noticed a gecko climbing the wall next to my bunk but found that to be common.

The 54th Aviation Company had about ten U1-A "Otters". Our call sign was "Big Daddy", the aircraft had crimson circular logos on each side of their engine cowlings with large yellow number 54 overlaid with silver aviation wings in center. Across the top arc in white lettering was 'Otter Air Service' below the emblem in white was 'Big Daddy', the lower arc, in white, read 'Utility Airplane CO.'

Missions varied but the 54th was mostly a taxi company stopping at remote ARMY sites throughout the day with passengers, mail, and freight to load and offload. We covered the lower half of South Vietnam, III Corps and IV Corps.

One mission was to fly a specially equipped Otter with a mounted camera hole in the belly to do mapping. Two individuals flew these missions and were usually gone days at a time. We also dropped 'Chieu Hoi' leaflets by the thousands in designated areas from time to time. These leaflets, part of psychological warfare, were an initiative to encourage communist Viet Cong soldiers to defect, offering them safe passage if they brought a leaflet with them.

Our young crew chiefs who flew with the missions were the bedrock of our operation, they kept those old birds flying. When missions were complete, the pilots made it to the club while the crew chiefs diligently worked off writeups which could take hours. Next morning, they were at their bird early prepping it for the flight. One crew chief I recall was Roger Luther who was exceptional. He and I made contact 40+ years later at an Otter Reunion at which time he shared memorable photos with me.

Roger Luther, U1A Crew Chief, 54th Otter Company with his aircraft -1970
(courtesy of Roger Luther)

It hurt to see my contemporaries' flying missions while I was stuck in maintenance doing test flights and assisting in maintenance operations. I did, however, make Aircraft Commander before any of those guys. I had an agreement with CPT Smeeks and later CPT Jones, if they would let me fly missions, I would work night shifts in maintenance. They agreed. One benefit was that I had a Jeep at my disposal!

The Otter was a beast to handle but in time, it became second nature. It was so large that in a strong cross wind, the fuselage became a weathervane requiring skill to keep it on the runway. Landing was done in incremental stages, eventually hand pumping the flaps to full 60-degrees when needed, on short, improvised dirt runways. The outer ailerons both extended down 23 degrees with full flaps. In a good wind, you could almost stop it on a dime!

We had one mission I flew a few times in which we landed on a dirt road near the village of Go Cong to drop off and pick up mail. The Vietnamese police would stop traffic when they saw us overhead. To depart, we turned around and departed in the opposite direction. As we climbed and circled back, there was a cloud of dust in our wake which engulfed those waiting behind the police barrier. I could not see anyone I knew to be there in that dust cloud. I felt sorry for that.

Engine Failures

Days were long but productive in the 54th. We all took pride in our daily accomplishments. We had a number of engine failures, however. Some come to mind. One morning an Otter taking off had a failure right after liftoff but made a successful landing at Bear Cat, a compound next to Long Thanh. They put the aircraft down in a helicopter landing area! Quite an accomplishment. On another occasion, Joseph Wright had to put his aircraft down, this is his story written to me about one of his engine failures:

"The interesting one was a cracked propeller thrust plate. my copilot remarked that it was hazy today. I looked out the side window and said it didn't look that bad over there. when I turned back the windshield was black. then the engine locked up. we were over Tan An, with generals and the head of nursing on board. We circled down and landed, I called home for a replacement aircraft. You came up on company frequency and said you were testing an engine swap and weren't too far away. We rolled out and managed to swing around at the end of the runway. we all got out and looked at the dripping mess (oil). One general asked how long we were going to be there, and I pointed out your plane on short approach to final. They were really impressed with how fast we got a replacement airplane down there. I never did tell them that if the prop had come off, with our loading I probably couldn't have controlled the airplane and we likely would have all been killed."

Del Hardiman

Close call - Engine failure

After taking off from an ARMY Ranger Camp, Tay Ninh East, a short, Pierced Steel Planking (PSP) runway; we, W01Lawton at the controls in the left seat, had an engine failure. I, also a W01, was aircraft commander in the right seat. At about 1500 feet the engine (our one and only) started running rough and losing power. I knew we were going down. We were near the mountain, Nui Ba Dinh (Devil's Mountain). Our option was to swing back toward Tay Ninh West (larger, paved runway) but we were not going to make it. I looked around and my attention was drawn to the fuel primer pump between our seats on the floor. The primer pump typically was used prior to engine starting to prime the engine with fuel. I thought what the heck, I started slowly pumping the primer and what do you know, we got some limited power back, so we continued toward Tay Ninh West. The partially powered engine was shaking the whole aircraft. I got a call on the intercom from our crew chief, Champagne (his last name) in the cabin who was yelling, "Sir this Major is trying to get out". I looked back at the door at our only passenger; a Special Forces Major who was ready to do a PLF out the back door (without a parachute). I yelled back at Champagne and said, "Let him go"! but he didn't go. We made it to Tay Ninh West and shut down. Looking at the engine, there was no sign of anything wrong. I called for assistance and Chase Smeeks came up in another Otter. He discovered the top of #2 cylinder had separated in flight and all our fuel air mixture was leaving from that cylinder leaving the other cylinders without fuel. We had been experiencing fuel starvation. Once we landed, the cylinder head was neatly back in place, and I didn't see it. The primer only shoots fuel in the top five of the nine cylinders, so when I used the primer constantly, I was shooting raw fuel into those five cylinders except #2 cylinder which was cracked and not producing. We had made it back on four cylinders! Chase said, good job, I'm going to put you in for the Broken Wing award but to my knowledge he never did. That procedure was not in the Emergency Procedures manual, but it worked. Ah those Spartan rebuilds! Spartan corporation had a poor record in overhauling those Pratt and Whitney engines.

Seeing my first dead casualties

Not long after being in country, I had a mission which included a stop at Vinh Long near the Mekong river. It was there that I saw my first dead. Covered bodies, five or six, stacked like cord wood in a truck with only bare

70

feet uncovered. I was told they were Vietnamese casualties from a prior night's encounter. That was a shocking scene, making me aware this was war.

C-119 Crash

One morning I had a mission to Rach Gia (Rock Yah) near the southern tip of South Vietnam. The runway clear, ocean visible off in the distance on a southern approach for landing. Airfield controlled by U.S. Army, palm trees adding to the scenery. Soon the other pilot and I noticed off to the right in the grass, a Vietnamese Air Force twin engine C-119 cargo aircraft lying limp with the right wing touching the ground. This was an attention getter. As we landed and our Otter rolled past the C-119 on our right, we noticed it had crashed into a large steam roller, one of those devices with two giant wheels to pack down dirt or pavement. The C-119 on landing, had departed the runway, swerving off to the right and impacted the roller. The aircraft was smoldering but largely intact. We taxied in, anxious as to what had happened. Speaking with two young Army Warrant pilots, the same as me, they told us their story. They had each been in small OH-6 "Loach" helicopters, holding at low hover side by side just beyond the steam roller waiting for clearance to take off after the C-119 landed. As they explained it, the C-119 touched down with its high wing landing gears. The right gear compressed in the strut on touchdown as it should have, the left remained extended. This caused the C-119 to veer out of control to the right. The two young Army Aviators told us, had it not been for that old steam roller, they would have been "goners"; it happened so fast they would not have had time to react. The C-119 would have come right at them. Luckily that roller was in the right place at the right time. I don't recall the condition of the C-119 crew, they had been evacuated by the time I arrived.

Pilot falling out of door in flight

Unbelievable! Our company, the 54th, was challenged to a volleyball match on the other side of Long Thanh airfield with the 210th battalion, our one and only time of doing so. While the game ensued, we witnessed two pilots in flight suits stop by with an incredible story. The two of them had just come from the dispensary. They related that they were flying with no passengers south along the eastern coast of South Vietnam enroute to Long Thanh airfield. The aircraft was a twin turbine U21A assigned to the

Command Aircraft Company. With just the two of them, they noticed a passenger door warning light on the instrument console. The pilot in the right seat elected to get up and check the door. When he attempted to secure the door, swoosh, the door fell open and the pilot went with it! Fortunately, his leg was caught on the door cable leaving him suspended in flight hanging on for dear life! The pilot at the controls could not get up to assist so they continued to Long Thanh with the other pilot suspended out in the airstream. Note, when parked, the door is mere inches from the ground while open, so the landing had to be made with utmost caution. Miraculously a safe landing was made, and the pilot survived albeit with a torn flight suit. From this incident, all U21A doors throughout the ARMY fleet had locking chains installed to prevent this from happening again.

Last flight of the season to Muc Hoa

Interesting memory. On this mission one of our stops was Muc Hoa, a Special Forces camp, located in the Plain of Reeds in the Mekong Delta to drop off and pick up mail pouches; it was the rainy season, and I would pronounce this being our last flight due to the runway conditions. The floating PSP runway had stakes on the ground up and down the runway to anchor it. If we sat, the runway would begin sinking and we would not be able to depart so we kept moving slowly while a military truck drove alongside to pass and receive mail. After that day, the runway was shut down until the water level subsided.

54th Utility Airplane Co.
Long Than North
Viet Nam
Sept. 1970

Pilots of the 54th. I'm second from the left back row. Our Commander MAJ Sutherland far right back row. (photo courtesy of Chase Smeeks)

Meeting my future wife

I did not go to Vietnam looking for a wife, the thought never entered my mind but fate again, stepped in. Our secretary to the 54th Commander, a Vietnamese lady, Miss Kim who I got to know with my frequent visits to her office, introduced me to a young 18-year-old secretary to LTC Baines, Commander of the Command Aircraft Company (CAC) on the other side of the airfield. The CAC had modern U21A twin turbine engine aircraft which flew VIPs. Her name was Nga, pronounced "Nah". She was shy and beautiful! In addition to being LTC Baines secretary, she also kept flight records for all aviation personnel. After getting a security clearance which her sister Mai helped her with, she took English and typing classes prior to getting her position. In total she was with CAC for three years. We met and in time got to know each other. Remember her preparing delicious fried shrimp for me! Now I knew she could cook! When I learned her older sister

Del Hardiman

Mai was married to an ARMY Major, now living at Fort Collins, Colorado, the thought of marriage entered my mind. In time, I asked her three times to marry me before she said "Yes"! Since I had a jeep, I would visit her at night outside the inner compound where her Vietnamese contemporaries stayed. It was in that jeep that we made plans. We hardly knew each other, and we both knew if this marriage was to happen, we would have to move quickly.

My future wife Nga (now Paula) busy at work in Command Aircraft Company, Long Thanh, Vietnam

Wife cost me a bottle of Johnny Walker Red

I spent time in Saigon with Nga's family when I could and was accepted by all. To get our marriage license, we filled out lots of paperwork through military channels as well as the Vietnamese government. ARMY CID agents visited Nga's neighbors to investigate her. Along with her sister-in-law, we took our paperwork to a Vietnamese office in Saigon for processing. Seems everyone was on the take, a bribe was necessary to move things along quickly, especially since we had limited time. We entered a large office with many desks. Nga's sister-in-law knew the process and asked I bring a bottle of Johnny Walker Red scotch whiskey. When we began our interview, she handed the bottle in a brown paper bag to the gentleman who would do our paperwork. All conversations were in Vietnamese. He took the bag and placed it in the lower left drawer of his desk. I noticed him discreetly open the bag and peer at its contents. Weeks later, we were notified our paperwork was ready for pickup. When we arrived this time, same routine, paper bag, again placed in lower left desk drawer, a view of its content, then we were given our approved paperwork. This time, however, the bottle of Johnny Walker Red only contained tea! Kudos to Nga's sister-in-law!

My favorite photo of Nga (now Paula), taken at Long Thanh Vietnam DEC 70.

Del Hardiman

54th Deactivated

The 54th got orders to deactivate by end of DEC 70. I would be transferred to Phu Loi in January. Late in the year, Missions were becoming less, personnel moving out, facilities consolidated. The Officer and Enlisted clubs were joined as one with the few remaining personnel. I flew many of our aircraft to Vung Tau to be turned in. They were in poor condition, so I suspect they were not salvageable.

Looping the Otter

I made ready for an afternoon test flight of one of our remaining Otters prior to turn-in, the revetments were mostly empty, no one around, there was a high overcast sky.

As My Crew chief Junk (his real last name) and I were preparing for the flight, just the two of us, Junk said: "Well Sir, are you going to do it?" "Do What?" I asked. "Loop the Otter, you always said you'd loop one of these someday." I thought about it for a minute then told Junk to go to the rear cabin and secure his toolbox, then come sit in the right seat. Off we went. I decided the way to keep engine torque over the top of the loop would be to start out with high pitch on the propeller (low RPM) in my dive to gain initial airspeed, then gradually increase propeller pitch as the loop proceeded and I was losing airspeed over the top. It's much like shifting into lower gears on a stick shift as you climb a hill. I went high to begin, much higher than necessary to be away from prying eyes. I remember looking at the altimeter at the bottom as I began the loop, it was 4,100 feet, up we went until we were looking up in the windshield over the top to see nothing but ground, then as we completed the loop, I pulled power back to keep airspeed within limits. At the bottom of the loop, I checked the altimeter once again and it read 4,100 feet. I had performed my one and only perfect loop!

Junk was so excited, he said: "Let's do it again!" but I thought once was enough. We landed, filled out the logbook and headed from the empty flight line to the club. As we walked in (the club) there was a discussion about looping the Otter of all things! The consensus among the group of pilots was that the Otter could not be looped! Junk and I looked at each other, our eyes met, we had just looped an Otter, but we dare NOT mention it. My career would have been in jeopardy. These many years on occasion, I've looked for Junk. Do not know his first name. It would be nice for him to back me up. I am sure he's told this story many times. Maybe he's tried to find me! Like they say, if you cannot corroborate a story, makes it difficult to persuade others it happened. It did!

Nga (Paula) and me next to one of the Otters I flew.

Turn in of last 54th Otter.

Time came to turn in the final Otter, 55-3253. Along with me on the flight to Vung Tau was Specialist Six (SP/6) McCollaum and SP/4 Moulton. Busy signing over the aircraft, I was not aware that McCollaum and Moulton had ventured off base to a nearby Vietnamese vendor and had a Zippo lighter inscribed as a gift to me (non-smoker). I was pleasantly surprised to be given this memorable keepsake which I treasure to this day.

CHAPTER 9
New Assignment – Phu Loi

January 1971, I reported to my new assignment, the 74th Reconnaissance Aircraft Company (RAC) at Phu Loi which had 0-1 Bird Dogs. This meant I would not be seeing Nga which left me melancholy. I was missing her deeply. My new assignment was, once again, assistant Maintenance Officer. I performed acceptance test flights and worked with the maintenance teams. We took care of Bird Dogs locally as well as 74th aircraft in outlying platoons when they came for scheduled maintenance. My new call sign was 'ALOFT ONE' which I was quite proud of. Occasionally I made mail runs to those platoons but no real missions which I longed for.

Suicide by Helicopter

Sunday afternoon, a helicopter reportedly crashed just outside the perimeter of the Phu Loi compound. Word came from within the club where I was having a late lunch, so I, along with others ventured outside to see what the commotion was about. I witnessed a line of military vehicles on the dirt road next to where I stood heading toward billowing smoke. I hitched a ride with others to check on the situation. One of those I met catching a ride was my friend CPT Murphy, who I had served with previously in the 54th Otter Company. CPT Murphy explained what he had seen. A large CH-47 Chinook helicopter lifted off the ramp tail first which was most unusual. It hovered then did a complete roll to the right to return briefly in the upright position. During the roll, CPT Murphy saw pieces of the left engine cowling fall away. The helicopter went to a right roll again but crashed inverted just outside the compound.

Now the question was who flew the Chinook and why. The aircraft had recently returned from a flight and had not been secured yet. To my knowledge the aircraft belonged to 213th Assault Support Helicopter Company known as the "Black Cats" of Phu-Loi.

A late afternoon company formation roll call was conducted; one sergeant unaccounted for. We were informed he had received a "Dear John" letter from his wife and was despondent. With his experience on the Chinook, it was determined that he was at the controls when the Chinook crashed. The aircraft was completely melted away leaving very little recognition.

Recovering Bird Dog at Loc Ninh

One day, I was called to recover one of our Bird Dogs at Loc Ninh airfield. Chief Warrant Officer O'Halloran, a friend, while making a steep left circling overhead 270-degree approach to final, crashed head on through the windshield of a Vietnamese two and half ton Army truck, killing both occupants. The 270 overhead was a means of getting down quickly presenting the least exposure to small arms fire. On this occasion, as O'Halloran, leveling out of the turn to final, left wing down blocking his view of the airfield, encountered the truck which had diverted unseen onto the runway. O'Holloran had two black eyes giving him an owl look but other than that he was bruised but ok. Since there was constant vehicle traffic next to the runway, the dirt was an orange powder. Our maintenance team rigged the Bird Dog for a Huey lift back to Phu Loi. During pickup, I crouched on top of the Bird Dog above the pilot seat holding the recovery straps to hook up with the Huey. In addition to the noise and rotor wash, there was so much dust I had only a few feet visibility, dust blowing in my eyes, clothing coated with the same. The Huey Crew Chief was hanging out almost upside down directing the Huey pilot who also had very little visibility in that dust. I can still see the crew chief only a few feet above me watching and giving the pilot directions. After a successful hook up, I got down and away; moments later, the Huey lifted the Bird Dog and departed back to Phu Loi. We got the job done!

During my few months at Phu Loi, Nga came once to visit. She and her 15-year-old sister Nhut had ridden two hours by bus to come see me. I signed her in at the security gate. It was Sunday and I was ecstatic seeing her! Nhut waited hours at the gate for Nga's return. Around this time, I asked for a one-year extension in Vietnam but only six months were approved.

Transfer to Cu Chi

I discovered the 74th had a hostile mission to which only 'Volunteers' were assigned. I was approved for transfer to The 3rd Platoon,74th Aviation Company Cu Chi to get back in the War Fight. New Call sign 'ALOFT 55'. That mission which I elaborated on previously was at Quan Loi in support of Special Forces Command and Control South (CCS).

At Cu Chi, assigned to the CCS mission, I had somewhat autonomy, my comings and goings were not tracked as was the case with other Aviators. I typically departed Cu Chi for the flight to Quan Loi where I flew in support doing Hi-Low missions, Loi Ho Vietnamese Special Forces insertions, standoff aerial support of those inserted and surveillance. All operations culminated over Cambodia. At times I would remain at Quan Loi for days, other times I returned to Cu Chi by nightfall. Soon I realized I had an option of returning to Cu Chi, get a fresh flight suit and head to Saigon to spend the night with Nga and her family when she was in Saigon. You ask, how was this permitted? I told my Platoon leader, CPT Harris what I wanted to do, his reply was "If you get caught, I know nothing about it." Soon my modus operandi found me routinely leaving Cu Chi at night in my Bird Dog enroute to Thanh San Nhut airport, Saigon. USAF ground support personnel were most accommodating, they hid my Bird Dog in an F4 fighter revetment behind an F4. I had a fake pass to get off Thanh San Nhut, grab a taxi and spend the night in Saigon. Early each morning I departed Thanh San Nhut heading back to Quan Loi. I called headquarters at Phu Loi to open my flight but told them I was departing Cu Chi when actually I was departing Thanh San Nhut. The Vietnamese controllers at Thanh San Nhut liked for me to make short takeoffs on the taxiway, they would say "ALOFT 55, you are cleared for short takeoff, short takeoff" at which time I departed from the taxiway, leveled off at 50 feet and headed north to Quan Loi. I flew over rice paddies, low enough to dip into the water with my tires, lift over the dikes then low again. All this was risky, but I was never discovered, at least no one reported me.

Close Call

with Vietnamese C-119 cargo aircraft

Typically, on these night trips to Saigon I followed the highway from Cu Chi to Saigon, always on the 'right' side of the highway at 1500 feet, all lights off to avoid small arms fire. One night, for some reason, I flew down the 'left' side of the highway. Suddenly, an aircraft passed me on the 'right' side of the highway, same altitude, lights flashing! Had I been on the 'right side, they would have flown right into me. I quickly turned on all my lights and kept that aircraft in sight as it entered south traffic to Thanh San Nhut. When I arrived, landing on the north traffic, I observed the aircraft of my 'Near Miss', already landed, taxiing on the other side. It was a large Vietnamese C-119 cargo aircraft. Fate took care of me that night.

Discretely visiting Nga

A few times, I flew back to Long Thanh where Nga worked, tied my Bird Dog down in a revetment and spent the night in the Vietnamese manned airfield fire department where they provided me a bunk. All this to spend a few minutes with Nga. Again, no one was the wiser, if they were, I was never reported.

On leave to Hong Kong

I took my one-week authorized leave in Hong Kong where I was given strict guidance from Nga on buying a diamond, what to look for to avoid flaws. This was a big deal for Asians. I had my wedding suit tailored at Kennedy tailors and a new pair of handmade shoes which I observed being made.

Marriage celebration

Our marriage paperwork was completed by June 4th, 1971 but we held our celebration later on September 4th, at the Continental Hotel in Saigon. There was no wedding since Nga's Grandmother had recently passed and according to custom, our marriage could not be held during time of mourning.

All arrangements for the wedding party were taken care of by Nga's family to include a seven-layered cake and lots of food served by hotel staff. My Commander, MAJ Bacon and quite a few officers from the 74th were in attendance, all wearing their summer dress. With Nga's family and friends and my military associates, we had a wonderful evening. Nga was dressed in a blue wedding gown; I in my newly tailored Hong Kong suit and brown dress shoes.

Some interesting events prior to the celebration. I flew into Thanh San Nhut (Saigon), changed into my new suit and shoes and caught a civilian jeep taxi heading for the Continental Hotel. We encountered such a downpour that water rose over the jeep hood and killed the engine. In short time, with no more rain, I rolled my pants up over my knees, shoes and socks in hand walked/waded two more blocks to the hotel.

Nga's brother Phuong was supposed to bring his band for entertainment, but they never showed up. Where were they? Strange. As it happened, they were all apprehended on the Saigon streets and forced into the Vietnamese Army that very evening! How tragic.

Paula and my, wedding reception Sep 4, 1971, Continental Hotel, Saigon, wearing suit I had made in Hong Kong by Kennedy Tailors.

Paula and I departed Vietnam from Tan San Nhut airport, Saigon, February 1972 along with our baby son Michael. Family members accompanied us in Paula's Uncle's small Mitsubishi truck. I was of the opinion my wife and son might never see her parents, brothers, and sister again. This brought tears to my eyes for the sacrifice she was making.

CHAPTER 10
Assignment Berlin

Paula, little Michael and I arrived in West Berlin on a four-year tour, September 1972. I had just completed the Rotary Wing Qualification Course at Fort Rucker, Alabama and the Aircraft Maintenance Officer Course at Fort Eustice, Virginia. Paula was busy as well; she had achieved her GED and U.S. Citizenship. Not bad for a short stay of six months in the States between tours. We were given living quarters in the U.S. Duppel housing area, a consortium of modern multistoried apartments in which 'everything' was provided. Our fifth floor, elevator accessed, three-bedroom apartment came with furnishings, complete kitchen with dishes and utensils. What a pleasant experience, coming from our worldly possessions loaded in back of our new 72' Ford LTD station wagon to a completely furnished apartment!

Berlin, only a few years prior was a city of rubble and recovery, some 110 miles behind the Iron Curtain. Post WWII it was divided up by the conquerors, Russia, Great Britain, and the United States. The British gave a portion of their sector to the French, resulting in fours sectors. The Russians (Soviets) had the eastern sector, East Berlin; British, American and French, West Berlin. My assignment was at Tempelhof Airport, hangar 3, home of the U.S. ARMY Aviation Detachment, Berlin Brigade. Tempelhof was under the command of the U.S. Air Force. At the time it was commanded by COL Gail Halverson, renowned as the 'Candy Bomber' who, as a young lieutenant dropped parcels of candy by small parachutes to anxious children when on final at Tempelhof during the Berlin Airlift of 1948-1949. The airlift

"Operation VITTLES" was a counter to the Berlin Blockade in which the Soviets cut off food and supplies to West Berlin in an attempt to gain control of the entire city. In time, other crews took up the candy drops culminating with more than 21 tons of candy in 250,000 small parachutes. Ref-5 Tempelhof, which no longer exists, was one of the "oldest" airfields in Europe. The Wright Brothers made a 15-minute demonstration flight there in 1908 viewed by some 250,000 spectators. At the time of my assignment, the hangar/terminal complex, was designed by Albert Speer, Hitler's architect, and armaments minister, to resemble an eagle but never completed. It was one of the largest buildings in the world, the hangar roof was approximately a half mile long, British and Pan Am airliners parked under the large overhang.

When I reported in, the Flight Detachment, assigned to the Berlin Brigade, had two DeHavilland U6A Beavers for clandestine surveillance of Soviet and East German facilities, three UH-1 (Huey) Helicopters and a twin-engine Beechcraft U8D. The UH-1s by prior treaty agreement were restricted to flights within the confines of the walled in western sector. At one time, I was told, Americans were flying helicopters down the streets of East Berlin while the Soviets were making low jet passes over West Berlin. The agreement stopped both activities. The U8D was the Brigade's connection to West Germany and beyond. In a short time I was checked out in all three types.

The U8D, by today's standards was minimally equipped for flights in icing conditions. It had inflatable deicing rubber boots on the wing leading edges and no electric windshield heat. My first encounter with these conditions was a flight coming back to Berlin from West Germany with Dave Hunt. In the clouds, sitting in the right cockpit seat I observed rime ice building up on the leading edges of the wings, soon the windshield was covered with ice. To a novice of flying in these conditions, I was a little concerned. I looked over at Dave and he seemed unconcerned. I thought if he is ok with this, I am trusting him. I learned you had to wait for the rime ice to build up before inflating the deicer boots. Too soon will allow a pocket to build up which would disrupt airflow over the wing, too late, the boots would not handle the ice. So, one had to learn to judge when to inflate the boots. We had heated air blowing internally on the windshields, but it would only melt a shallow hole in the ice at the lower part of each windshield. I learned we were ok and would land many times peeping through those narrow holes! Later, as aircraft commander, I enjoyed getting into these conditions with a new pilot. You could feel him squirming in the seat waiting on me to inflate the boots.

German winter flying in those days were challenging. On my second tour in West Germany, a friend reported a civilian aircraft one morning telling the German air traffic controllers in a calm voice he was icing up badly, eventually crashing, killing all on board.

Our U8D was replaced by a Beechcraft U8F with larger cabin, it did, however, have the same deicing package as the U8D. Later we traded up to a Beechcraft U21A, twin turbine which had electric windshield anti-icing. As mentioned, my tour in Berlin was four years (72-76). My remaining 18 months we received two U.S. Air Force 02s, same that had flown cover for me in Vietnam. The 02s, painted ARMY green, were Cessna 337s with twin piston powered engines, one on the nose and one behind the cabin. The 02s were intended to replace the U6s at some point. I was one of the first and very few qualified in the 02. The two Berlin U6s were the last in ARMY inventory, the last Fixed Wing aircraft with tail wheels.

Paula and Michael, spring 1973, in front of the then unoccupied Reichstag Building, currently   the seat of the German government.

Berlin – City of Spies

Many interesting times were had while assigned to Berlin, 'City of Spies'. I took German classes at night and even a course on Russian history. The city was a virtual museum of triumph and failure. In the UH-1's we flew the zigzag Berlin wall 365 days a year, The wall was some 102 miles in length, of which 64% was concrete. The remaining portion was a wire mesh type structure. Behind the wall were "death" strips, an anti—vehicular ditch, a high-speed access way, high intensity mercury vapor lights, an additional death strip with guard towers augmented with dog runs, and finally a warning fence. Along the wall, were some 243 watchtowers, 136 shelters, and 260 dog runs. According to CNN, History.com, 1 million landmines were laid by the East German Democratic Republic (GDR) around West Berlin; 5000+ people escaped East Berlin by going underneath or over the wall.

Another interesting fact. There were two metro rail systems in East and West Berlin. East Berlin had an 'S' Bahn system meaning it was a surface rail, West Berlin had a 'U' Bahn system which ran underground. The east S Bahn crossed over into the west near the city east/west border, but the occupants could not get off, they merely had a view of West Berlin from the elevated rail platform. The U Bahn belonging to West Berlin penetrated under East Berlin near the border but stops blocked in the eastern sector. I viewed the S Bahn on occasion, looking up at the passengers knowing they would love being in the west. What a paradox.

We joined British and French infantry forces in war games in the large Gruenewald Forest, supporting them with UH-1s. Simulated mock attacks were part of the games. Also, aerial tours of the city to VIPs and of course reconnaissance flights over East German and Soviet facilities in the U6 a vast area of a 20-mile circle from the city center. We provided aviation support to the three Berlin Brigade infantry battalions on their maneuvers in West Germany at Grafenwoehr and Hohenfels ranges. Typically, we took temporary loan of a UH-1(Huey) helicopter from one of the US ARMY aviation facilities in West Germany for this support. Our UH-1s were not permitted to leave West Berlin by flight.

Newly appointed UH-1 Test Pilot

When I arrived, being a newly minted dual rated pilot, both rotary wing (RW) and fixed wing (FW), as a qualified maintenance officer I would be doing test flights. No problem with FW but I had a total of approximately 80 hours of RW experience on my arrival, most with an instructor. I received a local orientation check out and began building flight time in the UH-1. I had excellent guidance such as to be cognizant in event of engine failure over a populated area with few emergency landing options. Always be looking for potential sites to land. These daily flights in the Huey built up my confidence level.

To perform my first UH-1 test flight, I waited until after 5:00 PM until most everyone had left for the day except my maintenance team to go out and do the test flight, the primary purpose of which was to determine whether the airframe, power plant, accessories and other equipment were functioning in accordance with predetermined requirements. A maintenance test flight is a demanding operation. Helicopters are inherently unstable. Rotary wing flight takes finesse and exceptional hand, eye and especially foot coordination. For any input counter inputs are required. It's not too unlike learning how to walk all over again until your feet learn to make those pedal inputs automatically.

It was a tense time; I was still gaining confidence. As it turned out, we had the first newly published Test flight manual (dated March 72) for the UH-1. I had my Technical Inspector (TI) SP/6 Booth in the left seat wearing his SPH-4 helmet as was I, read the checks as I did them for the first time! Some of the checks I performed were later taken out of the test flight procedures. In several ensuing flights, I performed sideward flight, out of ground effect hovering followed with a power off hovering auto rotation, Mast bumping checks at altitude which required a quick jerk of the cyclic stick forward then return to neutral looking for the bump to dampen out in four or five cycles. This was done in the forward right and forward left quadrants. Never felt comfortable doing those. This check was later eliminated due to suspicions of possible cause of some fatal test flight accidents. As a FW pilot, airspeed is your friend. One of the checks in the UH-1 was to, at altitude, slowly reduce airspeed to zero. Sitting up there watching airspeed bleed off to zero was quite, I can say now, unnerving, especially when you look down between the pedals 2000 feet below and notice you are moving slowly backwards over the terrain due to a head wind. A little more thrill than an amusement park ride! I did run-on skid landings in the sod next to the runway by initiating a power off landing, keeping airspeed and rotor RPM up by lowering the collective with a steep descent as I approached the sod on an imaginary glide path. You need to flare the nose up at just to right point, eventually pulling full pitch in the main rotor blades getting that final lift to cushion the landing. I had done this in flight school. As you are bumping along over the sod keeping a straight path while skidding to a stop, it would not take much of a wrong correction to flip the helicopter. Another test was to come to a three-foot hover and initiate rearward flight until sensing the rotors going into translational lift, then forward cyclic to come out of it. That was a little unnerving as well. Keep in mind, I was out there on my own doing these things for the first time. My pucker factor was maxing out, the TI, with white knuckles, kept telling me, "Mr. McFarland (my predecessor) never did this." I would say, "It's in the book" as I thought to myself, "Should I be doing this", while teaching myself to be a Huey test pilot. That experience bode well for me, my confidence improved and in time the Huey became one with me. Looking back as I write, I had too much pride to ask for help from some of our helicopter instructors who never knew what I did, unless Specialist Booth spilled the beans!

Engine Topping Checks.

Engine topping checks were required after engine or certain engine components replacement. I initiated these checks from the Gruenwald forest area out of way of incoming/outgoing air traffic. This maneuver required a slow climb to altitude until N2 (high pressure turbine RPM) dropped from 6600 RPM to 6400 RPM. Although, by regulation, Berlin controlled airspace was limited to 10,000 feet, a topping check would typically take up to and above 14,000 feet. In those days there was no means for controllers to track my altitude, so I broke the regulation, please do not report me! As you climb higher and higher, the controls become sloppy, the engine quieter and quieter. So quiet you could carry on a conversation without the aid of headsets. Twilight Zone stuff! Not a comfortable feeling. Once a topping check is completed at high altitude, it takes forever to get back down. When I did these checks, I would ask another pilot to go along, anyone I could find. On one flight, Benny Graves, a former instructor pilot at Fort Rucker flight school with thousands of hours in the Huey was at the controls in the left seat. As we passed through 7,000 feet, he asked me if I would take the controls. He said, "I've never been this high before"!

Today all maintenance test pilots attend extensive schooling before being qualified. The UH-1, a real ARMY workhorse, has long since been retired.

UH-1, Tempelhof Airfield, one of three I flew. Note: Pan Am airliners in background.

Paula giving birth to Patrick

December 28th, 1973, Paula gave birth to our second son, Patrick, born in the old American hospital. Being a holiday, there were no other patients, the hospital was empty with exception of the delivery team. As we waited, little Michael, a brave young lad now three sat alone on a bench downstairs waiting during the delayed delivery. So proud of him! I had the opportunity of witnessing Paula's delivery. A nurse told me Doctor Arban, doing the delivery had previously administered to Marylin Monroe. No way of confirming this.

Dropping skydiver over Tempelhof 1974 from my UH-1 during 'Open House' for Berliners. Helga Melman, civilian photographer was so brave, she hung out of the side, held by a harness to get this photo. USAF aircraft are on display. Paula, Michael, and Patrick are down there somewhere. (photo USAF Helga Melman)

Del Hardiman

Mom's passing

I received a call from my sisters Brenda and Garnell that Mom had passed away November 11th, 1974. It was not unexpected; Mom had been in poor health these last few years. I made it home before her passing for a 30 day stay to be with her while she was in hospital. We knew I would not be able to make it back for the funeral. By prior arrangement, they called to let me know after the funeral. So sad to lose my Mom just a month after turning 29.

When Patrick was one year old, we found a babysitter, very nice Mrs. Ponder, wife of a sergeant. Paula took an administrative job with the perishable warehouse which provided perishables to the commissary as well as to the U.S. Embassy in Moscow.

In our small group of Aviators (ARMY term for pilots) we had some who were rotary wing rated only. Those that were Fixed Wing were usually qualified in both rotary and fixed wing. I was an instructor pilot in the U6-A Beaver and as such transitioned two of the rotary wing pilots to fixed-wing which greatly enhanced their careers.

Herr (Mister) Hertl

We were fortunate to have at the detachment a Link flight simulator complete with an instructor. It was affectionally called the "Blue Goose". Herr Hertl was the Link operator and instructor. While in the Luftwaffe, he was one of few to have flown the ME-262, world's first operational jet powered fighter aircraft. Herr Hertl, small, gray haired, approximately 5'7", was liked by all. With a quiet demeanor he dressed in business attire, showing up for work carrying his familiar valise. At the end of the War, he ferried some ME-262's to Bremen, Germany to be shipped back to the states, and was the first civilian to be hired by the Berlin Brigade, his employment number was #1. Herr Hertl passed away while I was at the Detachment, deeply missed, leaving only his wife, no children. He never spoke of his time in the Luftwaffe.

Support of the U.S. Military Liaison Mission (USMLM)

Mentioned earlier, the single radial engine U6 was used for clandestine missions to observe and photograph Soviet and East German military installations in the politically sensitive Berlin Control Zone. This was in support of the U.S. Military Liaison Mission (USMLM). The USMLM was a high priority operation which those of us supporting it knew little about. By post WWII agreement, Soviet, British, French, and Americans were authorized a small contingent of vehicle ground deployment of intelligence personnel in each other's territories as a good will gesture or to keep each other honest. I once saw a Soviet mission car in our PX parking lot, perfectly legal. Mission cars were referred to as "smellum" cars, a takeoff of USMLM. The American mission cars, Ford sedans with an officer, NCO and driver venturing out at night near Soviet and East German military facilities, were sometimes chased. COL Otto Chaney, my Russian History professor, who spoke fluent Russian, and author of the book "Zhukov" was a member of the USMLM. He told us of being chased in the dark down dirt roads. Their only defense was a switch which turned on their brake lights giving the illusion they were applying brakes as they accelerated. The mission was headquartered in West Berlin but often operated from a mission house in Potsdam. All country missions were active from 1945 through 1990. Tragically, Major Arthur D. Nicolson, a USMLM tour officer was shot and killed on March 23, 1985, by a Soviet Army Sergeant. He was thought to be the last American death of the Cold War, the only USMLM 'American' officer killed in the course of duty. Nicholson Hall, located at the United States Intelligence Center in Fort Huachuca, Arizona is named in his honor. Ref-6

Soviet Potsdam Mission House

The U.S. Potsdam mission house provided by the Soviets was located beyond the western outskirts of West Berlin across the border in East German territory. The Soviets had a mission house provided by the U.S. in Frankfurt, West Germany. On July 4th, 1974, as a token of appreciation, I, along with my wife Paula, Alec Sayers and his wife Susie were invited as guests to the Potsdam mission house. Our escort was Marine Major Dominik Nargele. To get to the Mission House we crossed the historic Glienicker Bridge or "Freedom" bridge where the American U-2 pilot, Francis Gary

Powers and the Soviet spy Rudolph Abel were exchanged in 1962. The East German name for it was "Einheitsbruecke" or "Unity Bridge". It had concrete barriers to be negotiated slowly to complete the crossing. The mission house had one time been the home of a high-ranking Nazi. We were greeted by an American ARMY Captain, the house mom, as he was referred to, who gave us a tour but prior to entry told us not to discuss anything of importance since the house, was "bugged" with a monitoring system. They had removed some bugs but estimated there were more than 30 remaining. The cooks provided by the Soviets were eastern spies we were told. The Captain told us a *great story*! It seems the food initially received from the Soviets was rank, barely edible, so the Americans provided their own for some time before coming up with a plan! The U.S. was providing good food to the Soviet mission house in Frankfurt, so they simply sent the raunchy Soviet food to the Frankfurt mission house and discontinued the American food. They told the Soviets they (the Soviets) were much too generous, and they wanted to share this wonderful Russian bounty with them. In no time, the food they received from the Soviets changed to good quality! After our meal, we went out onto the back lawn to talk beyond reach of the house bugs. As we spoke, we were observed by an East German gray patrol boat lying at rest nearby on Lake Wannsee. I observed personnel in the boat training their binoculars on us which told me we were monitored in and outside of the house. A great trip I will always remember.

AAAA recognition

The ARMY Association of American (AAAA) which most of us were members tracked U.S. ARMY Aviation throughout the world. It published a monthly periodical and sponsored the most sought-after Aviation units of the year award. Immensely proud that the selected 1975 American Detachment of the year in Germany was the Berlin Brigade Aviation Detachment! Ceremony of presentation, along with that of other Aviation units was held in Berchtesgaden, West Germany.

Meeting Hannah Reich and Sergei Sikorsky

Our detachment had regular AAAA events such a tour of the Schultheiss Brewery, where hundreds of German and military personnel sought refuge up to May 2, 1945, prior to surrender to the Soviets on May 3. Ref-7 We did wine tastings and dinners as well. On one occasion, our distinguished guests were Hannah Reich and Sergei Sikorsky. Hannah, a former Nazi, set more records in Aviation than can be covered in this writing. She tested many new German aircraft during WWII, compiling more than 40 altitude records both in powered and unpowered aircraft. In the final days of the War, she landed a small Fi 156 Storch in the Tier Garten near the Brandenburg gate to meet Hitler in the Fuhrer bunker. She was one of the last to see Hitler alive. I found Hannah, trim, with a pleasant smile, to be a gracious lady. Sergei was the son of Igor Sikorsky, a Russian-American, acclaimed by most as father of the helicopter and first four engine aircraft to include flying boats. The list of his aircraft designs is endless. Sergei's achievements are laudable as well. Drafted in 1943 he worked in the Coast Guard Helicopter development unit that trained helicopter pilots in rescue hoist operations, litters and pilot techniques. Ref-8 He eventually became spokesman for Sikorsky aircraft one of today's prominent helicopter manufacturers. During their introduction, little was said of their prior life's work, so it was later I realized I was with Hannah Reich that evening only a few miles from where she had met Hitler for the final time those many years before.

Sergei Sikorsky and Hannah Reich (Photo – Del Hardiman)

Kidnapping

February 27th, 1975, Peter Lorenz, head of West Berlin's Christian Democratic party was kidnapped by the 'June 2' Movement to gain release of members of the extremist organization. He was held captive for a period of six days. The city was under lockdown with cars being searched in an effort to find Mr. Lorenz, whose whereabouts were unknown, he might already be dead. The abductors were thought to be at least two men and a woman. Mr. Lorenz's was the first kidnapping of a government official by extremists in Postwar Germany. Ref-9 After days of negotiations, the Bonn government acceded to the demands of the terrorist group. Former Berlin Mayor and clergyman Heinrich Albertz gave himself up as a hostage negotiator shuttling back and forth to South Yemen to help gain the release of Mr. Lorenz. Ref-10 I had the opportunity of flying Rev Albertz in a UH-1 from Tempelhof to Tegel Airport in the French sector amid his shuttles. As I looked back at him, dressed in suit with tie, I observed this brave man's worn features having endured days of stress. At Tegel airport, I stood behind ropes as Rev. Albertz, joined by Henry Kissinger, U.S. Secretary of State, gave a statement addressing the situation then to continue his journey. Mr. Lorenz was released in good condition at midnight, March 5th in the Wilmersdorf district of West Berlin after demands had been met.

Communist Agitators

Several instances of my tour, communist agitators came from the eastern sector, perhaps several hundred with red flags waving, shouting, and demonstrating. Not much came of these, once they dispensed and traveled back to the eastern side, life was back to normal. On one occasion, I was at Tempelhof on my side of the fence when just feet away on the other side we were faced with these protestors, yelling, and seemingly attempting to tear down the fence. My recall was that sea of red flags. This was my only life experience with rioters and at the time, not knowing what the ultimate outcome would be, a little unnerving.

West Berlin Police Force

West Berlin had a well-trained police force, it was said this was more like an Army than a police force. They had the capacity of controlling most any situation, which was rare. The police were not permitted aircraft, so we flew them from time to time to check out requested locations.

Del Hardiman

Flying German civilian technicians

I had an interesting mission, flying several German civilian technicians around a prominent radio tower in a UH-1 not far from Tempelhof. As I circled tightly, they were taking readings. We did this for two days in succession. A few days later, I, along with Manfred Uding, my crew chief, who was a German in the U.S. ARMY were invited to a dinner by those we had flown at their facility. Attending were our hosts, Manfred and me. We were feted with German Eisbein and Sauerkraut. Eisbein, a German delicacy usually served in winter, consisting of a cured portion of pork upper hind leg. It was a meal I remember well. Our gracious hosts, after dinner, asked Manfred and me if we had heard of RIAS? I had not. It stands for 'Radio in the American Sector' they proudly proclaimed. The radio station of which we were helping them check their antenna had been in operation for years transmitting into Poland and other eastern bloc countries. They asked, who do you think pays for RIAS? Again, I did not know. They proudly said, "You do"! We are funded by your U.S. Congress. Afterwards we were given a tour of the facility. They proudly showed us their 'backup' transmitter which was a Nazi holdover from WWII. Painted dark green, it consisted of four trucks with trailers, aligned, each containing a portion of the radio station. The inner walls opened, connecting the four trailers, which became a single room amply fitted for use. We walked into the enclosed container observing the many aged radio devices, all seemingly in pristine condition. They told us, though it dated back to 1939, the station was fully operational.

Aerial Tours

One of my achievements most proud of is writing the aerial tour of West Berlin. There was a tour already, but it was word of mouth passed on from others. I took it upon myself to research the tour making corrections and putting it down in written form as a template for others. In all, my tour identified 74 points of interest along with commentary. The tour was such a success that dignitaries visiting the Berlin BDE would frequently ask that it be added to their visit. We often had wives on board. Passengers wore headsets as we weaved and wagged our way across town and along the border wall pointing out points of interest. The tours were about 40 minutes. Those pilots checked out for the tour spoke by rote over the intercom as they maintained controls. I had a passenger ask once at the end of a tour if that was a recording! We were that good. Additionally, I spent two days in a UH-

Dangerous Enclosures

1 with an Armed Forces Television (AFTV) cameraman on board to film these points of interest. Some of note from my presentation were:

- Brandenburg Gate built in 1791. It was through this gate in 1806 that Napoleon marched his troops following the defeat of Prussia at Jena.

- Fuehrer Bunker, where Hitler spent his remaining days. It is also the site where the Reich's Chancellery Building once stood.

- Teufelsberg "Devil's Mountain": It is estimated that at the end of World War II there were some 3 billion cubic feet of unsalvageable rubble in Berlin. Much of this rubble was carried to this location, mostly by women and children, to build the mountain. It was used by American Intelligence to construct a high-tech monitoring structure on top. Most of these personnel were fluent in Russian.

- "Victory Column", built in 1873 to commemorate the Prussian victory over the French during the Franco— Prussian war of 1870-71. The column stands 193 feet high and the figure on top is the Goddess of Victory. Embedded in the column are cannons captured from the French.

- Olympic Stadium and Mai Field. Built for the 1936 Olympic games. seating capacity for approximately 100,000 people. it was here that the black American athlete, Jesse Owens, won his four gold medals.

- Checkpoint "Charlie", the only authorized crossing point into East Berlin for allied personnel.

- Spandau Prison - The only remaining inmate was Mr. Rudolph Hess, former Deputy Fuehrer to Hitler, serving a life sentence. The prison was guarded on a monthly rotational basis by all four powers. On several occasions, I observed from above, Mr. Hess making his lonely walk around the prison inside the confines. He died August 17, 1987. The last two prisoners to be released in 1966 were Mr. Von Schirach and Mr. Albert Speer each having served twenty-year sentences. Mr. Speer was author of the bestseller "Inside the Third Reich" of which I have an autographed copy.

- <u>Tegel Airport</u>, in the French sector, was quite unique from the standpoint it was built during the Berlin Airlift of 1948-49 and it was only some 92 days from the time the first spade of dirt was turned until the first aircraft landed there. Women were instrumental in its construction. Upon completion Tegel had the longest runway of any airport in Europe in excess of 7,000 feet.

- <u>Spandau citadel</u> dates from the 16th century, but the Julius Tower itself dates from 1317 when it was a watchtower and dungeon. This moated castle was once a fortress, later a prison and in the 19th century under the Prussian kings, the treasury of the Prussian Empire.

- <u>City of Potsdam</u> (in the distance). It was here in July 1945 that the "Tripartite" Conference was held. Three powers were represented, the United States, Britain, and the Soviet Union. The U.S was represented by the late former President Harry S Truman.

CHAPTER 11
Back to the States

In spring 1976, Paula, Michael, Patrick and I headed back to the states. I would be attending the Warrant Officer Advanced Course at Fort Rucker, AL and afterwards my degree completion for a BS in Aeronautical Studies at the Embry Riddle off campus facility also at Fort Rucker. All in all, I had nine months more or less out of the ARMY system, a good reprieve. We left Fort Rucker in the fall of 77' with orders to Randolph Air Force Base, San Antonio, TX for the Fifth ARMY Flight Detachment. Paula was pregnant with our son Benjamin so her sister Mai, married to ARMY Major Bob Burke, stationed at Fort Bragg, N.C. recommended she come to Fort Bragg for the delivery which we did. I went on to TX and came back for Paula and now our three sons two weeks after little Benjamin was born.

Once again, thankfully in a flight detachment with dual rated assignment, that is, flying both fixed and rotary wing aircraft. In time I became the detachment aviation maintenance officer. We had seven aircraft, two UH-1 Hueys, three twin engine Beechcraft T-42s, two U-21s and a Beechcraft C-12A. An honor to serve 5th ARMY for three years. We primarily supported General staff and additionally, medical personnel from Brook Army Medical Center paying calls on a regular basis to ARMY installations throughout South Central U.S.

5th ARMY Flight Detachment aircraft, Randolph AFB, TX. (photo Del Hardiman)

Hijacked Cherokee

While assigned to the 5th ARMY Flight Detachment, I joined the Air Force Aero club to get my Airline Transport Pilot's license in their twin-engine Cessna 310. My instructor was a quiet spoken thin set man by the name of Roy, I no longer remember his last name. Roy told me an incredible story of which he was involved. It was of a hijacking and killing when taking a man, his wife and 12-year-old daughter on a chartered flight in a Piper Cherokee from a small airport just east of Randolph AFB, TX near San Antonio to Houston Hobby Airport. The man, his wife and daughter boarded the small Cherokee late morning and they departed for Houston on a clear day. Roy was in the front left seat, the father in the front right seat of the four-seat aircraft, wife in rear left seat and daughter in rear right seat. The flight took them along I-10 heading east. This would have been about a one-hour flight. At some point in the flight, the mother pulled out a pistol and said she was going to kill her husband and maybe all aboard. Roy pleaded with the wife, telling her he had a wife and children and didn't want to die. Her husband persuaded his wife not to shoot but wait until they landed. Roy switched his transponder to the 'Hi-Jack' mode (7500) to alert FAA flight following. Flight following asked Roy to confirm the transponder squawk and he confirmed "Yes". By sending out the transponder squawk, the others on board did not know he had alerted the FAA. The wife seemed to have calmed down. When they arrived at Hobby Airport, a non-controlled airport (no tower) at that time, Roy stated he landed and taxied up to the fuel pumps and to his chagrin, not a sole was in sight. He shut down the aircraft, the husband opened the right door and stepped out on the wing. He lent a hand to help his wife out of the aircraft and at that time she pulled out the pistol and shot her husband in the chest, killing him. Within seconds, the aircraft was surrounded with police who apprehended the wife. The police had been hiding, out of site. The incident made the local noon news. Roy was interviewed live on TV. He went on about his business, returned to the small airport and gave instructions that afternoon to a student. His boss came up to him that afternoon and said "Roy, you are on TV, why didn't you say something"! Roy said that he was in shock he guessed and just continued on. When he got home, his wife too had seen him on TV and was quite upset. That night he said he lay in bed on his back eyes wide open, unable to sleep. Sometime later he was interviewed by a magazine and given $1000.00 dollars for his story.

Airborne - Lost Communications

From June 22 through July 11, 1979, Bruce Barefoot and I were temporarily assigned to the Fort Sheridan Flight Detachment located at the Glenview Naval Air Station, Glenview, Illinois, a suburb of Chicago. The reason for our duty was to relieve some pilots of the detachment who had excessive leave accrued but with pilot shortage unable to take it. We flew numerous missions as second in command in the unit's C-12 aircraft. Following is an accounting of one such mission which proved a little challenging.

July 9th, I accompanied Craig Laing on a flight to Pittsburg, PA to remain overnight. During the night the area experienced heavy rain.

July 10th, early morning, Craig, and I pre-flighted our C-12 (78-22136) and readied our next flight which would be to Stewart Field, (SWF), NY the airfield serving West Point Military Academy. This flight would be under Instrument Flight Rules (IFR) due to the weather.

On takeoff, as we rotated to start our takeoff climb, we experienced a loud squeal in our headsets; so loud we both jerked our headsets off. We realized we would not be able to communicate with Air Traffic control (ATC) even without headsets. What to do? We set our transponder code to 7600 to let ATC know we were experiencing communication failure. 'Lost Commo' procedures was clearly defined step by step on the back of each pamphlet of approach charts one of which I held on my lap. In this case, we were to fly the original course previously assigned by ATC but at the Minimum IFR Enroute Altitude (MEA) listed. While Craig flew, I made calls 'in the blind' at each required location, hoping our transmissions were received. On and on we flew, in clouds, from one way point to the next. Now we would need to shoot an instrument approach to Stewart Field without any advisories. We initiated the approach, breaking out to see the runway and landed without incident on our 1.4-hour flight.

As we taxied onto the ramp, I noticed two gentlemen in civilian dress suits standing nearby. I deduced they were from the Federal Aviation Agency (FAA). Were we in trouble, would our licenses be in jeopardy?

When we exited the aircraft, one of the gentlemen came up to me with a smile, saying "We heard your transmissions, good job", then shook my hand. Fate had once again taken care of me, in this case us.

The Beechcraft mechanic assigned to the Airfield showed us a wet communications board in the nose compartment. The small board was horizontal in a tray with a small amount of water, no doubt from the previous night's rain. As we rotated for takeoff the water shifted, shorting out the board and our ability to communicate.

Departing Randolph AFB

Paula and I bought land and had architectural drawings for a new home not far from Randolph but under the Presidential administration at that time, interest rates soared to 20%! The house did not get built; I asked to return to Germany which we did in spring of 1980. Little did I realize this would be my last assignment flying the UH-1, a helicopter I greatly missed over the years.

CHAPTER 12

Coleman Army Airfield, Mannheim, Germany

We departed for Mannheim, Germany, as mentioned, in the spring of 1980, dropping off our beloved brown Irish Setter Rex with friends in Tallahassee, Fl. From Tallahassee, we turned in our Yellow Mercedes sedan at the Charleston, SC ocean terminal, then caught our flight from Charleston to Frankfurt, Germany. Our family of five, Michael, Patrick Benjamin, Paula, and I were to have six years on this assignment.

We moved into Benjamin Franklin Village one of several military housing villages near Mannheim-Kafertal. Michael and Patrick were enrolled in the Department of Defense (DOD) school system which was taught by mostly American civilians under contract. The schools were much the same as their American counterparts, with clubs, sports, and youth activities. Benjamin was still too young for school but next year was enrolled in kindergarten.

Paula was a stay-at-home Mom for several years then continued her professional career with Headquarters Combat Equipment Groupe Europe (CEGE) located nearby. In good weather she rode her bicycle to work. Her duties, as equipment manager, included monitoring and transferring combat equipment for US troops deployed to Germany for Return of Forces to Germany (REFORGER) exercises. CEGE sent Paula back to the States to attend Logistics training at the United States Army Logistics University, Fort Lee, VA where she was the honor graduate.

Each of the boys played on soccer teams, Michael lettered in High School Soccer and Track and Field, competing with other American schools in Europe. He exerted great effort in Cross County running.

Michael enjoyed the Boy Scouts, earning the rank of Eagle Scout. His scout troop, with adult supervision, rode bicycles one summer from Mannheim to Paris, camping along the way, no small feat! They caught the train back home, however. We took many trips with the scouts visiting the French Maginot Line erected as a defense from Germany and Michael climbing glaciers in Switzerland among others. Our whole family was involved with Michael's scouting, I drove the troop on many occasions in a military bus the ARMY let us use. Patrick was my right-hand man!

70th Transportation Battalion

On arrival at Mannheim, I processed in to the 70th Transportation Battalion at Coleman ARMY Airfield. The 70th, under previous designation, originated in Metz, France prior to its move to Coleman ARMY Airfield in 1956. It consisted of Headquarters B Company and control of two major ARMY airfields in Europe, the 207th at Heidelberg and the 56th at Coleman. I was assigned to the 56th. Eventually I became the Company Fixed Wing Maintenance Officer qualified as Pilot in Command of both U-21s and C-12s. The 56th had UH-1 and OH-58 rotary wing aircraft as well, but I flew only fixed wing. There was also a CH-47 heavy lift helicopter company and the 7th Signal Company with U-21's at our small airfield. It was a beehive of activity most days.

I enjoyed my times over the years transporting passengers throughout Europe. My call sign was 'Lord 38'. After three years or so, my son Patrick came to me crying saying I was never home. That troubled me. Usually, I departed for work before the boys were up and came home too late to have time with them. Out of concern, I asked for a transfer back to Berlin which was not approved. I was moved up to take over the position of B Company, 70th Transportation Battalion Fixed Wing Maintenance Officer for my remaining three years. In this capacity, I managed a team of German civilians and Non-Commissioned Officers (NCO's). We supported all U-21s in the European Theater. C-12 maintenance was by Beechcraft contract, but I performed test flights on the C-12's and U-21's. My hours were more regular, and I continued flying missions for the 56th. Fondly remember at times coming in on a regular day only to find I was put on a last-minute mission I had not planned for. It was a wonderful distraction.

Close encounter with Danish F-104

On a multi-day operation in a C-12 passing through Danish Airspace, I received a request from Danish Air Traffic Control. They asked it we would mind Danish fighters use us as a training target. I replied yes, since I had this done by USAF in F-4s before. We were at 12,000 feet, sky clear. Typically, you would see the fighter(s) coming at you from either your 10 o'clock or 2 o'clock position so we were peeling our eyes looking for them. While looking, I was distracted by an object to my left. Holy cow, there was a Danish F-104 neatly tucker under my left wing! The pilot had his oxygen mask pulled away and gave us the biggest smile of white teeth imaginable! Our crew chief, Specialist Geisler, quickly handed me her camera. The F-104 pilot saluted, then kicked in afterburner, making a horrendous noise and vibrating our aircraft as he pulled away, I got two camera shots of him. The crew and passengers were thrilled!

Danish F-104 begins pulling away as seen above our left engine cowling (Photo, Del Hardiman).

Photo captures the Danish F-104 as it eclipses the sun. (Photo, Del Hardiman).

Signing off logbook in Stuttgart, Germany after recent test flight on RU-21H

Fatal Accident

Saturday, September 11, 1982, I walked over to Flight Operations to file a flight plan for a test flight. The airfield was void of any activity with exception of a recently departed twin rotor CH-47 from the 295th Assault Support Helicopter Company. When I walked into Flight Operations, I observed Rena, our German dispatcher, pulling weekend duty, in a state of distress. Rena, short in stature, medium cut sandy hair, mid-thirties, was pacing back and forth behind the counter saying, "They were just here and now they're all dead"! What, I inquired? She was referring to the recently departed CH-47 I had observed earlier which had crashed, killing all on board. This was to have been a festive occasion, celebrating Mannheim's 375th anniversary. Thousands of spectators were on hand to watch hot air balloons and free-fall exhibitions. After boarding at Mannheim, the skydivers' intent was for the CH-47 to climb to 13,000 feet and set a world record of the largest connected circle of free-falling sky divers ever attempted. As thousands watched, the CH-47 reported troubles and was quickly descending to land on the nearby autobahn. At 600 feet, the two rotors meshed causing catastrophic damage resulting in the crash killing all skydivers from Germany, France, and Wales along with seven U.S. troops and five crewmembers. Witnesses reported the rear tail rotor had detached. In fact, it was later determined the forward transmission had failed causing the forward and rear rotors, no longer in synch, to mesh resulting in the aft (rear) transmission pilons and blades to separate. As a result of this accident, it was revealed procedures for cleaning the transmission oil jets were inadequate. All CH-47s with the same transmissions were grounded pending corrective actions.

In memory that fatal day, a carved stone obelisk engraved with names of those lost sits near the airfield entrance.

Meeting Peter Pan
Operation Flintlock 83

Pete Daly, crew chief Terry Lightener and I, Aircraft Commander of C-12 (22944) departed Sculthorpe, England May 16, 1983, first stop Zaragoza Spain to refuel. From Zaragoza we flew to Marrakech, Morocco in North Africa with stops at Casablanca and Rabat both in Morocco. We were part of an annual Allied *Operation Flintlock,* our passengers were Colonels, participants of the operation.

We overnighted in a plush hotel which I believe was part of the Holiday Inn chain. My attention was drawn to the many brass items in the hotel lobby.

Early next morning, around 6:00 AM, after swimming some laps, I was the sole hotel occupant at the pool. As I sat in one of the poolside recliners, under a cloudless blue-sky, I noticed a Chinese gentleman walking around the pool, dressed in dark blue business attire with a camera slung from his neck. For some reason I got the feeling he wanted to start up a conversation, which we did. He informed me he was born in China and was taught English by missionaries. He mentioned the horrors of witnessing Japanese soldiers beheading innocent Chinese civilians picked at random in the city streets. He discussed Chinese culture and sang several tunes from different regions to demonstrate the different dialects. At one point, he mentioned he was 79 years old. Well, I said, that cannot be, you look nowhere near 79. He said, "Here I can prove it, look at my driver's license". I looked and his California license which indicated he was 79 but the name on the license was PETER PAN! What gives? He told me he was an actor and had been in motion pictures for quite a few years. When it came time to give himself a screen name, he chose the name Peter Pan because he liked that character so much. He had been in the movie "How the West Was Won", "When Harry Met Sally" and was the last person in the prison cell of the final "Barney Miller" TV comedy series. He was also the Chinese hotel clerk character of a flea bag hotel Charles Bronson secluded himself in for 'Death Wish II'. He stood there and reread his lines from that scene when Bronson checked in. He pointed his finger at me, as if I was Bronson and said, "I don't want no twouble here, you hear me I don't want no twouble!" As it happened Peter Pan was on a tour of the Middle East with other senior citizens. To keep in shape, he practiced 'Tai Chi'. Later I saw him with his group of mostly Caucasians, he looked too young to be with them. He said he lived with his daughters in California and invited me to visit him if ever I was in the area. A special day to remember!

Next morning, May 18th we departed Marrakech for a non-stop flight to Stuttgart, West Germany.

Racing another Army U-21 from Shape HQ, to Coleman ARMY Airfield.

I enjoyed self-created challenges competing with unsuspecting adversaries. On two separate occasions, I manipulated catching and passing another ARMY aircraft departing ahead of me, both of us going to same location. Once I overtook an aircraft, same models, by searching altitudes for favorable winds and in time slowing passing the other aircraft to land before them. Bragging rights! My favorite was a race from Coleman ARMY Airfield, Mannheim, Germany to Supreme Headquarters Allied Powers Europe (SHAPE) near Mons, Belgium. My friend, Karl Nagy of the 7th Signal Company and me of the 56th Aviation Company, also in a U-21A, both with a crew of two pilots, departed at the same time to pick up passengers in SHAPE. We landed within minutes of each other. When I noticed Karl kept his engines running at SHAPE, I knew the race was on! He wanted to beat me back to Coleman! Karl departed ahead of me, both of us on instrument flight plans tracking the same airways. I listened as Karl made frequency changes ahead of me. I called ahead on a separate frequency to Ramstein Air Force Base requesting to proceed through their tactical controlled airspace with direct flight to Coleman which they approved. When Karl reached Nattenheim, his course took him due east toward Frankfurt. Knowing Karl could no longer pick up my calls, Frankfurt Control handed me off at Nattenheim to Ramstein which sent me to a lower altitude short cut to Coleman. As far as Karl knew, I was still behind him. I let my passengers know what I was doing to their delight! I landed at Coleman, discharged my passengers and was standing in front of my aircraft when Karl taxied by with his passengers. I made a point of looking at my watch as if to say what took you so long? He never knew what I pulled off and never asked but I had the pleasure of winning that day!

Close call

Instrument approach to Berlin

September 26,1983, after completing test flight of U-21 18080, I was enroute from Coleman ARMY Airfield to Berlin in that aircraft with a maintenance team which would be replacing a left wing on U-21 18014. Weeks before, Dick Fegreus, an instructor pilot, had landed on Tempelhof's (Berlin) runway 09L during a scheduled mission. On landing, the left landing gear of 18014 collapsed, sending the aircraft off the runway to the left in the grass damaging the wing. It took several weeks to get a replacement wing which our team would be installing. Arriving at Berlin Tempelhof Airfield, we made an Instrument approach to runway 09R. The sky was overcast with limited visibility. CPT Mike Proulx, flying the aircraft from left seat, having recently transitioned from UH-1 helicopters to U-21s with limited experience in the U-21 was following my lead. As Pilot in Command, I had tons of experience at Tempelhof, stationed there previously from 72-76. SSG Karl Grote, my good friend and senior team lead was in the passenger compartment along with the team. This approach had a Non-Directional Beacon (NDB) associated with the approach which was a letdown point on the approach. Unusual but there was another NDB a few miles west of the one just mentioned. I was overconfident since I knew this area like the back of my hand. I directed Mike to begin his descent over the farther NDB, thinking it was the outer marker (other NDB) designated for the approach. During descent, we were not flying into the glide path which one would expect. As we continued our descent, I received a tap on my shoulder from Karl who told me he saw trees close below. Instantly, I realized the situation and applied power, climbed to join the 'correct' outer marker to intercept the glide slope for a normal landing. No harm, no foul. If Karl didn't have years of aviation experience and was not too timid to speak up, we most likely would have flown into buildings ahead surely killing all on board at that speed. Like they say, "Flying is hours of boredom mixed with seconds of stark terror". This one was on me, my fault. Karl saved us that day.

Camping in Europe

Our family enjoyed summer camping trips. We toured widely…Venice, the Pisa Tower, Anne Frank's house in Amsterdam, Omaha Beach a week after the 40th anniversary of the D-Day invasion June 6, 1944, by the 1st and 29th Infantry Divisions.

To see Paris, we camped two times in Maisons-Laffitte, 20 miles north of the city. From there we caught the train to downtown Paris to enjoy Versailles, Notre Dame Cathedral, the Louvre Museum, and many other points of interest.

Family at Leaning Tower of Pisa, Italy. L/R, Paula, Michael, Benjamin, (foreground), Patrick in rear.

Del Hardiman

Meeting General Westmoreland

Once, we visited the Luxembourg American Cemetery to see General George S. Patton's burial site where, at his wishes he was buried with his men. We arrived at the cemetery late on a Sunday afternoon, there was only one car in the parking lot. While observing the many memorials prior to visiting the cemetery, I noticed a single individual walking up from the cemetery towards us. He was in civilian attire wearing a sport coat. As he neared, I recognized him; it was General W.C. Westmoreland. He had been visiting graves of some of his WWII fallen comrades which I thought was most meaningful. The General, now retired, stopped, and spoke to us for a moment or two. As I stood holding Benjamin in my arms, I told the General of meeting him once at Fort Rucker when he invited a few of us to sit at his table in the chow hall. He somehow convinced me he remembered. General Westmoreland had Commanded U.S. Forces in Vietnam and later U.S. ARMY Chief of Staff. When we returned home, I took out an encyclopedia to show the boys the man they had seen in real life.

On a side note, General Patton died of head injuries sustained in December 1945 from an automobile accident nine days earlier a few miles from Coleman ARMY Airfield where I was stationed.

Benjamin getting lost in Venice

Venice has a special memory for our family. On this occasion, we were camping south of Venice. We traveled by water taxi one morning from our campgrounds to St. Mark's Square in Venice, a favorite spot to begin our day sightseeing. Along with us was another couple, Harry Francis, his wife Kim and their two daughters ages 10 and 12. Our older two boys were about the same age as the girls. After we disembarked from the water taxi at St. Mark's Square and while making plans and arrangements of belongings, our youngest son, four and half year-old Benjamin, occupied himself chasing hundreds of pigeons nearby. When we started our tour of the city, we looked around and NO Benjamin! Long story short, we spent at least five hours alternately taking turns (all four adults) walking, walking, checking, checking. Finally at an hourly check with the police around 2:30 P.M., I was told there was a small boy being held by some tourists. Could it be Benjamin? My son Patrick (9) and I accompanied a policeman quite some distance, over canals through Venice housing (Could not believe he had gone this far). Finally, we entered a circular court and saw Benjamin! He was with a young family, father, Italian, wife, British, along with their two small children and the father's Italian mother. The gentleman who spoke English, surmised Benjamin was lost but had to chase him down to hold him. Benjamin did not want to be with strangers. To calm him, the couple gave Benjamin a coloring book and a Coca Cola while they held him. He seemed no worse for wear; I was so relieved! I was thinking the worst, that he might have been kidnapped. The Italian grandmother did not speak English; she called Benjamin "Bambino", Italian for small child. We took pictures and graciously thanked the couple! By the time of our return to our relieved group, Benjamin had a new name, "Bambino". Now in his 40's, we still sometimes call him "Bambino".

Close call

Sucked near the ground by a CH-47 cargo helicopter

Spring 1985. A few weeks prior to my trip ferrying a RU-21H from Stuttgart, Germany to Fort Hood, TX, I dropped off an RU-21H at 330th Aviation Company at Stuttgart and brought another back to Coleman ARMY Airfield to have fuel ferry tanks installed. My friend and pilot, Barry Lewis accompanied me. In most cases, I asked someone to ride along to complement the crew. Barry was not qualified in the RU-21H but operated the radios while I flew from the left seat.

As we neared Coleman Airfield, Barry asked if he might take the controls and shoot a Ground Controlled Approach (GCA) from the right seat. The visibility was good so why not? Our GCA was by a controller (German in this case) giving heading, altitude, and course corrections to bring us down the glide slope by radar. This was good for the controllers and pilots to hone their skills.

While Barry was responding to the controller, I noticed a large CH-47 helicopter not far ahead sling loading a heavy concrete block. The CH-47 was obviously on a training mission. On short final, as I watched, the CH-47 diverted to the grass sod to the left of the runway hovering to drop his heavy load. Rotor wash from a CH-47 can be catastrophic to a fixed wing aircraft and controllers are taught to keep safe separation between the two.

On short approach, we encountered a tremendous down wash pulling us uncontrollably toward the ground and the CH-47! I grabbed the controls and applied full power, from there my memory draws a blank. I remember seeing blades of grass and that's all. We gained control and circled back for landing.

Afterwards, I ran into my friend Buddy Dietz at the snack bar who had been in a UH-1 sitting at the far end of the runway with a student. Buddy had observed the whole event, he told me our R-U21H went close over the top of the CH-47 and that our wings were perpendicular to the ground as we did! I could not recall this. From this very close call, I filled out an Operational Hazard Report (OHR) in essence pointing out the airfield tower and controller's unprofessional conduct.

CHAPTER 13

Ferrying U21h's from Germany to Fort Hood Texas

As Fixed Wing (FW) Maintenance Officer in the 70th Transportation Battalion, I supported all twin turbine U-21A aircraft in the European Theater. I had a crew of German mechanics and ARMY Non-Commissioned Officers (NCO's) who were the best. We performed Field Level maintenance, tearing down, inspecting, and repairing as needed. Upon completion, I spent hours rigging the stubborn PT-6 turbine engines followed with comprehensive test flights prior to returning aircraft to owning agencies. We also supported RU-21H Special Electronic Mission aircraft (SEMA) assigned to the 330th 'Guardrail' Aviation Company stationed at Stuttgart. These were used for electronic eavesdropping and surveillance in support to the 7th ARMY, Germany. Once you saw one of these you would not forget it. Loaded with antennae protruding from wings and wing tips, they were a spectacle to behold.

In 1985 the RU-21H's were replaced by RC-12D's, a much improved, larger Beechcraft 200. The RU-21Hs, approximately 7 aircraft, were scheduled for return to Fort Hood, TX. Since, in my position, I was the only non-330th Aviator qualified in the aircraft, the 330th Commander, in coordination with my leadership, asked if I would assist in ferrying these aircraft to Fort Hood. I enthusiastically accepted.

Prior to our flights, all crewmembers took a five day 'Cold Water' survival course in Plymouth, England. My group attended the first week of April 85'. Intent of the British taught course was to make us cognizant of imminent death in the cold North Atlantic after ditching if survival skills were not

119

enacted immediately. We were reminded our hands could, in the extremes, become useless clubs after five minutes exposure. It was instilled upon us to inflate our emergency single man raft, be on board and covered from the elements without delay. The survival kit had fresh water, rations, and survival radio. Once in the raft, the British had a marvelous means of evacuating the inevitable water from the rough sea after inflation, better, I thought, than our American rafts. All buttoned up, out of the elements, hopefully someone would pick up our emergency calls.

Proof of training concept was brought to bear when we were dropped in the English Channel with survival kit, a green canvass container approximately 2'X2'X2' with a D-ring to pull and inflate the raft. It was a real confidence builder to get that exposure and go through the numbers to complete survival tasks. Recall, when first hitting the cold water, it was all I could do to keep from taking a deep breath while under water from the shock. The North Atlantic would be much colder.

Our flight of three RU-21H's ferried from Stuttgart, Germany to Fort Hood, TX was from 10-16 June 1985. These aircraft, as was all European U-21s, were recently painted by my shop with light gray CARC (Chemical Agent Resistant Coating) paint. For additional fuel, my maintenance shop installed two large metal fuel ferry tanks temporarily for each aircraft in the cabin on each side of the center aisle. I was Pilot in Command of aircraft 15886, along with a young Captain and crew chief who would be taking care of each three aircraft along the way. This was a five-day trip with overnight stops in Kinloss Scotland, Keflavik Iceland, Sondrestrom Air Base Greenland, 60 miles north of the Arctic Circle, Pease Air Force Base, NH, and then Ft. Hood, TX. In Keflavik, it was still daylight at midnight! Once we were in frigid conditions, we wore cold weather suits and over Greenland donned oxygen masks while at 14,000 feet. I did something none of the others did. Seated in the left cockpit seat, I tied a 15' green nylon strap around my waist, the other end secured to my survival kit. Figured if we had to ditch, I would open the overhead escape hatch, throw my kit into the water, and follow it out. The kit, prior to inflating would sink; with lanyard attached I could pull the kit to me. Others would manage in their own way.

While over Greenland, I happened to look down to my left and observed the tracking station we were flight following with in the snow-covered terrain.

Dangerous Enclosures

Something I had never seen before, next to the station was a four-engine turboprop C-130 cargo aircraft on skis. Suspect they were bringing supplies to the station. In Sondrestrom, we spent the night at the Artic Inn, U.S. Air Force billeting. The runway, situated deep in a fjord had been built in the 60's, my Brother-in-Law James Weatherman had a hand in the construction. I was later told by my friend Jim Murdock that he too also worked at the airfield one summer.

On the flight from Sondrestrom to Pease AFB, over the North Atlantic, we were out of range of navigation aids for about an hour, just dead reckoning, hoping we were still on course. Good feeling when we once again picked up navigation signals.

As we neared Fort Hood on a Sunday, recall listening to Dave Dudley's song, popular at the time, "Six days on the road and I'm gonna make it home tonight"; seemed apropos for our trip. Later in my career(s), I would cross the Atlantic many times non-stop in corporate jet aircraft.

Keflavik Iceland donning cold weather gear in prep for flight over the cold Atlantic to Sondrestrom
Air Base Greenland.

Meeting same man in two different countries in less than a month

May 14th, 1985, long day in U-21A (18019) taking us from Coleman ARMY Airfield, Mannheim, Germany to Biarritz, France then to Seville, Spain with final stop at Naval Air Station, Rota Spain. It was late when we put the aircraft to bed and headed for the Officer's club for dinner. We inquired at the bar about getting to town. There was a gentleman in civilian clothes, sitting on the second stool from the left who turned to us and said he was leaving for town and would give us a lift. Turned out the city was very close by. We thanked him as he dropped us off at our hotel.

Fast forward to June 12th, I'm on the second stop of the trip to ferry one of three RU-21H's from Stuttgart, Germany to Fort Hood, Texas as previously mentioned. This stop brought us to Keflavik, Iceland. I ventured into the Naval Officer's club and to my surprise, seated on the second stool from the left was the same civilian I had met in Rota less than a month before. What are the chances! I walked up, tapped him on the shoulder and said: "We gotta stop meeting like this!" He was surprised to see me as well. I learned he was a contractor checking out equipment on Naval bases. Surreal!

Genoa, Italy, Achille Lauro Hijacking

October 4th, 1985, Gil Vasquez, and I in C-12 22564 had a flight to Genoa, Italy to drop off personnel on a CH-47 Chinook recovery mission. With time on our hands, after lunch, Gil and I took the opportunity to do some sightseeing. We noted a single cruise ship in the harbor. One day earlier, an Italian cruise ship, the **Achille Lauro**, had departed from that same spot (October 3rd) to be highjacked by four Palestine Liberation Front (PLF)terrorists off the coast of Egypt October 7th. The hijacking took on worldwide attention when it was learned the terrorists had selected 69-year-old wheelchair-bound Jewish-American Leon Klinghoffer to be killed first. They threw Mr. Klinghoffer in his wheelchair overboard after shooting him. Mildred Hodges was the second selected to be killed. The hijackers were eventually taken into custody and sentenced in Italian courts. Ref-11 The hijacking left a lingering impression on me, noting I had been in the same location as the **Achille Lauro** 24 hours after its fateful departure.

CHAPTER 14
Crete – Three Unusual Circumstances in One Day

(U.S. Bombing of Libya, (2) mouth to mouth resuscitation to a stranger and (3) meeting a former WWII British POW with tales to tell)

Monday, April 14, 1986

Little did I know what would transpire on this trip to the Greek island of Crete. Fellow pilot Gil Vasquez, myself, and Julio Deleon our crew chief, departed Coleman ARMY Airfield Monday morning, April 14th, 1986, to pick up ARMY passengers at Frankfurt Rhine-Maine Air Base. Our aircraft was an ARMY C-12A, tail number 22944 a twin turbine Beechcraft. Our passengers, Colonels, from the 32nd Army Air Defense Command (ADCOM) would observe firing of U.S. ARMY Air Defense missiles off the Greek island of Crete.

Departing Frankfurt, my log shows a 3.9-hour flight on this leg. We climbed to over 20,000 feet crossing the Swiss Alps enroute to our first destination, fuel stop at Naples Capodichino International Airport, Italy. Our southern course took us off the west coast of Italy. We were in contact with German, Swiss, Italian, and Greek air traffic controllers along the way, all, in accordance with International Civilian Aviation Organization (ICAO) guidelines, spoke English. We logged 2.5 hours on our second leg to Chania, Airport, located near Souda Bay on Crete. In total, we logged seven hours for the day.

At Souda Bay, after our passengers departed, C-12 refueled and secured, we were driven to our hotel for a three-day layover. On prior trips, crews stayed at the Porto Veneziano Hotel in old city Chania but this trip we checked in to a hilltop hotel, the name I no longer recall. It was very nice with all amenities expected at that time.

Tuesday, April 15, 1986
(Three unrelated events)

This day brought three totally unexpected, non-related events. (1) U.S. Bombing of Libya, (2) mouth to mouth resuscitation to a stranger and (3) meeting a former WWII British POW with tales to tell. Each event, as it happens, took place in the hotel restaurant. What are the chances!

This morning I went to the restaurant for breakfast; I observed two wall mounted black and white screen televisions, both on different channels streaming videos of sheer pandemonium, civilians running around among what looked like bombing debris. I could not determine the circumstances since I did not speak Greek. When I paid my bill, the cashier, knowing I was American, asked me what was going on. When I told him I didn't know, he gave me a sneer and said, "Oh Sure!" He later told me at one time he lived in New York for six years. I learned President Reagan, in retaliation for an April 5th bombing in West Berlin which killed two U.S. servicemen, ordered major bombing raids against Libya, leaving 60 dead.

It dawned on me that I had witnessed LTG (retired) Vernon Walters, then an attaché, for the Reagan Administration arrive at Coleman Army Airfield Sunday morning April 13th, day before the Libyan air strikes and our departure. Walters was brought in for a short visit with Helmut Kohl, then Chancellor of W. Germany. Kohl's home was not far from Coleman Airfield. I always suspected that short drop-in by Vernon Walters to visit Helmut Kohl was to appraise him of what was about to happen.

Around 1400, (2:00 PM) same day, the 15th, I was again at the restaurant, this time for lunch. From my table not far from the breezeway to the outdoor pool, I observed individuals pass by in swimsuits headed for the pool. A gentleman caught my attention; he was tall with years on him, adorned in a long striped multi-colored robe walking proud and erect.

125

In about 15 minutes a panicky young man in swimsuit, ran into the restaurant, looked around, seeing me, who he assumed to be an American I think, gestured for me to come help. I followed; in the pool, lying face down, was the gentleman I had observed only minutes before in the multi-colored robe. People were standing around looking at him but no action, they didn't know what to do. I jumped into the pool, which was shallow at that point, got help moving him to a poolside lounge chair and immediately began mouth-to-mouth resuscitation. He vomited food into my mouth numerous times which I spat out but continued. Soon a young man was assisting by giving chest compressions. He told me he was a doctor. We both continued working on the gentleman while deciding how to get him to a hospital.

There were no emergency services, so we carried him, with assistance, in the lounge chair to a small dusty landscaper's pickup truck for a drive down the hill to the nearest hospital. The gentleman was tall, and the truck so small, his legs extended beyond the truck bed. All the time, both the doctor and I continued our emergency procedures.

At the hospital, the last I saw of the gentleman was when a technician began using a defibrillator on him.

When I returned to my hotel, I inquired about this gentleman, who was he? I learned he was Norwegian in his 80's on holidays with his widow's two elderly sisters. After learning of his passing, possibly by heart attack, I went to the sisters' room to apologize for not being able to save him. One of the sisters told me their brother-in-law was always looking out for them. They thanked me for giving them the details. So sad for their loss.

That evening, Gil, Julio, and I were seated at the restaurant for a late dinner. We chatted with a couple seated next to us, a chat which lasted hours. We enjoyed each other's company. The gentleman was a former British soldier taken prisoner by the Germans at the very spot we sat! After the war (WWII) he relocated to the States and at the time, he and his wife lived on a farm in New Hampshire, next to Senator Warren Rudman's farm. He was a retired furniture designer and had renovated a horse barn into seven guest rooms which he was quite proud of. We were told this was each's second marriage. He and his wife had both lost their previous spouses. She had been married to a U.S. diplomat stationed in Greece years before and of course he was taken prisoner here. She had lived in Greece with her husband so they both had a Greece connection. The gentleman was devastated that this hotel was now on what he felt was hallowed ground. When I mentioned the famed highly decorated British fighter pilot Douglas Bader who had 22 aerial victories, doing so with prosthetic legs, not to mention his escapades as a German POW; he was amazed I knew of Bader.

By the time we broke away it was 2:00 AM in the now empty restaurant. Before I leave this subject, I was enthralled to be told by the gentleman that, as a POW, he spent time in the same prison camp of which the famed movie THE GREAT EXCAPE was based on. In the movie, tunnels named Tom, Dick, and Harry were tediously dug in secrecy by POWs to establish an escape route. He told us much about prison life, He said it was not too difficult to go from prison to prison. You swapped places with someone from one of the other prisons and answered by his name at roll call. That way you could visit friends. What a fabulous evening! A wonderful couple. They invited us up to go skiing if we were ever in the area.

CHAPTER 15
Departing Germany – Second Tour

Time to pack up and return to the States. Patrick and I, along with our Dalmatian Dog 'Lady', departed from Frankfurt enroute to Fort Belvoir Virginia on 12 JUN 1986; Paula, Michael and Benjamin, Saturday the 14th. Our original scheduled departure was Friday the 13th for the entire family but... even though I say I'm not superstitious, why chance a Friday the 13th airplane ride!

Looking back, I had some great experiences and some not so great in the previous six years. Certainly, I enjoyed the support of many, in addition to my commanders were my extremely dedicated maintenance team over those years. We worked like a well-oiled machine. In particular, my deep gratitude to SFC Karl Grote Non-Commissioned Officer in Charge (NCOIC) replaced by SGT Michael Kelley as NCOIC, both excellent maintenance managers who kept things on schedule. Also the team consisted of, SGT Malabed, SSG Gregg and the German maintenance support staff: Messrs. Gepperth, Local National Supervisor who never saw a problem he couldn't solve, Angerman, Weiser, Marjanovic, Heaschmidt, Debese, Boutin and Pflaum. These men could strip an aircraft down to bare bones or disassemble if necessary. There was usually a couple to accompany me for sometimes hours of engine rigging in the runup area and on my many test flights.

PART II

The Early Years – two near death experiences

CHAPTER 16
Reflections of My Childhood

As I sit in my comfortable office in our spacious three-story house of some 5500 square feet, situated on six acres of forest and beautiful lawn with affluent neighbors of doctorate degrees, retired general officers, politicians, and professionals, I look at my many plaques, photos and mementoes on the walls which reflect on many of my life's stories. There is also a large room in the basement with walls covered with more the same. Why do I keep these? They are to remind me that a 'Devine Hand' was always there, intervening, helping me along the way. My wife Paula and I, married 50+ years, planned well, you might call us frugal which left us in a comfortable position.

It wasn't always that way. My younger years were in perpetual poverty. My father, an abusive alcoholic husband, I was told, left my Mom with three children, never to be seen again. I was so young at the time; I have no memory of him, but my two older sisters Garnell and Brenda did. Aunt Pauline, my father's sister and her husband came to visit my mother from time to time.

My Dear Mother was left to do the best she could. She took in sewing, baked over 20 pies each weekend for her sister's husband's restaurant, raised a garden each year and canned fruits and vegetables for winter. I had no idea at the time, we were receiving a pittance of welfare money to help, I believe it to be $35.00 per month.

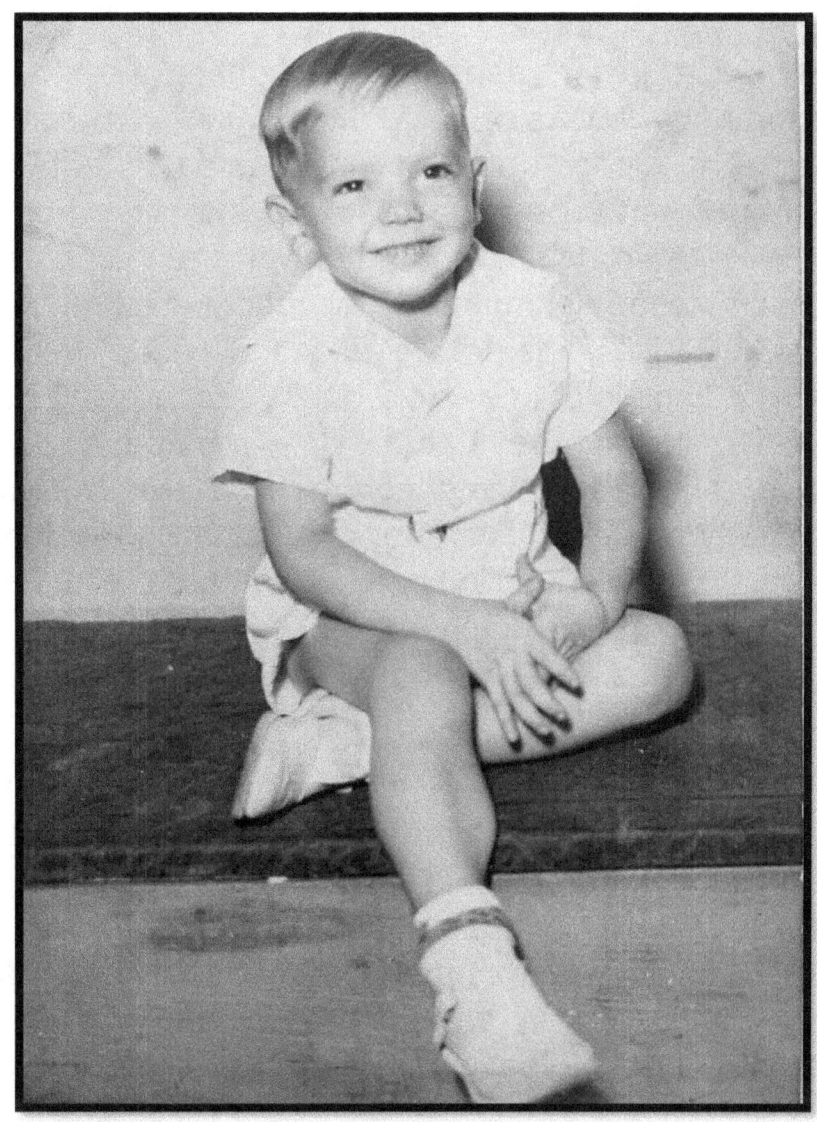

Age 3

The home we lived in was a rental with absolutely no insulation. If you opened the one and only closet door in our house in Mom's bedroom and peered up, you would see shingle tiles covering the roof frames, no insulation. The house had no underpinning so in winter a strong breeze would raise the linoleum rug in the living room with cool air chasing away the warmth. We stuffed folded newspapers in the windows and doors to keep the 'cold' out. To save heating, Mom let our coal burning stove in the small living room burn out after she tucked me in for the night. One night I screamed for her when I felt a mouse under my covers. She came and dispatched the mouse. In the morning, after lighting the stove, she would come get me from under layers of quilts after which I rushed to the warmth of the living room. The kitchen door was closed to save heat. We turned the water off at night from an outside valve to prevent pipes from freezing. At night, we poured water in pots, placed them on the kitchen table to have water in the morning when getting ready for school. Next morning, we used an ice pick to break the ice in the pots to get to the water. There was no toilet or bathroom, no automobile or television, only a secondhand radio. My early baths as a child were in a number 10 tub. When you needed to 'go' you went to the Out House, a small wooden shed which covered a large hole in the ground to catch body waste. Toilet paper was usually newspapers or pages from catalogues, I was always afraid in the night that I would be bitten by a snake as I sat there. From our kitchen window, in summer, you could see one of several cotton fields owned by Mr. Alton Watt and his brother Joe, two senior citizen bachelors.

Alton owned the house we rented which was situated on a short dirt road. He was highly educated, still attending night courses, in his 60's. I enjoyed sitting on the front steps of the dilapidated home he and his brother shared, helping me with my math. They had another brother, Neri, who was Georgia Secretary of Agriculture. I was told they owned quantities of property in an adjacent county. I was scrawny and thin, remember a neighbor talking to Mom of her concern about my being so skinny.

Interesting story: One of the Watt's two large mules which Joe used for plowing, ran away; Alton elicited me and my kid neighbor, Kenneth Bass, several years my senior, to accompany him in his old Studebaker pickup truck to help search for the missing mule. During the search, at one point on a slight bluff near a bridge, we got out and what did we see; below on a railroad track coming towards us from our right, was the mule running down the center of the track, ears pinned down, looking like a thoroughbred; close behind was a locomotive with cars trailing! The mule soon leapt to the left off the tracks but continued its pace as the train slowly passed it, both disappearing under the bridge!

Dangerous Enclosures

Later that afternoon Alton discovered in the afternoon newspaper a mule was at the downtown fire department for the owner to claim. Must be his! Kenneth, and I went with Alton to the fire department to fetch the mule. The two of us were to lead the mule home on a harness. Alton demonstrated to us that the mule would not step over a curb so to get it on the sidewalk we would need to lead the mule from the street to a driveway entrance. We led the tall mule for an hour of so back home. It was an exciting day for two young boys!

I sometimes snuck into the barn where the two mules were in their stalls. It was so serene to be with those beautiful animals and silently commune with them.

Spring, 1971, while on 30 days leave from Vietnam, I took this picture of Mr. Bert Bass, Kenneth's father, with his mule plowing. Retired from almost 40 years working for the city, one of his enjoyments was plowing as he did in his youth. Near left (not seen) is the house with the metal roof (mentioned below). Across from it (not seen) is the house I grew up in. The visible house is the Parlier family; the dirt road I mentioned runs in front of the house.

Our house, one of three on the road, was an upgrade from the one we originally lived in across the road. We moved to that house when I was three coming from an apartment. Our meager furnishings were carried in the back of a large truck with steel lining, most likely a coal truck, which we stood in on the short trip. After our belongings were taken into the house, I proceeded to get back on the truck when Mom told me "This is our home now". The house had a metal roof. One night during a hailstorm, it was so loud and frightening, Mom cradled me and my two sisters in her arms in the front room on the couch and prayed out loud for God to spare us.

We had an ice box on the back screen porch to which large blocks of ice were delivered. That was prior to having a refrigerator. The iceman came in from the rear whether anyone was home or not to drop off ice. On the front porch, we had a four cornered colored cardboard, 8 inches square, which had a flexible wooden fan handle cradled in an empty milk bottle. Whichever size block ice was requested, 25, 50, 75 pounds was positioned at the apex of the cardboard to let the iceman know what was requested. Milk was delivered to the front porch in quart sized bottles. There was a garden in back (most houses had gardens) which Mom planted vegetables, pumpkin, and watermelon.

Mrs. Aiken, a widowed neighbor, led her black milk cow daily from its barn, located behind our house, to a pasture nearby. She drove a heavy metal spike in the ground which the cow was tethered to as it spent the day grazing. At noon Mrs. Aiken would bring her cow a pail of fresh water, then take her cow back to its barn in the late afternoon. I anxiously looked forward each day observing this ritual.

Our neighborhood had lots of children to play with, many of WWII veterans; we also had several WWI veterans who readily accepted kids. It was not uncommon to walk right into any house in the neighborhood unannounced. Doors were never locked. There was a retired couple, Mr. and Mrs. Summers, living not far away who always graciously welcomed me, usually rewarding me with homemade cookies.

On one occasion, I ventured into their barn; I enjoyed hiding in the barn to be near their cow. Unexpectedly I heard Mrs. Summers coming to milk her cow, I scrambled to the barn loft and hid. Mrs. Summers did not see me as I peered secretly between cracks from my perch observing her as she gently spoke to her cow as she milked.

Being post WWII children, our parents had endured the 'Great Depression'. In school, beginning first grade in 1952, all were equals, no one knew of our circumstances. I had classmates not much better off than me but others whose father made good wages, with 'stay -at - home' moms who showed up at school regularly to help with class events. My lunch through the 3rd grade consisted of two banana sandwiches, no mayonnaise, just bananas between two slices of bread every day. At some point, the school intervened and started giving me free lunches. I don't think my classmates were aware I was getting these free lunches. Those meals were warm and nutritious.

My teachers were wonderful role models. Each showed an interest in me. Why? What were they seeing in me? Did they show the same to others? As I progressed through elementary school, wearing shirts made by my Mom, I learned school was my sanctuary. I often arrived early from the three mile walk and ventured down to the boiler room where I sat and talked to Garvin, our school janitor.

Mrs. Lucy Dowell, my third-grade teacher, in her 60's, taught us cursive handwriting. She and her husband had no children. Through the years into my adulthood, she and I corresponded. I always stopped, along with my family, to see her and her husband each time I came back home. I visited her in a nursing home not long before she passed away in January 2002 at the age of 99, ten months prior to her 100th birthday which would have been October 2nd. Her husband passed at 102, still with a current driver's license a year or two before her. After her passing, her grandniece, who lived in northern Virginia, brought me the lamp Mrs. Dowell wanted me to have which she read by for decades. I have a snake plant (Dracaena trifasciata) she gave me some forty years ago, still doing well. Each time I sign my name, I think of her, she was the one who taught me.

My wonderful third grade schoolteacher, Lucy Dowell and husband on one of our visits with them.

In time I had been selected by my teachers on at least four occasions to have my picture taken by Mr. Fry, photographer and columnist from our hometown newspaper, The Record and Landmark. In one fifth grade class photo, I stand, smiling at the camera next to a four-foot-wide plastic replica of the U.S. Capitol building with a photo of President Eisenhower mid frame on the wall. How had I been selected? I was promoted to Captain of our school Safety patrol. Why was I selected? Coming from such poor beginnings, these small steps of recognition gave me footing for pride in accomplishments and that there was more to life than from whence I came. I owe so much to my teachers!

Fifth grade photo in Record and Landmark local newspaper. Shirt made by Mom. (photo by Fry)

My school principal at N.B. Mills elementary, Mrs. Annabelle Boyd who also taught my afternoon fourth grade class, gave me a brand-new bicycle! It was a straw color with light blue trim lines on the fenders. What a surprise! Why did she give it to me? As far as I knew, I was the only one she had given a bicycle to. I was bursting with joy! I'm sure the teachers were aware but don't believe my fellow students knew it was Mrs. Boyd who gave me the bicycle.

When I arrived home with the brand-new bicycle, my Mom was sure I had stolen it and insisted I take it back. It took some time to convince her it was a gift from Mrs. Boyd.

In another photo, I am seen wearing my Safety Patrol harness, standing by my bicycle with other students looking at me with the inscription, "Delbert Hardiman center, gives students a lesson in bicycle safety measures".

That bicycle opened doors for me, I had the opportunity to use it on my first of two newspaper routes.

Being poor had its challenges, one needs work of some type to bring in money. In my younger years, I washed dishes on weekends at my Mom's brother-in-law's restaurant, shined shoes on Saturdays for a short time at a local shoe shop. All in all, I kept my circumstances private. When given a ride home one night from an elementary school event by the parents of a fellow student, I had them let me out at a house a few blocks from home, then walked the rest of the way. Didn't want them to see where I lived.

Lest I forget my first love, Eloise Helms who arrived for 5th and 6th grades; her mother was a teacher at our school. It was purely puppy love, but I was smitten. Unknown by us at the time, our teachers were aware of our affection for each other. I was so shy, rarely had the courage to speak to her. We exchanged gifts for Christmas, to her a box of chocolate covered cherries, to me a plastic model of a Navy battleship. On a school field trip to Raleigh, our state capitol, Eloise, and I were on two separate buses; eventually the buses were stopped, and the teachers put us on the same bus seated together because I was so hurt not being near her. Eloise and I are together in two of the aforementioned newspaper photos. Our only date was at the State

Theater to see the 1956 movie *Anastasia* starring Ingrid Bergman and Yul Brynner; Eloise was accompanied by our dear friend Gayle Poole. I sat in the row directly behind them!

In middle school, Eloise and I went to separate schools, and I was out of the picture. We graduated from the same high school and though my breath was taken away each time I saw her, I never took the opportunity to get reacquainted.

After all these years, Eloise is a grandmother, happily married as am I. We have corresponded these past many years on each of our birthdays, reminiscing of those puppy love days. We are both still in touch with our dear friend Gayle Poole.

CHAPTER 17
Testifying in Court as a seventh Grader

In Junior high school as it was called then, grades seven through nine, I experienced an interesting event. As a seventh grader, while classes were out for morning recess, I noticed a man come through a gate from the adjoining street. He was thin, poorly dressed, maybe 30 years old; he wandered over to the student bicycle parking lot and inquired about the bicycles. By this time, I had a larger 'used' black Schwinn bike I used on my afternoon newspaper route and became suspicious of his intentions. When the bell rang to go back to class, I hid to observe him in the brick walled two story staircase which had large openings. With students back in class, he got on one of the bicycles, lit his pipe, and rode away out the gate. I went to Mr. Donnelly's office, our principal, to report the theft. The police were notified and in no time, he was tracked down and caught.

Hard to believe, I was asked to go to trial to point out the man who stole the bicycle. I was only a child but rode my bicycle to show up alone at the county courthouse. Judge Fred Hedrick, who was blind, asked a few questions of me to determine my competence; after which I pointed out to the prosecutor the man who had taken the bicycle. He was sentenced to one year in prison due to prior convictions.

Side note: Years later, while driving home on highway 21, from my job with the N.C. Air National Guard in Charlotte, I noticed a man on the side of the two-lane road with his thumb held out, 'hitch hiking' to catch a ride. I recognized the man right away as the one I had testified against back in the seventh grade. I stopped and gave him a ride. We held small talk as I drove; he had no idea who I was. I wondered what he would have thought if he knew he was sitting beside that boy responsible for him going to prison.

High School Band

In the summer prior to eighth grade at D. Matt Thompson Junior High, I attended summer Band classes at our Senior High School; Mr. Bryant, an older gentleman, was the director. I had been given a 'used' clarinet by my cousin Alton McCollum, a young high school band director in another town. My progress was impressive to Mr. Bryant, who recognized several of us with gifts of small packets of candy and invited me to join the senior high marching band. Next fall, as an eighth grader, I was in the Senior High marching band playing 3rd clarinet. My neighbor, Johnny Krider, a student there, gave me early morning rides in his 49' blue Ford convertible to practices held in the football field under Mr. Bryant's supervision. After practice, I caught a bus back to Junior High. I enjoyed the band tremendously but to Mr. Bryant's disappointment, I eventually let my clarinet playing drop. I was not willing to put in the time at home practicing, practicing. Mr. Bryant was one of my paper route customers and I thought the world of him.

Junior High School Football

I played Junior High football but without a father figure for encouragement as many others had, I did not excel. My Mom was able to buy me a pair of football shoes, but I soon outgrew them. There was no money to buy larger shoes.

CHAPTER 18
Early Exposure to Aviation

The reader, no doubt contemplates my early days in Aviation but for now would like to inject my first experience with flight as a 12-year-old. It would be some years later at age 15 in which I was imbued with excitement of airplanes and events which forever changed my life.

My first visit to our small city airport was with my neighbor Johnny Krider who had me sit sidebar on his bicycle as he pedaled the two of us on a summer day some four miles from home to the airport. That was my first time seeing an airplane. Later, another neighbor, Danny Lippard and I raked leaves to earn the two dollars for a ride in a small yellow, tandem seat Piper Cub. Small as we were, Jim Matthews, the local aircraft mechanic at the time, placed us both in the rear seat, tucked under one safety belt. Jim, in the front seat, hinged the door open to the right-wing latch with the left window also open. There was no activity at the airport other than us. Looking out at the ground almost close enough to touch I was mystified as we began our takeoff, wheels rolling faster, the ground moving ever faster beneath us, then liftoff as we left earth for my first time. Wind in our faces, trees getting smaller; the 65 horsepower Continental engine noise muted our conversation other than a shrill of exhilaration. My heart pounded as we soared higher. The aircraft did not feel sturdy as it bounced gently in the wind. I could see farther than ever before in my young life, miles of space out under those yellow wings. Jim controlled the aircraft with a stick between his legs, making turns, showing us points of interest. On our return, descending for landing, trees getting larger, the blacktop runway reaching up to us as we gracefully touched down once again, wheels rolling. I was smitten, I had ventured into the beyond, experiencing flight for the first time!

Afternoon Paper route

Eighth grade saw me with a large paper route. I traded in my used Schwinn bicycle for a new red Jaguar Mark II which I purchased for $100.00 on a payment plan from Riddle's Bicycle and Hobby Shop. I customized my new bike by changing out the standard handlebars for long 'steer horn' bars; along with that I put an oversized metal meshed basket in front over the wheel. Additionally, I had two canvass bags one on each side of the rear wheel. This arrangement was typical for most paperboys.

Being a paperboy was opportune as I developed skills in management and teamwork. After school, I reported to the downtown newspaper rear loading and dispatch facility where papers by the hundreds were coming off the noisy press, busily collected and identified in batches by young Bobby Wilhelm, a newspaper employee. The smell of freshly inked paper was in the air. Like clockwork, identified stacks of newspapers were placed on long tables to be rolled. Rural adult deliverymen were the first to get the papers while paperboys assisted them rolling their papers. It was a beehive of activity, well-orchestrated with the sound of the press in the background, we developed quite a skill in taking a stack of papers, tightly rolling them wrapped with a rubber band; like a machine, we knocked out the batches in no time. Then came our turn. Each of us purchased our own box of green rubber bands which would last for a week or two. We had fun as well. Earl Kuykendall, one of the older boys would come whisper the name of someone in each boy's ear as we were rolling our papers. Earl would loudly do a countdown at which time you would turn and shoot a rubber band at the person he had told you to. What a surprise when 15 boys turned and shot you while you aimed and shot at the one Earl had told you to! Only Earl knew who was on the hit list. We were all friends from different backgrounds and schools working as a team. The sooner you rolled your papers and loaded your now heavy bike, the sooner you would be on your way.

At the end of the day, my patrons dutifully waited for their daily newspaper which, in those days, brought news of community and world events into kitchens or living rooms. In some instances, they were disappointed by my late arrivals. After leaving the Record and Landmark newspaper building, bicycle loaded with 150 tightly rolled papers, I sometimes stopped by the downtown Hefner's Café on East Broad Street or maybe stop to play softball with kids while my deliveries waited. When asked why their paper was late, I usually told them we had problems with the press, a little white lie.

One thing I took pride in was being able to pedal down the center of the street, no hands on the handlebars, accurately slinging papers left and right to land, if not on the porch, certainly close by.

There was an older gentleman, Mr. Phelps, who managed the paperboys. It was he we reported to at his window in the dispatch room. He was a retired Navy Petty Officer as I recall, by now a gray-haired curmudgeon who laced every sentence with profanity. He had his good side but coming from a background without profanity, it took its toll on me. One day as he spewed his words at me, not for any reason, I made a decision; I had had enough, so I gave Mr. Phelps my collection book and told him I quit. David Rives, a friend two years younger who rode occasionally with me and knew the route took it as my replacement. With no income, I sold my beautiful Jaguar Mark II for what I owed on it, roughly $30.00. That was my last bicycle.

Side note: David Rives family had a nice cabin on Lake Lookout and an outboard motorboat. Earlier, I got to know David while we were both in Boy Scout Troop 2 at Race Street Methodist Church. David's father and he came by in their old blue jeep with boat in tow to pick me up on several occasions to join them on the lake for the weekend. Mrs. Rives and their daughters Shirley and young sister Sally joined us at the lake; that was my first experience riding in an outboard motorboat. What a thrill, I am eternally thankful for their thoughtfulness to this poor kid who lived on that dirt road.

CHAPTER 19
Line Boy

In the spring of my 9th year in mid-school I hitchhiked to my local airport as on other occasions to watch with fascination, airplanes come and go. This particular day was different, however, one that would change my life forever. Unknowing, I had been observed by Jimmy Miller and his young nephew Mason Linker who, along with his uncle, ran Miller's Aviation. Don't remember which, but one of them approached me to ask if I would be interested in a job as 'line boy'? What was a line boy? Whatever, I thought to myself, who do I kill to get the job! A line boy was needed to replace Mike Branch, the current line boy who would be going to college in the fall. After explaining what my duties would be, I eagerly accepted! I would be refueling local and transient aircraft, writing tickets, washing aircraft, taking care of the terminal building, and putting aircraft away at end of day. It was a dream come true, I was ecstatic and couldn't wait to let Mom know!

During the summer I was to work five days a week with a salary of $28.00 per week but I was there seven days a week! I was offered flying lessons by taking $10.00 a week out of my salary. How thrilling, couldn't believe this unexpected surprise, this I also gladly accepted! Life took on an entirely different meaning, no more scratching to put money in my pockets. That job changed my life forever, it opened many doors and offered a future. My logbook shows I had my first flying lesson June 14th, 1961, age 15.

Jimmy, returned to manage the airport in 1960 after having managed it with his brothers in the early 50's.Mason and his uncle Jimmy were the kindest, most respectful people I had ever met, friendly, smiling, encouraging. Their attitude rubbed off on me but who wouldn't be that way if one could be around all those airplanes!

Side note: Some years ago, my friend Jim Murdock and his wife Jenny, presented me with a book, saying, "I think you'll like reading this". Jim (Murdock) has known me for over 60 years going back to my youth as a line boy. The book, *Hangar Sweepings, reflections of an airport Bum*, copyright 2009, by Harold Mills was a page turner, I found that someone in the late 30's/early 40's had worked as a line boy at the nearby Rowan County Airport experiencing so many things I could relate to albeit with what is now considered antique aircraft. He presents a treasure of North Carolina aviation history, stories, some of which I recall being told by then gray-haired hangar rats, those who come to hang out at the airport.

I learned some interesting facts about my boss Jimmy and his younger twin brothers Harold and Howard.

Harold Mills tells the story of 1942, during WWII, civilian pilots, mechanics, office workers, all took their own airplanes to a string of coastal airfields to fly anti-sub patrols out over the Atlantic in which he says is one of the great, untold stories of WWII. German Submarines (U-Boats) were sinking ships within sight of land up and down the east coast. In no time, several thousand civilian pilots, part of the newly formed Civil Air Patrol, flying all sorts of small aircraft were assisting the ARMY, Navy, and Coast Guard who, at that time did not have enough boats or airplanes to patrol the sea lanes. Jimmy and his uncle Marvin Overcash were two of these. Marvin became somewhat of a celebrity when he and Rhonda Story (male), flying an overladen 90 horsepower Stinson 105, dropped a jury rigged 100-pound bomb, suspended between the landing gear, on a U-Boat as it was descending beneath the surface. They didn't sink the sub but had marked it for Navy PBY's (flying boats) to come finish the job. Marvin received an Air Medal but never wore it. The Navy took over the coastal patrol by 1943 and Marvin joined the ARMY for the duration of the war. As a young kid, I met Marvin several times at his small gas station across the road from the Miller Brothers farm runway near Mooresville, North Carolina but had never been told his story.

Dangerous Enclosures

According to Harold Mills, in his book, Jimmy bought the Miller farm from his grandmother where he and his younger twin brothers operated a grass strip right after WWII. Harold and Howard, for a brief time were in the Aviation Cadet program at age 18 but were mustered out at the end of the war before they could pin on silver wings.

After Christmas of 1945, Harold, and Howard, aided by their GI Bill eligibility, attended the Spartan School of Aeronautics in Tulsa Oklahoma to get their A&E (now A&P) maintenance certification. While there, they discovered that surplus Army Air Corps training airplanes were being sold off, acres of surplus Fairchild PT-23 trainers south of Memphis, TN. They went to investigate resulting in the purchase of a PT-23 for $382.00. Harold and a pilot friend flew the PT-23 back to Tulsa where he and Howard made repairs to make it airworthy. With little piloting skills, the two brothers were given some navigation guidance on how to lay out a course for home. On December 21, 1946, they finished their A&E mechanics course and departed for home back to Mooresville the next day.

By 1948, Miller Brothers Airport was an official flight school, with a hangar and menagerie of Piper Cubs, Aeroncas, Cessnas, two Stearman PT-17's and a Fairchild 24.

Eventually, the Miller Brothers took over operation of the Statesville municipal airport, Jimmy was manager, Harold was chief of flight operations and Howard ran maintenance. They had twelve airplanes. In 1954 Harold and Howard left Statesville to fly for Piedmont Airlines. Jimmy left the airport operations at the same time. Harold and Howard began with Piedmont flying DC-3's and eventually Boeing 727'and 737's. Harold passed away with brain cancer at age 50, Jimmy was killed when he crashed his Piper Aztec in a field nearby after departing his farm on a foggy morning, October 2nd, 1979. Howard lived to 95.

I hitch hiked to my new job, sometimes walking much of the four-mile trek on Buffalo Shoals Road which took me interestingly past the Bostian rail Bridge. It was at this bridge on August 27th, 1891, in morning darkness that a train with passengers, having left Statesville at 2:30 a.m., went off the bridge taking the lives of 23 people with scores more injured. The five-span concrete bridge towered some 60 feet above 3rd creek. There were no

147

hospitals at the time, so survivors were taken back to Statesville to be cared for in private homes. Thousands came to see the wreckage. Ref-12 In earlier days, I had walked the bridge and climbed down under it to see notes left behind through the years. Some said the bridge was haunted.

With my new job I met interesting people, every day was an adventure and looking back I can regurgitate facts about so many of those old airplanes. I learned to 'prop' airplanes, that is, stand in front of an airplane and pull down on the propeller to start the engine while someone else was in the airplane at the controls. This was a delicate undertaking, you had to make sure to be clear of the turning propeller, after engine start, not to lose an arm! Saturdays and Sundays saw many small airplanes come in for gas, most did not have starters, so I 'propped' them by hand after refueling. As a young teenager, I think I must have propped more airplanes than anyone active in aviation at that time. Not a bad start for a 15-year-old.

After school, I walked home, left my books behind, walked up the short dirt road to Buffalo Shoals road and put my thumb out to catch a ride to the airport. I caught rides with people on their way home from work. They got to know me and gladly stopped to give me a lift. After a few hours of work, there was always someone at the airport to ask if I needed a ride home.

As years went by, If not in school, I was at the airport, advancing my aviation career. I was given more and more responsibilities; I wish to pause for a minute to draw a scenario of my environs as I tell stories of those years, stories, I feel need to be told.

The Statesville Municipal Airport, as it was called in my time, was owned by the city, located west of town out in the country just off Airport road. Entering the airport confines, on the left one would see an open 'T' Hangar. The T Hangar allowed small aircraft to be tied down tail first into stalls four or five on each side.

Arriving at the gravel parking lot one would notice left front, the red brick, single story terminal building separated from the blacktop aircraft parking ramp by a gated four-foot chain linked fence with two concrete walkways leading out to the ramp. A covered walkway from right to left, led from the parking lot to terminal building. To the right was a single-story red brick Civil

Dangerous Enclosures

Air Patrol building. In the distance, on the right, was a single tin clad metal hangar opening to the ramp. Adjoining the hangar in the rear was a maintenance shop where repairs, inspections and rebuilds were conducted. In the far end of the ramp were two fuel pumps, one dispensing 80/87 Octane fuel, the other 100 Octane. Beyond the gas pumps, was a grass field for tying down aircraft that were not hangered. Leaving the blacktop ramp was a gravel taxiway leading behind the hangar to a second hangar in the rear. The paved, blacktop ramp had a short taxiway opposite the front hangar leading to the left joining runway 28/10. A left turn onto the runway brings you a short distance to the threshold of runway 28 clearly visible from the terminal's large windows. A right turn brought you to the intersection of a second runway 2/20. The two paved runways were almost perpendicular to each other, runway 2/20, the longest at 3,650 feet. Near this intersection on the far side of the runway was a bright orange windsock inscribed with the letters 'Gulf' in dark blue lettering. Aviation gasoline was purchased from Gulf Oil Corporation that provided the windsocks. Replacing a worn, faded windsock gave me a sense of pride. The terminal building was modern for the time, with brown textured tile floors, large viewing windows on the runway and ramp sides. Vinyl maroon-colored upholstered couches were built-in around the wall below the windows. A red Coca Cola soda machine which dispensed bottles of Coke, stood centered on the right, a 'Lance' cracker/peanut vending machine next to the far end wall. Covering the wall left of entry was a large map of the United States with a long string and mileage indicator. One could swing the string, anchored at Statesville on the map, to anywhere in the U.S. to get a rough idea of direction and mileage for flight planning. Beyond the map was entrance to a small office where airport operations were conducted to include a radio with a 122.8 Unicom frequency for advisory communications with incoming and outgoing aircraft. The office had roll-out vertical windows facing the ramp and parking lot. There was also a closet with a control box for runway lighting. A small bar existed on the left beyond the office but in my time, it was never used; it did come in handy, to sit on the stools, carry on conversations, do flight planning and maybe a game of checkers. To the far end, left side, were Male and Female restrooms. There was also an entry/exit door on the far end. With no air conditioning, the terminal was wide open in warm weather.

This would be my world most of my teen years. As you read the following stories, please keep this scenario in mind.

My boss, a young Mason Linker, 1963, in the office on the radio giving advisories to local aircraft.
(photo by Randy Gilleland)

Mystery man

Summer activity at the airport during the week usually found me fueling an infrequent transient aircraft, washing an airplane at the front of the hangar which I did with bucket, hose, ladder, and long brush, answering phone calls when neither Jimmy or Mason were around and occasionally clean the terminal building. I have fond memories of when our mechanics, Virgil Outlaw, John Gibson and a few others took morning coke breaks in the terminal building. There were always stories! One of the routines was to see whose coke came the farthest distance. Each bottle had the name of a distant city on the bottom. The string on the wall map would be the judge of whoever had the bottle farthest away and subsequently win the challenge. One morning, they were discussing a gentleman from Statesville who would be joining up with his WWII buddies in Indiana for a reunion. How exciting that would be. Not long after the mechanics returned to work, I was alone, feet propped up on the office desk when the phone rang. It was a call from an individual saying that he was going to a reunion in Indiana and inquired if we could get him there. Wow, this must be the man we had just talked about! I assured him, yes, we can take him to Indiana, this would be a real plus for our small operation! The gentleman said he wanted the airplane exceptionally clean to make a big impression on his friends. I assured him the aircraft would look great. He said he would be arriving around 1:00 PM. After he hung up, I ran down to the maintenance shop where three mechanics were busy. I told Virgil, we had a charter flight and asked him to get prepared for the flight. My boss Jimmy was not available at the time and Virgil sometimes took these flights. Virgil went along with the story, and I hurried to get our Piper Tri Pacer cleaned up. I washed it down and got under the belly to clean it immaculately. Around 11:00 AM, Jimmy arrived in his Cessna 172. As soon as he exited the aircraft, I was waiting to tell him the good news! He went to the maintenance shop, then back to the office. Around noon, I checked, and Virgil had not yet changed clothes and prepare for the flight. I was getting worried. As 1:00 PM got closer, and no one seemed to take any action, I ran the conversation I had had with the 'potential' charter and the voice seemed familiar. It suddenly came to me, that was John Gibson's voice, I had been had! I walked back to our maintenance shop, looked around and then down to John Gibson, lying on a small maintenance dolly doing some work. He looked up at me and asked, "Has the gentleman looking for a flight arrived yet?". I said, "Yes" and I'm looking at him! It was you! Everyone had a huge laugh at my expense I might say. They were playing with me since I didn't seem to have enough to keep me busy. Found out that Jimmy had been let in on the scheme, that is why he did not seem to show interest. Great fun and humorous memories of my experiences as an airport Line Boy.

Tricking two ARMY National Guard pilots

On another morning break, there was conversation of some geographic similarities of the Statesville and Salisbury airports, particularly water features, lakes, and rivers. After the break and the mechanics returned to work, we had an ARMY National Guard Beaver (U-6A) land and taxi up to the fuel pumps. The single engine green colored Beaver with tail wheel had a 450 Horsepower radial engine. Two pilots exited the front cockpit, one from each side, both wearing, what I refer to as Fidel Castro caps, standard issue at the time. They had two high ranking officers seated in the rear. One pilot got me off to the side and asked: Is this Statesville? A little bit of mischief popped in my head as I remembered the recent conversation comparing Statesville and Salisbury airports. My reply to the inquiry was, "No, this is Salisbury" at which time, to my surprise, the other pilot, somewhat disturbed, looked his companion in the eye and said, "I told you so"! Then I told them, to their relief, "Yes, this is Statesville". The devil made me do it!

Side Note: Later, as an ARMY Aviator, I would fly many missions in the Beaver from Berlin Tempelhof Airport over Communist East German territory.

Flying Banners

Many have seen banners towed behind small aircraft overhead along the beach, sporting events or large festivals. As a 15-year-old, not yet flying, on a bright summer day, I observed a J-3 Cub make a low pass with a banner in tow over the mowed grass area to the right of runway 2. The pilot released the tow line to the banner, now lifeless fall dormant on the grass. It was a thrill to see, sort of a mini airshow, my first and only encounter with a banner. The pilot returned to land and in short order taxied up to our fuel pumps. After fueling and a Coke break, the pilot asked if I might hold the banner for his takeoff when he once again continued. Of course, I said, what do I do! I went with him as he taxied back to the grass strip. The resting banner was quite long, perhaps 100 feet. The leading edge was secured to a 10-foot wooden pole which was tethered to the aircraft by a very long rope while in flight. The pilot said I was to hold the pole in a vertical position as he took off and snatched the pole from my hands. After checking the banner to make sure all was in order the pilot arranged the lengthy rope to takeoff on the far side of the banner with me holding the pole! I watched him accelerate nearer and nearer, zooming by, gently lifting into the air, then swoosh, the banner was snatched from my hand! The lifeless hue of colors was once again trailing its message for all to see as I watched it disappear over the horizon. So exciting!

Weekends

Dangerous Enclosures

Families made a weekly Sunday event of coming to the airport with children in tow after church. They were dressed for church, joining other families. Fred Bustle and family, Fred Nesbit and his teenage son Jonathan. Harold Williams, WWII veteran, owner of a Tempco Swift, brought his two sons, while his daughters usually stayed home, Jim Miller (not my boss), Gary Foster with wife and children. Gary and Bobby Poole were co-owners of a small Luscombe, Jim Murdock, shared ownership of a Luscombe with Robert Brawley. Others included, Houston Ballard, Jesse Lentz, Vester Boone, Andy Pendleton, Calvin Burrell, Joe Hornbuckle with family and many more.

Fred Nesbit, a Pearl Harbor survivor had been an ambulance driver that Sunday morning, December 7th, 1941, when the Japanese attacked. He told of seeing Japanese pilots dropping bombs but initially thought they were Americans who sometimes dropped duds for practice. He thought, uh oh, somebody's in trouble, they've got live bombs, then he saw a "Jap" airplane come by low overhead with the red meat ball on the wing, close enough to see the pilot in the cockpit. After the melee he told of picking up some souvenirs which included a Japanese sword but the duffle bag he kept things in was stolen.

Saturdays, brought a few who shared ownership in airplanes to meet with fellow owners to wash their aircraft, join in conversation and back on Sunday to take their family for a flight. It was my job to get their aircraft out and ready.

Annual Fly in breakfasts

Once a year, a number of owners would select an airfield, usually (Florence, SC) to fly to and join in a Sunday breakfast. A gaggle of airplanes, some slower than others would depart at the same time, on one occasion one slow pilot arrived too late to join in the breakfast. It was fun to hear their stories when they returned.

Airport visitors and pilots ranged from businessmen to self-employed who came to learn to fly or be a part of it. Everyone was courteous, they treated me well, I was in the mix, taking care of their airplanes and yet the same age as some of their children.

153

Del Hardiman

Mason Linker trickery

While yet a neophyte to aviation, my boss Mason, a young 23-year-old, let me sit in the front left seat of our blue and white Piper Tri-Pacer N7032D, a four-seat fabric airplane with nose wheel. He let me handle the controls, my sister Brenda, seated in the rear, maybe her first airplane ride, would be impressed with her young brother's piloting skills. The Tri-pacer had dual controls joined to a yoke behind the instrument panel anchored to a flexible pully below the floor which had direct input to the tail elevators. As we flew, the controls in my hands began slowly pulling forward, causing the aircraft to descend, I pulled harder and harder to keep us level, didn't want to make a bad impression on my sister. As I pulled back harder and harder, suddenly, there was no more pressure, and I jerked the controls back hard causing the aircraft to shoot up. This was so embarrassing as I didn't want to frighten my sister! Mason, in the right seat, looked at me and asked, "What are you doing"? Once reestablished and leveled off, the same situation occurred, then I noticed Mason had his left foot on the yoke down below pushing it forward causing the nose to go down. When he saw I had noticed, we had a good laugh!

Wayne Lowe, Benson Gyrocopter

Amusing unplanned events sometimes happened at our small-town airport. One I remember with hubris is the Sunday morning attempted flight of a Benson Gyrocopter by Wayne Lowe. The Benson could be described as a pilot seat mounted at ground level on three wheels with two wooden rotating helicopter type blades affixed on a vertical shaft behind and above the seat and a tail fin some length behind the seat. In the early sixties, the Benson gyro copter was immensely popular and was very maneuverable with or without a pusher propeller engine, thousands of sets of plans were sold over a thirty-year period.

The technique was for the pilot to reach up overhead with one hand and get the rotor blades turning, then be towed by a vehicle which, with forward speed would enhance faster rotor speed to produce lift. The pilot had a handle with which he could tilt the rotor toward the direction he wished to go. Having a pusher engine with small propeller, mounted behind the pilot seat, there was no limit to where one could fly or go. The gyro copter at our airport had not been there long as it waited on a pusher engine. As mentioned, it

154

could still be towed. So, this Sunday morning, as was often the case, small talk transitioned into activity. Wayne, short, slight beer belly, always jovial 35-year-old bachelor was one of the three owners of this Gyrocopter. He was either coerced or decided on his own to get the Benson out for a safe fun run down the runway, what could go wrong; it seemed simple even though Wayne was not a pilot and had never flown a gyro copter. A plan developed; Wayne would be towed down the runway with a ski rope behind my boss's black Ford pickup truck. Our small-town airport was the perfect setting for such operations. Driver of the Ford was Fred Nesbit, as mentioned earlier, a Pearl Harbor survivor who came most Sundays along with his 14-year-old son Jonathan. I guess Fred was in his mid-50's at this point; always dressed well, had a constant tremor in one arm from nerve damage sustained by a motorcycle accident he told us. A handful, including myself watched from afar as Wayne was lined up, ski rope attached to both the gyrocopter and the Ford pickup. Wayne got the rotor turning and gave the signal for Fred to proceed down the 3650-foot runway moving away from us. In no time, Wayne was airborne, tethered to the Ford, rotor blades turning, it was a marvelous site! Then tragedy. Fred looked up and noticed a small aircraft on final approach coming in their direction. Should have been no problem, just decelerate, let Wayne come back to Mother Earth and make a controlled exit into the grass to clear the runway. Well, Fred did not take those actions (guess a pre-brief would have been in order), he made a hard left veering turn off the runway and Wayne, now a passenger, was yanked to where he had not intended to go! Wayne had not anticipated this and doubtful he would have known how to react anyway. He lost control and smashed into the ground shattering the gyrocopter's wooden blades. Not injured, Wayne bore no ill feelings toward Fred, but the opportunity for that particular Benson Gyro copter to fly never came again.

Ike (Ikey) Kennerly

I've always wanted to capture stories whether they are mine or others. This is a story told by Ike (Ikey) Kennerly from west of Statesville. Ikey flew in from time to time in his Cessna 180 for gas. I loved this particular story and asked him to tell it several times. Ikey was a small, short guy, rusty complexion and happened to have been a glider pilot in WWII. Can no longer remember but he was more than likely involved in D-Day invasion. When Ikey was a young soldier at Fort Benning, GA., he once went Away Without Leave (AWOL). On his return to post, he hitch-hiked back. A green military sedan stopped and picked him up. He was joined in the back seat with none other than GEN Omar Bradley! It was winter, cold, the sedan had little heat, so he shared a blanket with the General! There he was, AWOL, sharing a blanket with one of America's highest-ranking Generals! He was scared to death, but it all worked out and the General was none the wiser. When Ikey told that story, he was that young soldier again. Those true stories, slightly embellished, meant so much!

Runaway Super Cruiser

I had just enough experience with taxiing the many aircraft at our airport to be confident enough to demonstrate my talents. On this summer day, my boss Jimmy's brother Howard, a captain for Piedmont Airlines was on one of his frequent visits and asked if I would bring a Piper Super Cruiser up from our 'T' hangar for him to use for a while. Gladly I walked down to the hangar, untied the Cruiser and pushed it out of the dirt hanger floor onto the grass. I got into the Cruiser's front seat and began looking for the starter button but could not find it. I had the key turned to the 'on' position, but where is the starter? In my mind as a fifteen-year-old, I wanted only to get that aircraft started and taxi it up to Howard who was standing off in the distance on grass talking to another man, waiting. Where is that starter! Oh, well, I knew how to get the aircraft started by 'Propping' it. This is done by turning on the magneto switches in the cockpit, exiting outside and carefully pulling the propeller by hand until the engine started. So, that is what I did. I set the parking brakes and put some chocks in front of the wheels to hold the aircraft once I had it started. This should be a good plan. I set the throttle to idle, turned on the magneto switches, exited and began pulling the propeller, no start. I went back to the cockpit, cracked the throttle a little more, still no start. Back to more throttle, which by now was opened quite a bit. This time, the engine started but to my fright as I stood there off the side, the engine began revving faster and faster. The wheels were straining against the chocks and suddenly jumped over the chocks! I grabbed the right wing strut and held the right side with sheer might as the tail wheel aircraft and I made a complete right circle, engine pulling. I held on by planting both heels into the ground. Gradually I was able to work my way back to the door, reach in and pull the throttle back! All this in a manner of seconds. Knees shaking, I got into the aircraft and taxied up to Howard and the other individual. I'm sure they witnessed the whole thing but said nothing. That was close! Just another uneventful day. Later, I got in the aircraft and discovered the starter button. If only I had known its location in the first place.

Houston Ballard

My logbook shows my first flight, June14th, 1961 was in Houston Ballard's PA-11 (N4865M), an upgraded version of the Piper J-3. Phil Loftin gave me the ride. Houston's PA-11 was white with green engine cowling. Interesting side note. Houston, an excellent aircraft mechanic purchased his aircraft and rebuilt it from a wreck. One day, I was standing in our office looking out at the ramp, when a strong breeze came up, I witnessed the PA-11 parked at the gas pumps, lift off and fly backwards across the ramp, gently setting down next to the chain link fence, tail touching the fence! No damage to the aircraft. It happened within seconds, and I just happened to see it!

Houston, in his early 50's, was quite slim, standing around 6 feet, black hair, a man everyone enjoyed being around. He worked in town and would come to the airport in the afternoons either taking his PA-11 for a flight or spending time hanging out in the maintenance shop. Houston had an FAA Airframe maintenance certificate and told of rigging the very first Douglas C-47 cargo aircraft to be used for dropping airborne troops. On D-DAY, June 6th, 1944, C-47s dropped over 13,000 paratroopers during the invasion of France. Ref-13 Houston and his wife Irene, a nurse, the first anesthesiologist in our county, were married 63 years; they had one daughter, Pam.

Years later, I visited Houston, then retired, at his home introducing him to my wife Paula and sons, Michael, Patrick, and Benjamin. Houston displayed his large collection of Charles Lindbergh memorabilia which included Lindbergh post marked envelopes and stamps, a hobby he was quite proud of.

Gifton (Gif) McCreary

For several years, on occasion, Gif McCreary would stop by the airport in a Bell 47 Helicopter. He was slender, late 30's, sandy hair, over six feet tall. His helicopter was the same model used in the TV show M*A*S*H. A North Carolinian, Gif's routine was to spend the winter in Texas rebuilding a 47, return with it, then during the summer hopping passengers at major events such as the Charlotte Motor Speedway. As a licensed A&P mechanic with Aircraft Inspection Authority (IA); I believe the only one in the state at that time, he was authorized to sign off certain civilian helicopter maintenance as requested by other A&P mechanics. At the end of season, he would sell his helicopter, then go back to Texas. The times I saw him, I was enthralled! Once he gave me $2.00 to clean the large chin bubble of his helicopter!

Bell 47 like the one Gif flew into the airport early 60's (photo courtesy Airliners.net)

Early training flights

As mentioned, $10.00 a week came out of my salary for flying lessons, but I had to beg a licensed pilot to fly with me to get my training. Only the day I soloed did I have a licensed instructor. During the summer I got flying time in our yellow J-3, N2028M. On one of my first flights, I coerced John Gibson to go with me. Solo position for J-3s is the rear tandem seat. John was in the front seat, seemingly uninterested in my back-and-forth taxiing. From the rear seat, visibility was obscured by the cockpit and engine so one had to swivel back and forth to see ahead. When I gave the J-3 power, we went off the runway into grass on the right side of the runway, John never touched the controls but let me struggle from behind. When I got airborne, John, jokingly looked back at me and yelled, "I didn't come out here to go rabbit hunting"!

Red Grant doing Bat Man jump at Statesville Airport

One sunny morning I found myself standing next to a recently arrived non-English-speaking Hungarian refugee. Hungary, at the time was under control of the Communist Bloc of nations, getting out was not an option but his brother had helped him escape only weeks before. His brother was a photographer doing a photo shoot for True Men's Magazine stationed out of New York, so he brought his brother along to assist. We stood near the windsock; the non-English speaking Hungarian and me. I was asked, at 15, to trigger, on his command, a cable button attached to the tripod mounted camera with a stove pipe lens aimed skyward as Red Grant exited from a towering aircraft above from which Red would jump, outfitted in a bat man suit. Red and his manager, former manager of defunct Mackay Airlines which operated from Fort Lauderdale Florida throughout the Caribbean, agreed to meet the photographer midway from New York and Florida. They put their finger on the map to decide where to join for the jump. As it happened, the point was our airport in Statesville, N.C. Red was short in stature, late forties, graying red hair; he told me he had jumped behind enemy lines in Europe during WWII. He also told me of the number of people doing the bat man jump, some were dead or no longer performing this dangerous stunt; he was one of the few who still did. If the jump was not performed correctly, he explained, arms or legs could be broken with fatal results. I was dumbfounded! He wore a red jump suit with white helmet and goggles, black webbing was sewed from legs to arms and between his legs. With extended arms and spread legs, he appeared as a giant red and black bat. The team requested we provide two airplanes to record the jump, one for Red to exit from, the other to chase him with the photographer. The Hungarian and I were to take photos from the ground. I remember the shuffling sound of Red's walk out onto the ramp to the small Piper Tri Pacer that would carry him aloft. The left rear door had been removed for his exit. Red had a parachute harnessed to him for late deployment after his soaring bat jump. I recall his manager and worried friend commenting that Red was getting too old for this. As I looked skyward with tension and abated breath toward the jump plane overhead, at first, I could see a speck separating from the aircraft getting larger as Red screamed downward making maneuvers while the chase plane followed. Excitedly, I pulled the trigger time and again as the Hungarian with trained camera called out. Eventually Red's parachute deployed, and he landed safely nearby. A delayed whooshing sound followed Red's high-speed dive. All went well, regrettably there were only a handful of witnesses. It was yet another unplanned thrill I experienced as a youngster at Statesville Airport and another day's work for Red who instantly became my hero! Did not have the opportunity of seeing the magazine article, but perhaps there was a photo I had partially been responsible for! Now days daredevils routinely perform Bat Man jumps pioneered decades before by men like Red but with aid of high-tech innovations.

P-51

One Saturday a doctor from Wilmington, N.C. landed in his P-51, taxied up and parked for the night. Sitting there on the ramp, the aircraft was an attention getter! I was told stories of the P-51's reputation for winning the war against the Germans but this was my first time seeing one! Next afternoon, the doctor came out to preflight and depart. Some asked if he would mind giving us a little show? His reply was that this aircraft was costly to operate and that he would not be giving us a show. He fired up the engine, which had an unmistakable sound, taxied out, made his engine checks and was gone. A little disappointed, we watched him disappear out of sight then turned to walk away. Moments later, we heard the P-51! It was coming down the runway towards us like a rocket just feet above the runway! As the aircraft zoomed past, the doctor pulled his P-51 up in a shallow climb doing barrel rolls until out of site! Breathless, we had had our airshow!

John White Moore

Fond memories of John White Moore who told great stories of being the Sheriff of our county from 1934 to 1943. When I knew him in early 60's, he came regularly to the airport, never short of something to say. He raised black angus cattle on land he owned nearby. I accompanied him several times to feed the cattle; on one I lost my treasured high school class ring which John found in the cow's feeding trough and returned to me.

John, the son of a doctor, was a Teddy Roosevelt looking type without the mustache. He had been a pilot in his younger days, buying his first airplane in 1927, hauling passengers out of fields. I believe his pilot license number was below 100 meaning he was one of the first to have a license. He was a graduate of NC State University and had a brother, as I recall, who was a surgeon at the Mayo Clinic in Rochester, Minnesota. In a Charlotte Observer interview with his wife Margaret White Moore, she stated: "Those who knew John Moore in the early years of this century declared he would never reach manhood. They said the adventurous youth would be kicked to death by one of the horses he rode helter skelter across Iredell County countryside".

John told many stories of chasing "moonshiners" in the thirties. He said the 'shiners" had a technique of spraying coal oil on the exhaust from their car as he chased them which smeared his windshield with black smudge, the coal oil was also laced with pepper so when he stuck his head out the window to see, he got pepper in his eyes. On another occasion, there was a man bringing "moonshine" whiskey to the courthouse to sell! The man wore a long coon skin (raccoon fur) coat in which he hid the whiskey. John said he approached the man, who he knew, and told him, "I know you need the money to feed your family, I'll let you go this time, but if I catch you again, I'll have to arrest you". Just one of many memorable individuals I had the opportunity to meet while a kid at the airport.

Johnny Crowell

Johnny Crowell (1893 – 1983) was a senior citizen who stopped by every other month in a J-3 Cub to refuel. He flew low, over electric power lines, inspecting them for Duke Power Company. Johnny, slim, soft spoken with white hair, always dressed as a gentleman. At the time I knew him in the early 60's, he appeared to be at or near 70. When he exited the Cub, he would put on his trademark fedora, always wearing a bowtie. Others at the airport knew him but I did not. It was later, after researching him that I discovered just how famous he once was. I knew only that he came, spent time, often taking lunch with us at a local restaurant. He visited a few times in his black 56' Ford Thunderbird hard top with port hole windows. In the T-Bird was a scattered assortment of aircraft parts in the trunk and right seat. I appreciated the fact that he flew from the rear seat and had a modified front seat on which was secured an Olivetti typewriter to type his reports. It was said he could type while flying the aircraft at tree top level, using his knees to control the aircraft. Must have been true, otherwise why have the typewriter at his fingertips! I was thrilled to watch him depart, he took off and remained just above the trees soon disappearing over the horizon! He was a member of the "Quiet Birdmen" (QB), a secretive club founded in 1921 by WWI pilots, its membership continues today by invitation only.

His QB Profile states "At the age of 29 (in 1922), Johnny purchased six surplus WWI JN-2 Jennies at Southern Field, Americus GA. Some he sold off and ferried the rest to Charlotte NC. He left a few for Charles Lindbergh, also a QB member, to buy in 1923".

During the 20s and 30s he and WWI ace, Elliott White Springs became popular and successful Barnstormers.

His QB epitaph states, in part, "Johnny" Pioneer, aviator. Charlotte's first licensed pilot and first airport manager. Barnstorming pioneer in aviation. Set world records in aerobatics. Logged 2.5 million miles in 100 types of aircraft. Inventor and gentleman".

In 1938, at Charlotte, Johnny set a record for quickest outside loop in his Great Lakes 2TIA. His time, 55 seconds for four consecutive outside loops which were opposite normal loops.

QB profile continues: One of his stunts was to fly with both arms tied in plain view while demonstrating "hands off" flying. In one show, the local Sheriff was recruited to tie Johnny's hands so that he could not reach the controls of his aircraft. Johnny then taxied to the runway and performed: a take-off, a loop, a snap roll, a spin with recovery to a point, landed and taxied back to crowd center, his hands visible above the cockpit rim the entire time.

Some of Johnny's patents were (courtesy QB) a Training Device for Aviators, a tensiometer, thermostatically controlled choke for the Ford Model T and an automatic spark advance. His best-known invention was the Three-Castle-Locknut which became a standard in the US auto industry.

Johnny's son, John Edison "Jocko" Crowell was a WWII P-47 fighter pilot with the 366th Fighter Group. His highest rank was Lieutenant Colonel, awards include Air Medal with 2 oak leaf clusters, Distinguished Flying Cross and purple Heart.

Dangerous Enclosures

Johnny was yet another memorable individual I met as a youngster at my hometown airport.

Closing for the evening

Putting aircraft away in our two hangars each evening was one of my responsibilities. Mason, my boss, was proficient taxiing into the hangar with wings very close to the hangar walls. That impressed me. In time, I too would taxi small aircraft into the hangar, spinning around only a foot from the wall. I did it with precision and complete confidence. Great depth perception.

First time seeing a UH-1 (Huey) helicopter

*Most of you remember the venerable UH-1 Huey helicopter, loved in Vietnam as was the Jeep of WWII. Some 16,000 of these were built by Bell Helicopter Division. It was a multipurpose utility helicopter which served this country well and paved the trail for today's Army Air Assault/MEDEVAC fighting teams. More than 7,000 Hueys saw action in Vietnam. Of these, 2,202 "Huey" pilots were killed and approximately 2,500 aircraft were lost, roughly half to combat and the rest to operational accidents. Ref-14

Following is my Huey story:

In the summer of 1961, we had an unusual ARMY helicopter land but, in this case, it did not go to our fuel pumps but hovered over to the edge of the black top ramp and sat down near the chain link fence which separated ramp from the airport terminal building. I had never heard that sound before, it had the sound of a jet mixed with the whop, whop of the rotor blades. After shutting down and the rotors stopped turning, the pilot exited who I recognized immediately as CPT Billy Redman, a native of Statesville on active duty in the U.S. ARMY. I had known of Billy mostly from his reputation. He was the only child of Walt and Susie Redman, proprietors of a small café in town. I frequented the café from time to time and saw Billy first there. He was young and handsome! His parents were so proud of him. Billy stopped by from time to time in various ARMY aircraft and always purchased fuel. My first aircraft to refuel was a Beechcraft U-8D Seminole Billy brought in on a stop to visit his parents. (Billy retired as a LTC from the Active Army and later became a state senator). On this day, Billy told me, "Can't buy any fuel today, this thing burns kerosene (slang for jet fuel), there are only five of these in the ARMY. I'm taking it to Fort Rucker, Alabama." Billy's father, Walt came

163

out to pick him up which gave us 'gawkers' time to check out this strange helicopter. As it turned out, I too would become an ARMY Aviator, trained at Fort Rucker but this was the first time, at age 15, I had heard of Fort Rucker or seen a Huey. Someday, not knowing at the time, I would grow up and fly Hueys. When Billy returned and fired up the Huey, one of only five in the ARMY, the ignition made that familiar popping sound so well known by anyone who's ever flown or ridden in one. As Billy departed over the horizon, I noticed there were two indentions in the soft hot pavement where his skids had rested.

After my tour in Vietnam, I was trained in the Huey at Fort Rucker. On a trip home in 1972 enroute to my next assignment, I stopped by the airport where I had worked as Line Boy and pilot for years. Before I could walk out on the ramp which I knew so well, a young Line Boy stopped me at the gate and told me I was not permitted beyond the fence. I did not tell him the job he had, I once had. As I stood there something caught my eye, the two indentions of Billy's skids were still visible in the black top some 11 years later! It caused me to pause and reflect on all that had taken place since those marks were left there in the summer of 61'.

Many years later, after a tour of 22 years in the ARMY, pilot for NASA and later as a civilian, the Systems Manager of all UH-1s in the ARMY National Guard, I processed the turn-in of the last Hueys in the Guard. October 7, 2009, I attended a ceremony at Fort Meyer, VA in which the 'Last' operational National Guard UH-1 Huey was on display at the parade field. The ceremony was enriched by numerous dignitaries to include Medal of Honor recipient LTC (Ret.) Bruce Crandall who had distinguished himself in Vietnam at the Battle of the Ia Drang Valley, saving countless lives in the Huey. I take pride in knowing I might be the only one to have had the opportunity of being a part of the memorable Huey from its early beginning until its last days, some fifty years.

CHAPTER 20
Air Shows

Air shows are exciting! We had a number of them when I was a kid at the airport. Crowds came to see these festive events. Transient aircraft came as well; parked uniformly in the grass, a beautiful site. Occasionally one might see something unusual. On one occasion two men, a retired Air Force Colonel and his retired sergeant brought a PT-19 all metal WWII open cockpit two seat trainer to the show. It was beautifully polished to a high luster. They were so concerned for its safety they slept under the wings the night before the show for its welfare. Usually the airshow participants arrived Saturday, the day before the Sunday show and I, among others, was busy taking care of whatever tasks they requested. I remember driving to town to pick up corvus oil sold by Texaco which the stunt pilots used to spray on their hot exhausts to create the white smoke. These were vintage biplanes with modified radial engines, each had its own distinctive bright colors, in some cases with names and logos. On the day of the show, the airfield was closed to transient aircraft, strictly controlled by the FAA. Once, one of our local pilots, Harold Simpson in his Tempco Swift was kept away from landing until halftime of the show. When he was cleared to come in, he responded with "Roger, Swift 09 Victor coming in on one engine". He only had one engine! The show would not be complete without a dynamic fast-talking announcer who cultivated the audience's knowledge of events overhead, with commentary about each aircraft, the pilot, and historical facts of interest. On more than one occasion Haskell Deaton was the announcer who was also a ventriloquist, the only one I ever saw. I recall him asking me the name of Doodle Brown who was writing a receipt for gas in our office. Haskell stood near Doodle and said, "Hey Doodle", Doodle looked up out the open window briefly then back to writing. After the second call "Hey Doodle", Doodle looked out again and said, "I'll be there in just a minute". It sounded as if the caller was indeed outside!

I was thrilled to be on the "inside" permitted to be among the pilots and their aircraft. Some notable airshow pilots I got to briefly know were Bennie Walker, Bob Nance, Hal Krier, Chuck Hilliard, Mel Robinson, our own Virgil Outlaw and Baxter Slaughter, the Flying Farmer. There was a beautiful trim young lady, Gail Black who did wing walking. Wing walking was a thrill to watch, Gail wore a black suit with goggles and cloth helmet while standing strapped to a metal 'T' frame anchored on the center of Bennie Walker's top wing. As he looped, rolled, made low level inverted passes while trailing smoke, Gail was standing prostrate up there with her arms extended like wings, that took guts! Thrilling to watch! During the week Gail was a schoolteacher.

Bennie and Bob were Piedmont Airline Captains who teamed up, Bennie in his open cockpit Stearman, Bob in his Great Lakes and on some occasions Joined by Virgil for what they called the 'World Air Show'. These aircraft, with the exception of Virgil's, had inverted carburetor systems which allowed the engine to run while inverted. Virgil's Stearman had a stock 220 Continental engine without the inverted system, so when he went inverted, the engine quit running until he rolled it back upright. Mel Robinson's Stearman had a huge R1340 650 horsepower engine, the largest I ever saw on a Stearman. Hal Krier, in his Great Lakes Special was well known throughout the country as one of the top American aerobatic pilots. He was later inducted into the International Aerobatics Hall of Fame. He represented the U.S. in competitions in Spain, Russia and Germany. Ref-15 Charles "Chuck" Hilliard flew a souped-up J-3 but was known for flying other aerobatic aircraft. Baxter Slaughter, dressed as a farmer in bib overhauls would sneak into an idling J-3, jump in, and fly it off the ramp, leaving the pilot running behind him while the announcer, in hysterics yelled that some farmer had stolen the aircraft! Baxter's stunt made it appear he did not know how to fly and was about to crash as he demonstrated almost impossible feats; it was another highlight of the show. Throughout his career, Charlie (Hilliard) was recognized many times for his aerobatic excellence, including the International Council of Air Show's Wilkinson Sword of Excellence Award and induction into the International Aerobatics Hall of Fame. He was the first American to win the

World Aerobatic title Ref-16. Sadly, accidents and death followed these heroes of mine. Mel Robinson was killed a few years later in the mid 60's near Lakeland, Florida when his Stearman had a structural failure. An aileron tab linkage broke, setting up a flutter and left-wing separation. Charles Hilliard was killed April 16, 1996, also in Lakeland, Florida at the Sun 'n Fun fly-in when his Hawker Sea Fury flipped over while taxiing after having completed his airshow routine.

Age 16, Standing next to Bennie Walker's Stearman during a weekend air show. Note other biplanes in the rear. I might be wearing Bennie's cap and goggles.

Virgil Outlaw's Stearman

After the day's work, Virgil would take his Stearman with Red/white sunbursts on the wings out of the hangar; we'd pull it by hand over to the gas pumps for 20-Gals of 80/87 octane fuel. I would hand prop the 220 horse Continental and Virgil, in the rear open cockpit tandem seat, would be off doing his airshow practice routine. On a few occasions, I got to ride along as a young teen to experience the thrill of G forces. On one occasion I stood in the middle of our small ramp with my hands raised like you do when directing an aircraft to park except I was holding my hands up to get Virgil's attention. He noticed me and made a gun run, swooping down on me at high speed. As he closed in, our eyes met, Virgil, his ever-present smile encapsulated in his cloth skull cap. Feeling an impulse to dive for cover but I didn't, Virgil made his low pass just feet above me and as he roared back into the heavens I saw him look back with that smile! For a second, it appeared I had just been strafed by Charles Lindberg who Virgil resembled.

Virgil's Fatal Crash

Sadly, Virgil took off a week to do some crop dusting in eastern North Carolina, the cub he was flying stalled and crashed, crushing him between the engine and his full load of dusting material; He died instantly we were told. His wife Marie and little two-year-old daughter Jenny were living in a house trailer at our airport when this happened. All who knew Virgil were shocked. He was from Wilson, N.C. having brought his wife Marie and little daughter Jenny to Statesville to open his shop. We were all saddened to hear of Virgil's passing. I stayed behind while my fellow airport workers attended Virgil's funeral. Virgil's Stearman sat in our hangar for some time before being sold, a reminder of former, happier times. He was liked by many, an A&P mechanic, stunt Pilot and a hell of a great guy.

Virgil Outlaw in his Pitts Special he had for a while; wife Marie can be seen in house trailer door. (Photo courtesy Max Tharpe)

First Solo

Sunday, October 22, 1961, I was scheduled to solo on my 16th birthday, I could hardly wait! But as fate sometimes happens, there was an aircraft accident at my boss's airport on his farm earlier that morning. It seems Doodle Brown had taken a Piper Super Cub up with a Davidson College Student. They crashed on takeoff, but the left wing cushioned their injuries by impacting in a slight ravine. To my knowledge, the student was injured which, as I recall, might have prevented him from flying again.

169

Eleven days later, NOV 2, 1961, my boss Jimmy, soloed me in our J-3 N2028M. The day was gray, overcast, around 4:00 PM. Jimmy went around the pattern with me a couple times, then got out and directed me to make three circuits by myself. Witnessing my solo was Dr. Eckley who had part ownership in a Piper Super Cruiser. By tradition, a piece of my shirt tail was cut, my name, date of solo, written on the cut cloth and placed on a bulletin board along with other recent 'solo' shirt tails. I now had a pilot's license but still did no driver's license! My joy was unbelievable, look how far I had come!

Shirt tail cut signifying date of my solo – age 16.

N2028M as it is today, still flying, still owned by the Miller family.

Fear of Flying

My first spin was by accident on one of my early solo flights as a 16-year-old in our yellow Piper J-3 Cub. I was practicing stalls from the rear seat which is solo seat in a cub. It was impressed on me to learn stalls from my boss's brother Harold, a Piedmont Captain who took me out for some training. Later, while doing my stalls alone, west of the airfield, I unintentionally got into a left spin. It terrified me, I let go of the controls and grabbed the front seat, which previously always had someone there riding along with me, this time no one was there. The J-3 came out of the spin on its own, I made up my mind that this was all of aviation I wanted so I reached up and turned off the engine ignition switch, why I don't know. I glided over to the airport and made a dead stick landing on runway 20 then brought it to a stop off the right onto grass. I got out and walked back to the terminal building, leaving the J-3 alone in the grass. When Mason asked where the aircraft was, I told, as best I could, what happened and that I did NOT want to fly anymore! He put me in his black 57 Ford Thunderbird and drove me back to the J-3. He made me get back in and propped the aircraft. He insisted I go fly which I did. Looking back over my many years of flying in many regions of the world, I thank Mason for what he did. Had he not, my life would have been completely different. In time, I overcame my fear of spins, in fact I did them on a regular basis on other aircraft as well. I perfected a technique of doing spins at night, which scared the dickens out of my friends. At night there are no visual references to judge by, so I used car lights below on the newly completed Interstate 40 for reference. No one but me was the wiser. Spinning out of control in complete darkness is not for the faint of heart and there were usually screams of fear but I had that reference below me which made it routine. It was a thrilling challenge. To this day, I do not know of anyone else who did spins at night!

Side Note: As a 17-year-old, Jimmy trusted me (now with Private Pilot license) to fly his 72-year-old mother Della and 12-year-old daughter Chris to Myrtle Beach, S.C. in his Cessna 172 (N7912X) to join the family on vacation. Now, I ask myself, would I trust my young daughter (if I had one) and aged mother with a 17-year-old pilot?

First Car

My first car was a green 1948 Plymouth coupe which I bought from Ben McCoy an ROTC student who took lessons at our airport. Ben, whose ambition was to be a doctor, noticed I liked the car which had been given to him by his Aunt. It was in pristine condition. Ben asked if I wanted the car and if so, he would sell it to me at a lower price than he was asking. That was $150.00 which I did not have. Jimmy bought the Plymouth for me but I had to pay him back. I drove the car home and turned in the license plates, since I did not have insurance. It sat in our dirt driveway for 10 weeks while I saved enough for the insurance which was $155.00, $5.00 more than I paid for the car. I would come home after school and crank Plymouth, listen to the AM radio, and dream of legally driving it someday. This was the first car in our family. I can still smell the interior, so proud to have a car to drive to school in my eleventh grade!

Night landings in a cow pasture

On occasion, I would fly to Jimmy's farm, in Mooresville which was not much more than a cow pasture. I had flown there with Jimmy landing at night in complete darkness, landing lights bringing the grass/dirt strip into focus at the last minute. I asked Jimmy how he did that! He pointed to his uncle Marvin's gas station across the road which had a lighted neon dairy sign in the window. He used the dairy sign to judge by. I too became proficient in using that sign at night. I flew a Cessna Sky Hawk, a Cessna Skylane and Piper Super Cruiser into and out that cow pasture at night on a few occasions. This would help me in my future ARMY flying.

Gibby and Randy

Two of my closest friends in my youth at the airport were Gibby Jenkins and Randy Gilleland. We were high school buddies, Gibby and I going back to the third grade. We were also in the Civil Air Patrol in which we shared many wonderful experiences. They, and occasionally one or two others enjoyed hanging out with me at the airport particularly when I put away aircraft for the evening. I developed a routine of taking the J-3 for a short night flight before putting it away. With no one around, we did some things that might have got us in deep trouble but were never caught. The J-3 had no lights, so it was illegal to fly it at night. Gibby was the only one with guts to ride along with me, he sat in the front seat holding a flashlight on the airspeed indicator as I took off into the darkness around the pattern, once flying over town, another time over the county fair. When we came in for landing, it was anyone's guess if I could pull off a descent landing. I thought as long as I could see the airspeed indicator and align with the runway lights, I could make it. No visual cues for depth perception. On several occasions I took aircraft off and landed on grass in front of the T-hangar to put an aircraft up for the night. We still reminisce about these events but have kept them to ourselves all these years. Who would believe it anyway? Just the beginning of my risk taking.

Completing Mike Branch's last 200 miles of his 6045-mile trip across the U.S. in his clipped wing Cub, N30551, Sep 13, 1962.

Mike Branch, my predecessor at the airport had a beautiful blue and white clipped wing J-3 Cub (N30551) with a sunburst wing paint scheme. It was hangared at my boss Jimmy's farm near Mooresville, N.C. A clipped wing cub is a normal J-3 Cub with approximately 42 inches of each wing removed (clipped) inboard next to the airframe. The shorter wings made it acrobatic with a sporty look. According to Mikes account, **A Boy's Great Flying Adventure**, December 2008, in the summer of 62' Mike set out in his Cub to fly across the United States to California and return using only charts, compass and a constant vigilance for landmarks. He departed Miller Airport, Mooresville, NC on July 31, 1962, his 6045-mile trip, and 82 flight hours would take him on a circuitous route southwest through western Texas, along the Mexican border to California where he stopped for a few days to visit his uncle and family at Rutherford, CA. Next, he flew north along the west coast to Washington State, then easterly to South Dakota from there southeast toward N.C. The Charlotte Observer newspaper requested Mike make a collect call each day to give a synopsis of the day's events which were reported daily in the newspaper as a human-interest story. The Cub was slow, so his trip with many stops along the way, took him 38 days. On Mike's return, he made it back to Island Airport, located on Dickinson's Island in the Tennessee River near Knoxville where he parked his Cub. Due to the weather and fall college classes starting at N.C. State, Mike had to leave his aircraft and take a bus back home, unable to complete the final 200 mile leg of his journey.

On the morning of September 13, 1962, Jimmy, on a trip with passengers, dropped me off at the small island airport to bring Mike's Cub back to Statesville. I was sixteen and only a few times had flown solo anywhere. Jimmy, from the start, placed more and more responsibility on me. I remember him telling me to just "follow the river" to get home, then he was gone. I looked over the airplane and observed a five gallon can of aviation gas strapped to the front seat. I was told, to make it, I would need to find an airport near Asheville, N.C on my way east, land and put the five gallons of gas in the gas tank located between the cockpit and the engine. I propped the airplane to start the engine, then climbed into the rear seat. There was no control tower, it was still early morning, bright and clear weather, so I taxied out, made my engine checks then applied full power on the Continental 75 horsepower engine. I had no electrical system for radios or navigation. Climbing up, I was already over the Tennessee river, so I kept it under my left wing as I proceeded east. In about an hour, I began looking for an airport to stop and refuel. I found an airport, but there were large white X's on each end of the runway meaning the airfield was closed for operation.

Continuing, I located another small airport near Asheville, in western North Carolina. I landed and put the five gallons of fuel in the nose tank. So far so good! I departed and located the river again, by now it was called the Catawba River. Western North Carolina mountains were very scenic, I had a bird's eye view sitting up there alone in Mike's Cub; the river continued onward with several man-made lakes below. In time I recognized the region below and turned toward my hometown airport. Back in my comfort zone, I landed and taxied in. I wanted to make sure I got someone to sign my logbook stating I had arrived 'Solo'. Ms. Betty Thigpen signed my log "Arrived solo Statesville, NC". My log indicates the trip took two hours and fifteen minutes. It was an honor to complete the last leg of Mikes momentous journey!

Side Note:
On Mike's return, the city of Mooresville had planned to have a reception and parade with the high school marching band. A parade was held in Mike's honor anyway. Mike later flew his Cub back to Island Airport, then back home so he could say (to himself), yes, I completed my trip.

Ray Barr

On a mid-week summer morning of July 1963, a red and white Piper Cherokee 140 landed and taxied in. The Cherokee was a single engine, all metal four-seater with low wings and tricycle landing gear. The pilot, a middle-aged gentleman, opened the door over the right wing, climbed out on the wing and stepped to the ground. He went into our terminal, soon returning to the ramp with a coke in hand. I noticed he was looking around the hanger exterior as if searching for something. Our hangar did not have a city identifier which he was looking for. He came and asked, "What city is this"? I told him "Statesville", then he asked, "What State"?

His name was Ray Barr, recently retired Navy Commander from Florida, on his way to Bluefield West Virginia, his hometown but made it only to Statesville. The Cherokee was a new purchase and he had little training in it. Ray spent several days with us, hanging out at the airport, going to lunch with us; we got to know him and enjoyed his company. Not sure of his navigating skills, he asked Jimmy to fly him to Bluefield in his Cherokee. Jimmy, confident in me, a Student pilot, a month before I took my Private Pilot check ride, told me to follow them in our Cessna 150 (N6626T). I had very little cross country flying experience. On our flight, I kept the Cherokee with Jimmy and Ray in sight in the distance, knowing if I lost them, I would be in deep trouble! Once they went between two clouds which closed momentarily ahead before I got through. My heart rate increased as I continued into the clouds and thankfully made it through to see them still ahead above the mountains! We made it to Bluefield, said our goodbyes and returned to Statesville. I now had more experience of cross country flying.

Close Call - flying with Jimmy Miller

In time, as you read some of my close call stories, you must be asking yourself, where in the heck did he learn to take chances and have them in the first place. I learned them from my experiences with other risk takers. Need to get somewhere, no problem, we will get there. At the time of late 50's and early 60's there was much to be learned about Aviation Safety. Risks were taken by many and accident rates back that up. This story I am about to tell falls in that category. I had the opportunity on occasion to 'ride' along on trips with my boss Jimmy who, as mentioned previously, operated Miller Aviation at my hometown local airport of Statesville, N.C. On this flight, I accompanied him as a young teen in his twin engine, white and green Piper Aztec, tail number N4727P to Bush Field airport in Augusta, Georgia. Trips like this were great experience for me. On our return, south of Statesville, I made a call to our airport to let them know Jimmy and I were south and would be there shortly. Jerome Eades who I will talk more about later answered the radio and told us the airport was socked in, clouds to the ground with poor visibility. As I recall, Jerome said, "I cannot see the windsock". As it happened, the weather was clear over the huge Lake Norman but north of the lake we could see the pall of weather before us. Jimmy, in the left seat, grinned at me and said, "Tell them we will be there soon". We descended to near tree-top level in the Aztec and continued. As we entered the weather, visibility was extremely poor. I was straining to see anything ahead when suddenly by reflex I grabbed and jerked the controls as a telephone pole, wires and all, appeared what seemed to be feet away out the right front in line with the right engine. We missed that pole by a whisper; it was there and gone beneath us in a nanosecond. Jimmy likely could not have seen the pole from his seat. It was strictly a reflex on my part, and I let go immediately afterwards. Jimmy looked over at me and said with a smile on his face, "Are you scared"? I don't think I made a comment and yes, I was scared! To this day I think I saved us. It was then that Jimmy realized we would not make it

176

in. He told me to tell Jerome we would divert to the Long Island Airport a few miles west across the Catawba River north of the lake. Long Island Airport could barely be called an airport, I had never been there. We landed on a wet muddy runway splattering mud on the aircraft. We could still communicate with the Statesville airport, so Jerome agreed to drive over and pick us up. Jimmy brought the aircraft home the next day and my job was to clean her up! I believe my many experiences of pushing the envelope in my aviation youth paid off in Vietnam.

Civil Air Patrol L-16

It was at the airport where I became affiliated with the Civil Air Patrol (CAP). At age 17, I received my Private Pilot's license by taking an FAA check ride given by Paul Wike from Charlotte. Having a Private Pilot's license, I was authorized as a Civil Air Patrol Cadet to fly CAP aircraft. During my two-week CAP summer camp at Shaw Air Force Base, SC, my wings were pinned on by COL Harp, the Shaw Commander in the base theater. Unexpectedly I was called forward not knowing what was happening. This was witnessed by several hundred other cadets who were there on our two-week summer camp. My photo was taken with COL Harp and a story, with photo put in the Shaw AFB newspaper.

The Statesville Civil Air Patrol Squadron had a beautiful L-16, a small, tail wheeled, silver colored fabric aircraft with the Civil Air Patrol logo on each side. After my check out I flew to several Civil Air Patrol functions across the state. When I taxied up as a kid in that L-16 I was center of attention until I showed my credentials proving I was legal. At that time, I was the only Cadet pilot in the North Carolina Civil Air Patrol

Civil Air Patrol Summer Camp at Donaldson Air Force Base.

Dropping a 17-year-old as a 17-year-old

We had a skydiving instructor, name I no longer recall, rent our aircraft from time to time for his students. I was so impressed and wanted to learn myself, even went so far as get my Mom's signature approval to jump. I practiced jumping from a 55-gal barrel making what I had been shown were Parachute Landing Fall (PLF) landings. One day, the instructor had a 17-

year-old kid who would be making a jump. He wore a cast on his left wrist and arm, an injury suffered from a previous jump. I, also a17-year -old, would be taking this kid up for the jump in a Piper Super Cruiser with the cabin door removed. I took the instructor up first to 3000 feet where he judged the wind by throwing a streamer out. He showed me a field below and yelled through the engine noise to "Drop him out over the corner of that field".

Here we were, two 17-year-olds sort of pushing the envelope. As we neared the drop point, I directed the kid to get out onto the step. I held his left cast covered arm with my right to help him hold on. As I held his arm, I felt the intense adrenaline from his body to mine. He watched my eyes and when I said 'GO' he let go, drifting down and away, for a second our eyes remained locked. As he fell, I chased him down to observe a good parachute landing on the airfield. I never had the opportunity to jump.

Doodle Brown and Sonny's Jump

I've mentioned Doodle Brown quite a bit. Doodle was what we might call an airport bum, someone who loves to be around aircraft. He was known to be 'Johnny on the spot', both at the Miller Farm airport near Mooresville and frequently on weekends in Statesville. It was not unusual for Doodle to pitch in on just about anything needing done. In his early thirties, about 5'7", fit as a fiddle to use that vernacular. Not sure what his weekday job was but Doodle had a close friend, Sonny. Where you saw Doodle, Sonny was usually there as well. Doodle trim and fit, Sonny overweight. Doodle decided to take up skydiving, not to be outdone, Sonny would take up skydiving as well. On a particular Saturday, Sonny, harnessed on a parachute, went up in our Piper Tri Pacer, left rear door removed for his first jump. Over the jump site, Sonny climbed out, foot on the step, hanging on the left wing strut, then decided, hey, I don't want to do this! Try as he might, he was too large with the parachute to get back in the aircraft. Finally, he had no choice but let go, making this his first and last jump!

Terry Eisenhauer-Wrong Way Corrigan

In 1927, Charles Lindberg became the first aviator to cross the Atlantic solo on a 33-hour flight in the Spirit of St. Louis from Roosevelt Field, Long Island to Paris- Le Bourget airport. Douglas Corrigan, who had worked on the Lindberg team also wanted to make that solo trip but was denied permission due to the condition of his aircraft. In 1938, he departed an airfield in Brooklyn, NY in what he said would be a solo flight to California; suddenly he made a 180 degree turn to end up in Dublin, Ireland, thus making the Atlantic crossing solo. Corrigan said he had compass problems and never changed his story. For this feat, his moniker would forever be 'Wrong Way Corrigan' as were many pilots later who lost their way. Ref-17 We had our own Wrong Way Corrigan; his name was Terry Eisenhauer. Terry, a 16-year-old, small in stature, sandy hair, planned his solo cross-country flight while working on his Private Pilot License. His intended flight was southwest. Terry departed in our Cessna 150, tail number N6626T on a Sunday afternoon. After hours passed nothing had been heard from Terry. He had read his plastic plotter backwards while planning his flight on his map. His instructor had not caught the error. His flight was actually northeast, 180 degrees opposite from his intended flight. Hours later, out of fuel, Terry landed at dusk in a peanut patch near Emporia, Virginia! He did such a good job that he did not put a scratch on the aircraft, only destroying six peanut plants! Terry was not injured with the exception of his pride. Next day, Jimmy went up to Emporia along with Houston Ballard, a historical figure in his own right. They pulled the small Cessna out onto the nearby highway put fuel in it and Jimmy flew the aircraft back to Statesville. Houston told us later there were power lines Terry would have crossed on his landing, and he could not see how Terry put the aircraft down in the field without hitting those power lines. Devine intervention? Thus, Terry was given the moniker 'Wrong Way Corrigan!

Charles Vinson (C.V.) Stewart

C.V. Stewart came to Statesville late 1961 as our chief A&P mechanic after the loss of Virgil Outlaw. C.V., often referred to as 'Stewart' brought with him his wife, daughters Gail, Vicki, and nine-year-old son Vincent; they lived in a house trailer on the airport not far from Stewart's shop. In his late forties, slim with receding black hairline, short mustache, Stewart typically wore white shirt and trousers the name 'Stewart' above right shirt pocket. He brought with him a highly respected reputation, none the least his ability to restore old or damaged aircraft. He began rebuilding old planes in 1945 in Portsmouth, VA. It's the woodwork and fabric which offers the biggest challenge, he said.

Hanging from the rafters at the renowned Steven F. Udvar-Hazy Center, National Air and Space Museum adjacent to Washington Dulles International Airport is a red Monocoupe 110 Special (N36Y) in which Woody Edmondson won the1948 International Aerobatic Championship Ref-18. Woody named his Monocoupe "Little Butch" which is painted on the cowling. C.V. knew and spoke of Woody often. Woody sold Little Butch in the early 50's to be owned by several individuals. In 1965 John McCulloch an Eastern Airlines Captain bought a 'wrecked' Little Butch and had it shipped to Naples, Florida, his hometown, to be rebuilt by C.V. (as told by C.V.), a Monocoupe specialist. McCulloch donated Little Butch to the museum December 29, 1981. Ref-19. It was undoubtedly recovered with new fabric again through the years. C.V. told me he always signed fuel tanks of the aircraft he rebuilt. On occasion I've visited the museum and wondered if C.V.'s signature is on one of the fuel tanks of Little Butch hanging high above.

Side note: Johnny Gibson, was enthralled with the Monocoupe; he purchased one from a mid-western state (no longer remember which state), removed the wings and towed it back to Statesville to refurbish. Of course, he had the Monocoupe specialist, C.V., to assist him.

Winter months saw less maintenance; to keep personnel gainfully employed, repairs and rebuilds of damaged aircraft were typically scheduled at this time.

LR. C, V. Stewart, Jimmy Miller, John Gibson (Photo Max Tharpe)

Three such repairs and stories of C.V.'s work follows:

McNeer Dillon

McNeer Dillon who owned a local manufacturing company had been an ardent lover of aviation since his youth from what I had heard he too had soloed at 16. At the time I knew and liked him, he had a small two place aircraft which he kept at the airport. McNeer would come on Sundays at times and take his lovely wife for a short flight. His aircraft, an Ercoupe, it was called, barely had room to carry a hat box behind the two cockpit seats. In time. McNeer found an old Stinson SR-9, a five passenger tail wheel aircraft with a large radial 300 horsepower Lycoming engine. The monstrous looking SR-9s were first flown in 1933. They had what was referred to as Gull Wings which looked like a large hump on top of each wing, in fact these were referred to as Gull Wing Stinsons. McNeer, with no experience in the Stinson brought the aircraft to our airport and hired our mechanic C.V. to completely rebuild it. After months of diligent work to include new fabric covering, McNeer took the Stinson out for touch and Go's a time or two to get used to the aircraft. It was something to watch, it appeared to be a handful to handle. One Sunday, McNeer brought his wife and another couple out to take them for a joy ride in that big Stinson to show it off. Belching smoke after startup, they taxied out and off they went. About forty minutes later they taxied back in. When the four of them exited the aircraft, I could tell something was wrong. Each had that 'fatal' look which caught the attention of others as well. McNeer asked for C.V. our mechanic to come out so he could tell him what had happened. While they were enjoying their ride, that large 300 horsepower Lycoming engine quit running. Stopped! Naturally, all onboard were thinking this was their last day on earth! Eventually the engine restarted as they were descending with the propeller wind milling. C.V. solved the problem within minutes. As he stood next to the engine, he noticed water dripping from the engine cowling. He told McNeer he had encountered carburetor icing which had cut the airflow to the carburetor, thus the engine stoppage. This is not uncommon, had he known to pull the carburetor heat knob, he would have been ok. From then on, McNeer' s wife and friends were never seen in that monster again!

Later, McNeer bought another old aircraft. It had been in a barn for years and the fabric was rotten. The aircraft had a number of identities such as a Twin Cessna, Bamboo Bomber, AT-17, and T-50. It was a twin-engine advanced trainer used to train pilots as they transitioned to B-17s and other multi-engine aircraft. If you ever watched the Sky King TV shows of the fifties, his earliest aircraft, the 'Songbird', was a Twin Cessna. C.V. used cotton fabric from McNeer's business to put temporary coverings on the wings to make it flyable to Statesville. A young man by the name of Dick Fromm as I recall, flew it to Statesville from the Greensboro/High Point area. Dick flew it leaving the gear down. I was at the airport when it arrived, excited to see it. McNeer' s twin Cessna, also a five-seater, was predominately made of wood and fabric. It was not designed for longevity but to meet immediate requirements of World War II training. C. V. rebuilt damaged wood and put new fabric on the fuselage and wings which took many months. It flew without incident.

A year or so earlier, I was given the opportunity to sit in the back seat of one of these as George Brown, an instructor from the nearby Salisbury airport, stopped by Statesville while doing training. Never forget seeing a chain, much like a bicycle chain, visible from the cabin floor, turning the gear mechanism to raise and lower the gear! Dick Fromm went on to be a Piedmont and USAIR Captain.

Flipping Joe Hornbuckle's Super Cruiser on its nose

On my return from Civil Air Patrol Summer Camp at Shaw Air Force Base, South Carolina one summer, I resumed my duties as Line Boy at the airport. My first day back, as usual I put away aircraft at the close of day into each of our two hangars. My last aircraft that evening was Joe Hornbuckle's Piper PA-12 Super Cruiser which had just been through a complete rebuild with all new fabric covering. Joe, a middle-aged businessman and a good friend had it painted in a beautiful deep red color with white trim. He and his family were quite proud of it. I got into the Cruiser which was on the front blacktop ramp and fired up the engine. I had taxied this aircraft a lot and knew its idiosyncrasies, one of which was the knowledge of poor braking. I gathered up speed and rounded the back side of the front hangar, heading to the rear hangar, now on gravel, I pulled the power back and intuitively applied full brakes which ordinarily would bring me to a slow stop. This time, however, in my absence, the brakes had been repaired so when I applied full brakes, the aircraft came to almost an abrupt stop which threw me forward on the control stick, the tail lifted and the nose went forward, the propeller struck the ground hard several times, Wham! Wham! before coming to a full stop. Then the tail fell back to the ground, and I sat there in bewilderment. My career flashed before my eyes as I realized what had just happened. I sat there in the airplane not moving, how long I am not sure, but it was a long time, eventually darkness began settling in. Our mechanic, C.V. noticed the airplane, which he had rebuilt, walked over to me, and asked what was wrong. I told him what I did and upon observation the propeller tips had sustained damage. C.V. told me not to worry, to put away the aircraft and go home. C.V., a master mechanic, trimmed two inches off the propeller tips and repainted the propeller. It was such a nice job; you could not tell there had been any damage. This was a secret kept between C.V. and me, no one was ever the wiser. Joe still had his Cruiser after I moved on. I am sure the shortened propeller diminished the performance of his aircraft, but he never knew. To this day I can see that propeller banging into the ground as I observed from the cockpit! I will always be grateful to C.V. for saving my bacon!

Sadly, in March 1963, C.V.'s wife died suddenly at their house trailer. Three children now without a Mom. She was only 45.

Some years later, C.V. remarried, his new wife Virginia became his assistant; from what I have read, she became a skilled mechanic. The two were a good match, together they rebuilt many aircraft. C.V. made the comment that at the time he and his wife were about the only ones left who liked working with wood and fabric. They spent two years in Africa where Stewart says he did a lot of work on one of the busiest airlines over there.

C.V. later was manager of the Lake Norman Aviation Maintenance shop near Mooresville. One day, he and his wife observed a Cessna 172 crash nearby after takeoff. C.V. rushed to the aircraft and pulled three men from the twisted wreckage. The aircraft was leaking fuel but did not catch fire. One man suffered compound fractures, the other two with contusions and abrasions. C.V.'s quick action saved the men from possible death had the aircraft caught fire.

C.V.'s legacy will forever be remembered by me. With a stroke of luck, after nearly 60 years, I am now in touch with his son, Vinson, 'C.V. Jr'., eight years my junior, a Navy retiree. A real treat recalling my memories of him as an eleven-year-old, sharing stories of his dad. C.V. passed away in 1982, age 68, buried in a military plot at Statesville Oakwood Cemetery. In the summer of 2023, I met with C.V. Jr. at the cemetery to visit his father's grave.

CHAPTER 21

Piedmont Airlines Martin 404 Landing at Statesville one evening by mistake.

How many exciting times can a young man have? What they say about flying, adjusted to my circumstances at the airport, "Days of boredom mixed with unplanned events of great excitement". One such event was when a Piedmont airliner landed at our small airport one summer evening by mistake! It was warm, clear skies, well past sunset. The single bulb of the tin metal constructed hangar light mounted high at the center apex on the front exterior shone brightly illuminating several owners of a Piper Super Cruiser as they dutifully busied themselves with light utility work on their aircraft. As was often the case, I was entrusted with closing the small terminal building at the end of the day; my boss Jimmy had long since departed for his farm in his Cessna 172. Lights for the two perpendicular runways were lit; the rotating beacon of white and green was slowly making swaths of light across the shadowy terrain. In those days it was not uncommon for owners to come after work and spend time with their airplanes. In total, there were 15 or 20 airplanes on the airport. At the end of the day, aircraft left on the ramp were stacked in the hangars usually by me. Those who kept their aircraft in our two hangars paid hangar fees, others kept theirs tied down in a grassy area off the side to the west beyond the fuel pumps.

Our attention was suddenly drawn by an unfamiliar aircraft sound coming from the west, landing lights on, beacon flashing; those who saw it at first surmised it was Farrell James stopping by in a twin engine Aero Commander which he sometimes did. As it neared and joined the traffic pattern for a left turn on final to runway **20**, we knew it was a large piston aircraft. We stopped what we were engaged in, fixated on the two bright landing lights coming in our direction but high. When it touched down, it was already some distance down the runway. We heard the engines roar as the pilot put the propellers in reverse pitch and bore down on the brakes. It looked as if the aircraft would not be able to stop at the end of this 3650 feet short runway which had a drop off at the end. I recall someone, saying, "He's not going to make it", then Harold Williams chimed in "He might make it. Well, he did make it but with only a foot or two it seemed from our vantage point looking out in the darkness. Having settled for a moment or two, the pilot put the aircraft in a tight right rearward turn to join intersecting runway **28** he had just crossed to make a very short taxi and left turn onto our ramp. It was then that we saw in bright red letters, **Piedmont Airlines** on the side. It was a Martin 404, a large twin reciprocating engine aircraft with full passenger load of 40! I had no idea what to do so I took charge as a young kid, walked out alone on the ramp which was barely large enough for this aircraft, raised both my arms to direct the aircraft for parking. As the aircraft turned left onto the ramp, aimed at me with two giant propellers turning, an arm appeared from the front left cockpit window waving me out of the way and I complied. The airliner inched forward then powered up the left engine to assist in making a 180-degree right turn. We feared the prop blast would damage aircraft in the hangar, but it did not. In short time, as our small group gawked at what we were seeing, the left engine shut down, but the right engine was kept at an idle. Then the exit door in the tail lowered, a uniformed pilot exited and approached me. His first comment was, "This is Statesville, isn't it?" I replied, yes and he said, "I was afraid of that, can I use your phone?" I led him to our brick veneer terminal building and the office, pointing to the phone. I walked out on the concrete walkway outside the office which had its windows cranked open. Without intending, I overheard the pilot's call. He asked the operator to give him "Park 50511" which I later surmised was the Piedmont Airline dispatcher. He said, "This is Posey Smith, I just pulled the biggest boner in the world, I landed at Statesville." For about 45 minutes the passengers remained inside the aircraft, which kept the right engine still running to have electrical power to restart the left engine. In time, another gentleman exited the aircraft, walked up the concrete walkway through the gate of our four-foot chain link fence to discuss the situation with Captain Smith. I learned this was Tom Davis, president of the airline! He had two guests on board with him. Posey said he and the first officer were enroute from Tri-City airport, Tennessee to Hickory, North Carolina which was about 25 miles west of Statesville. When they saw our rotating beacon, they "assumed" it was Hickory's airport, so they put their charts away and headed to Statesville, by mistake. They were high because Hickory airport is 368 feet higher elevation than Statesville. For that reason, they used up runway before touching down. Mr. Davis commented later that under the circumstances that was one good landing.

As soon as I got the chance, I called Jimmy at his home to let him know what happened; he headed back to Statesville in his Cessna 172. Mr. Davis wanted to let the passengers off to mill around while they were checking to see if the FAA would let them depart with passengers all the while the right aircraft engine remained idling. He told me to keep the passengers outside of the fence away from sightseers who had appeared out of nowhere. I looked at the parking lot and saw a cluster of headlights! Where had they come from, how did they know! Of course, it was not possible to keep the passengers from discovering what had happened. Eastern Airlines was on strike at the time, which accounted for a full load of passengers.

The FAA did not approve the aircraft taking off with passengers aboard, so two large buses were brought out to take the passengers to Winston Salem with exception of two young teenage sisters who were put in a taxi to drive them to Hickory. The purser, (male steward) went with the passengers in the buses. Some three hours after landing, the Martin 404 Piedmont airliner with only three on board, Posey Smith, his First Officer and Mr. Davis, president of the airline, departed using the same lighted runway in the opposite direction. Never forget the loud roar, the aircraft lights and the steep climbing left turn in the darkness as they made their way to Winston Salem. Jimmy had made it to the airport and was now gone. It was eerily quiet as I walked out to turn off the hangar lights and head home. Now on the dark empty ramp, I asked myself, "Did this really happen?" I have searched these past years while preparing this book but could not find any mention of this event. For those of us who were there that night though, we spoke of it often.

Saying Hi to MOM from above

Mom never saw me fly; she knew little of the experiences I had. Once, on an early flight some years later, I asked her to come out on the front porch with the porch light on so that I could pass overhead and she would know it was me, her young son. I changed the propeller pitch back and forth while passing overhead which made a distinctive sound. She had seen me above in the night sky but never in an aircraft.

Loren Edwards

Loren, slim, dark hair, in his late 20's, a charismatic individual, always happy, began his professional flying career at our airport. He had an Aeronca Chief, small two-seater single engine tailwheel aircraft hangered in Mooresville on Jimmy's farm. He became an exceptional pilot, eventually moving up to fly our twin radial engine Beech D-18s which were used for carrying 80 to 100 boxes of newborn baby chicks mostly throughout the south and southwest. As a 17-year-old I accompanied him to Keene New Hampshire on an instrument flight in one of the Beech's. On our return flight, we crossed into the New York sector control region. It was late at night, Loren, in the left seat held his navigation chart up close to check our routing, he slid the front left window back for some fresh air, when 'swoosh', his chart was sucked out the window! Now what? He calmly told our controller that, "believe it or not, my chart just got sucked out the window"! New York graciously gave us headings until we crossed into our next sector which we had charts for.

Loren was a trickster, on one occasion we were in a small aircraft near home low over water, heading toward the shore approaching trees to see who would grab the controls first! I chickened out and grabbed the controls as he laughed!

I picked Loren up one night in our Cessna 150, N6626T, and we headed back to the airport, visibility poor, in rain, we were hugging the tops of buildings over Statesville when Loren pulled the engine mixture control which cut off fuel to the engine; Loren yelled "Forced Landing"! I pushed the mixture back in immediately and we made it back. Loren was fun that way. I learned from him as with so many others. He later became Captain with Piedmont Airlines and eventually USAIR.

Willie Martin

When first meeting Willie Martin, I observed a young sandy haired man, slim, light blue eyes, mid to late 20's. He was accompanied by a friend that summer afternoon, I noticed he was quite friendly but also had a prosthetic hook with pincers on his left arm. I also noticed he was a little inebriated. As we stood outside our terminal building under the covered walkway, he asked if he might pay for an airplane ride. I took him up in our yellow J-3 which I believed to be his first flight; he was immensely impressed. He came time and again to hang out at the airport. I learned he was previously employed with International Paper Company in Statesville, where he lost his left hand in an accident.

In the Fall, I was in school, attending the local Mitchell Junior College, working elsewhere, no longer having contact with Willie.

Years later, after my 19-month tour in Vietnam, I returned to my beloved Statesville airport for a visit. The day I was there, a twin-engine Beechcraft Queen Aire landed, taxied in, and parked. To my astonishment, Willie was the pilot, a corporate pilot! How could this be! Somehow in the intervening years he obtained a commercial pilot license, most likely an instrument rating and multi-engine rating! It was such a thrill to learn of his many accomplishments! One can only surmise what he had overcome to meet his goals, proud of him is an understatement.

Willie took me to see his aircraft, he in the front left seat, me in the right, he demonstrated how he was able to control the yoke with his 'hooked' left hand while controlling the throttles with his right. Such a joy to see what can be achieved if the desire is there, dreams can come true.

CHAPTER 22
Aircraft Accidents

Dave Michael's tragic death. Near Salisbury, N.C.

A number of tragic deaths occurred while I was Line Boy and later pilot at Miller Aviation over the years. I start with that of Dave Michaels. Dave came to us as others had before and would later get into aviation. He was a retired Navy officer, a diver, an underwater welder to be exact; lean and still young in his early 40's. He had a lovely wife and two teenage sons which he gloated over. Never a dull moment when Dave was around, he continued wearing his blond, slightly greying hair in the traditional flat top military cut. Dave was a perpetual storyteller, laughter his trademark. He played the mandolin with aplomb, entertaining our small group with witty performances. Dave, in time worked his way up to flying our twin-engine Beechcraft D-18s of which there were two. The D-18 had twin 450 horsepower radial engines, low wings with a tail wheel. It could be configured to carry six to eleven passengers. Our D-18s, tail numbers N78N and N73E, stripped bare inside for cargo usually carrying boxes of newly hatched baby chicks throughout the south and southwest all the way to Texas. On occasion we had trips to Kennedy International and Keene, New Hampshire. Not rated in the D-18, I had several occasions to ride in the right seat with Dave. From the lucrative chick hauling, we ventured into hauling tropical fish from Florida to points north. These were the small fish sold at pet stores. Pickups were usually at Vero Beach Florida; the fish were in medium size plastic bags partially filled with water; oxygen pumped in to keep the fish oxygenated. Bags were encased in sealed 2'X2X2' cardboard boxes for easy handling. A typical flight might have upwards of 80 boxes.

On one of these flights, March 1, 1968, Dave departed Statesville for Vero Beach in one of the D-18s to pick up boxes of tropical fish and deliver them most likely to Greensboro, North Carolina. Accompanying him were two young men, one, Tom Porter, later to be a Piedmont Airline captain. They were typical of the time, eager to gain flight experience. We received a late afternoon call from Dave in Florida telling us that the aircraft had maintenance issues and he was renting a D-18, tail number N281FM, from the local airport. Next morning, I received a call to come to Salisbury mortuary to identify Dave's burned body. What happened? How could this be? Dave had crashed off the end of the nearby Salisbury airport. He was the only fatality, the other two were saved by the many boxes of fish. This is their story as I remember. On their way north, at night, the cabin got cold, so they turned on the Janitrol cabin heater located in the nose compartment which used the aircraft fuel for combustion. At some point heavy smoke began filling the cabin from underneath the instrument console in front of Dave who occupied the front left seat. They suspected the cabin heater was the problem but were unable to turn it off. To breath, Dave slid open his cockpit window sticking his head out for fresh air. The other two went back to the cabin situating themselves between the boxes. Dave desperately trying to control the D-18 as best he could, decided to land at Salisbury. They crashed just after midnight on March 2nd, short of the runway while approaching the airport making an emergency landing. Dave was killed in the accident only a few miles from where he was born and raised. His wife and two young sons were at home in Salisbury. Miraculously the other two sustained only minor injuries in the rear, crouching between the many boxes which acted like air bags. The aircraft was torn apart on impact and, as they told me, they simply rolled out onto the ground into the darkness. I was called to the morgue to identify Dave's body. I identified him by one of his heels which had a scar from a war wound. He had talked about the wound before and showed his heel to some of us. He was a hero, saving the other two by his sacrifice.

Paul Edinger

It was nice knowing an individual such as Paul Edinger, a thin, quiet, bespectacled individual 28 years old. He was an engineer recently assigned to the Kewaunee Technical Manufacturing Company in Statesville, a subsidiary of Kewaunee Manufacturing in Michigan from where Paul had come. I met his parents, wife Joyce, 24, and two children Paula (4) and Victor (1). They were special. In no time, Paul purchased a small underpowered single engine Piper Tri Pacer with intent to use it to return from time to time to Michigan to visit family. The Tri Pacer was a four-passenger, fabric airplane with a luggage compartment in the rear. Paul learned to fly his airplane and regularly came out in the afternoons to fly it in the short time I knew him. When asked to fly with him, for instrument instructions, Jim Miller (not my boss, Jimmy Miller), was appalled that Paul had been flying solo wearing an instrument hood teaching himself instrument flying. This was risky at best. When Paul made plans to use the upcoming 4th of July 1963 to fly to Michigan it was no surprise. Some days prior to the holiday, Paul brought his wife and children along with friends, a young married couple to clean the aircraft and prepare it for the trip. They were all happy. Unbelievably, they were planning on the four adults and two children to take the trip, all of them! Paul offered to drop the couple off in Kentucky on his way to Michigan and pick them up on his return. In retrospect it was not plausible to load four adults and two small children into the small four-seater. No one said anything or offered advice. On the morning of departure, I observed all six loaded into the aircraft along with baggage, a squatting landing gear hinted at the excess weight. I watched them taxi away and depart. Days later we got tragic news, Paul and all aboard including the couple he picked up on his return had crashed July 7th, 1963, near Hazard Kentucky. All aboard were killed. There was a state of shock for us at the airport! I envisioned memories of them just days before. We learned Paul had gotten into weather; it was suspected, lost control due to limited instrument flying experience. Those of us who knew Paul were deeply saddened but in retrospect, it was almost predictable. If only someone had talked to Paul. Later his brother stopped by to settle Paul's account. We of course expressed our deepest sympathies.

Pilot killed in Bonanza while taking off

One week, a gentleman flew in with a V-tail Beechcraft Bonanza. The Bonanza was a popular single engine, tricycle landing gear, all aluminum aircraft with lots of power. It was unique for having only two tail fins shaped like a 'V'. These were called "ruddervators". Quite a few crashed over the years, usually attributed to wealthy overconfident amateur pilots. The gentleman, who spent the week, had business in Statesville. One morning he departed early and crashed on takeoff, dying in the crash. Don't recall the finding of reason for the crash. The wrecked aircraft, with top torn off was brought back and put in the grass behind our front hangar. I was asked to show it several times. One of the deceased pilot's shoes remained on the floor below the control yoke. On one such viewing, I happened to notice a watch in the shoe which had not been there before. On close examination it was a Rolex. How did it get there? I surmised, someone had taken it initially from the crash, then had a guilt complex and secretly placed it in the shoe. Not long after the fatal crash, I looked out the window to see what I believed to be the deceased pilot walking in! Turns out, it was his identical twin brother. I gave him his brother's Rolex.

Jimmy and Robert Brawley Luscombe crash

Jimmy was riding with Robert Brawley on a weekend check ride in the small 65 H.P Luscombe Robert co-owned with Jim Murdock. After takeoff on runway 20 heading southwest, Jimmy pulled the throttle for a practice forced landing, but the aircraft engine did not recover in time before they crashed into trees off the end of the runway. I saw the crash and ran across the ramp, past the grass beyond the fuel pumps into the small trees where I saw them go in. As I was making my way in the trees, I met Robert rushing towards me, as we met, Robert never said a word, but kept going. When I reached the Luscombe tilted nose downward in the short pines, Jimmy was sitting on top of the fuselage above the cockpit, he smiled and said, "What took you so long?". The aircraft had only minor damage and C.V. had it repaired in no time.

Miller Aviation DC-3 crashing on takeoff

In time, Miller Aviation progressed into a multi-state operation. It happened by chance when we had a request to carry six boxes of live baby chicks to Douglas Municipal Airport in Charlotte to be dropped off at air freight. At the time the local hatchery shipped most of their chicks by ground which had a percentage of lost chicks. The hatchery and my boss Jimmy deduced the chicks could be delivered by air with much less loss. This led eventually to the purchases of two twin- engine Beechcraft D-18s for cargo. Miller Aviation evolved (as mentioned previously) into carrying baby chicks to multiple locations throughout the U.S. which, though only slightly lucrative foretold better things to come. I might add there were virtually no loss of chicks when carried by air. Eventually we picked up a retired Montgomery

194

Ward DC-3 (N525W). Jimmy went to Kansas, got a quick checkout, and flew it back to Statesville. It was a beauty with an executive interior, extended windows in lieu of traditional round windows. The interior was removed, making it compatible for cargo hauling. Jimmy was a seat of the pants flyer; one early afternoon he wanted to get the empty DC-3 ready, along with two others anxious to go (neither were pilots). We had a recently retired schoolteacher that came to work for us, his name was Bill Dulin, lanky with gray mustache, a WWII B-17 pilot. He liked being around aircraft again. When he heard Jimmy was getting ready for flight, the DC3 had a trace of snow covering the wings. I observed Bill with a ladder and broom cleaning snow off the right wing as best he could. Before he could get to the left wing, Jimmy said never mind, got to go! At approximately 1:45 P.M., February 29, 1968, He and his compatriots taxied out from the ramp and lined up on runway 28. The weather was cloudy with limited visibility. As they accelerated, I watched the tail lift off the ground then disappear from sight down the runway not yet airborne. I was about to turn away when I heard the crash! By the time I got to the aircraft, it was off the end of the runway in some small pine trees. No injuries except to the beautiful DC3. From what I gathered; the left wing did not lift off due to, I think, snow on the left wing disrupting lift. The official FAA report stated the aircraft had a left engine failure, but I strongly suspect it was the snow on the left wing. Years later, in Germany in the ARMY, I landed at a U.S. Air Force base to discharge passengers. There was light snow falling and I had a noticeably light covering on my wings. I attempted a takeoff but could not gain lift, so I aborted the takeoff. Taxied back and cleaned the wings, back for takeoff and I had lift. This reinforced my opinion of the cause of the DC3 crash back in 1968.

PART III

CHAPTER 23

Dangerous events and Close Calls of 1964 - 1967

Looking over my records and flight logs which I carefully documented, I became aware of just how many significant events and CLOSE CALLS I had during my senior year in high school and the remaining summer and fall. It was 1964 and by now I continued honing my skills as a pilot. I advanced from the age of 15 from being a 'line boy' pumping gas, washing airplanes to general all-around roustabout. From mopping floors and cleaning bathrooms I was eventually given full access to our operations of making billings and interacting with customers. My boss, Jimmy managed the airport along with his nephew Mason who retired years later from USAIR as Captain and instructor on Boeing 767s. As I advanced from Student Pilot to Private Pilot ratings, I was given more responsibility. By my senior year, I was flying, on occasion, Barger Construction Company's Cessna Skylane in which I carried one of their site supervisors to various locations in North Carolina and Virginia. I had numerous trips for Miller Aviation as well.

On several trips, if it was during school, I called my high school principal Mr. L. Dent Miller to ask for time off. Recall him asking in his deep voice "Delbert, do you think you can afford it"? I would tell him I wanted to pursue a career in Aviation at which point he would say "Go ahead but report back when you get in". I came back and, on several occasions, buzzed the school prior to landing at our airport.

In High School I was on the school wrestling team which won the Western North Carlina High School Athletic Association (WNCHSAA) championship, the first ever for our school.

197

Side <u>Note</u>: One of my friends, Bob Wasson, wrote the following in an email to friends, November 2, 2017:

Posted to All,

Some people are 'born to fly', and Delbert Hardiman is one of them. I flew with him in high school, and never felt safer. In college, I remember at least one time when we double dated in a 172 and flew to Charlotte at night for dinner. Our dates were impressed. Del frequently invited a friend and me on some of his commercial flights taking newborn chickens to their new homes in various states for a local hatchery but, sadly, I never had time to go. Good memories...

Bob Wasson

Mr. Miller, (my school principal), was one of my greatest mentors. He was encouraging, always asking about the Civil Air Patrol of which I was recognized by the North Carolina Wing and widely known. His confidence in me, led him to have Congressman James T. Broyhill nominate me to the U.S. Air Force Academy. I took and passed the written tests my fall year as a senior in high school.

I received a letter from Shaw Air Force Base, South Carolina, Subject: *Scheduling of Air Force Academy Candidates.* I was scheduled to report Monday, March 2, 1964, for the final two days of qualifying tests. USAF MAJ Harold Hartwig flew me from Charlotte in a chartered Cessna 210 (N3736Y) to Shaw. I passed the physical exams with flying colors.

I had a decision to make, had not planned on a career in the Air Force and had doubts about the rigors of the Academy. My career goals had been to be an airline pilot; I had several Piedmont Captains vouch for me. It was a foregone conclusion, at the time, I would make it to the airlines, but as you will read, that was not to be. Perhaps if I had a solid father figure at home to guide me, I would have elected to pursue the Academy, but I made the decision not to go, my thoughts were of my mother who needed my help. I thank Mr. Miller for his confidence in me to get me on an excellent path for my future but alas, the decision was mine.

CHAPTER 24
Close Call

Flight to Asheville, N.C. to visit girl friend

Saturday, April 4th, 1964, I flew from Statesville, my hometown in North Carolina west to Asheville, N.C. to spend a night at my girlfriend Jane Brown's house. I was in a small four-seater tail wheel, Piper Clipper, N5816H. Flight controls were dual stick and rudder pedals. This was my senior year in high school. According to my logs this was my fourth trip to Asheville. I had met Jane at one of my four Civil Air Patrol (CAP) summer camps which was a two-week event sponsored by the United States Air Force at Donaldson, Shaw and Myrtle Beach Air Force Bases, South Carolina. The flight to Asheville Regional airport was a one-hour flight. Jane's family picked me up for the seventeen-mile drive to her home. They were always welcoming and treated me like family. The next day, April 5th, I planned to return home, but the weather was not good, low clouds, some fog. My 'Get-home-itis' kicked in and I convinced myself I could make it back. Checking weather, cloud ceilings were reported to be about 4000 feet. I called back to Statesville, Terry Eisenhour, the 16-year-old filling in for me at the airport told me it looked like things were clearing up to the west, the direction I would be coming from. When word got out, I would be flying to Statesville, Jane informed me there were two North Carolina State University students who would like to catch a ride with me to Statesville, then proceed back to school from there. I said yes. The Clipper had two fuel tanks, a twelve-gallon tank in the nose and a leaking left wing 17-Gal tank. The nose tank gauge resembled that of an old 'A' model Ford. It was a bubble type indicating 4/4 for full, 3/4, 1/4, down to eventually 0/0 for empty. The left-wing gauge under the tank, near the front left window, was a graduated glass tube emanating from beneath the enclosed tank with markings indicated by a visible rod attached to a floating cork in the tank. These were sometimes referred to as boiler glass gauges. This aircraft had just been rebuilt and fuel leaked from the gauge. I filled up the nose tank and put five gallons in the left wing knowing that it would be my first to use due to the leak. At the time there was no radar so no tracking of me after my takeoff. I fired up with my two passengers, one beside me in the right seat and the other in the rear. I called the tower and asked for a 'Special VFR' departure which meant after my departure I would report clear of the airport and be on my way. Taxiing out, I was the only aircraft moving on the airfield. I was cleared for a 'Special VFR' departure and applied power to the 115 horse Lycoming. No sooner airborne than I was in the clouds and immediately realized I was in trouble. I did not have instrument training and the heading indicator began turning with me not being able to control my heading. I got one last glimpse of the terrain only to see I was now heading 90 degrees to the left of my intended course and in that direction were hills! With no instrument training, I could not control my heading, I climbed alternating slight left, then right turns to keep from losing the aircraft. This was very taxing, but I kept with it. It was like being in a compact car with zero visibility cruising at 100 MPH! Meantime, my two passengers had no idea we were in trouble. I felt that once I made it to the top of the cloud layer it would be clear on top, and I would be ok after that. I climbed through four thousand, five thousand, six thousand and at that point I could not get the aircraft to climb any more. I thought of carburetor icing, so I pulled the carburetor heat knob and the engine surged, I remember a momentary sound like that of a block of ice being put in a chipper. So, I continued my climb alternating headings back and forth desperately looking for the top of the clouds. At 10,200 feet barely climbing by now, I broke out on top! I was in what I will describe as a fishbowl in which I was at the bottom of the bowl. My heading, when I broke, out was 270 (West) opposite the direction I needed to go. Some miles straight ahead was a dark, nasty looking cumulonimbus cloud reaching thousands of feet above. I made a turn to the east not having any idea where I was. Somewhere during my climb, I ran the left-wing tank dry and switched to my 12-gal nose tank. As we headed east, I told my two passengers we were in trouble. I gave them the situation. We could stay up there and burn up precious fuel or venture back down into the clouds and hopefully break out somewhere under the clouds. I left it up to them to decide and they agreed to go down. Didn't make any difference to me, I had already made the decision to make the descent. Back into the clouds I had to control the aircraft making turns slightly back and forth again to maintain control. I knew enough not to get fixated on a heading; I had some knowledge of spatial disorientation. When that happens, the game is over. Again, this was quite stressful. At around six thousand feet we broke out between layers, clear in between, short relief but I kept my descent going. Burning my precious fuel, down to ½ indicated. By now I was keeping my easterly heading pretty good. In my mind I was probably south of my intended course, maybe even south of the North Carolina border. I turned my radio to 122.8 the standard non control airport frequency and picked up Statesville airport telling a pilot who was in the traffic pattern in our Cessna 150, N6626T, to make this his last landing because the visibility was getting bad. I called the airport and one of the weekend pilots, Jack White, answered and asked where I was. I took a deep breath and in my coolest response told him I was over Hickory coming home but actually I had no idea where I was. Little did I know there was concern at the airport. My boss's brother Howard, a Piedmont Airline Captain happened to be there as well. We continued our descent through the clouds and broke out around 2600 feet to the joy of seeing clear green terra firma below! Luckily, the student in the back seat handed me a map, had no idea it was there but grateful to have it. Now, to determine where we were! The land was green showing signs of recent rain. In the remaining hours of daylight, I made my heading northward and saw a large water tower. Water towers usually have identification on them so that would tell me where I was! I approached the tower and circled it, no name or markings, looked like it had just been painted. Looking further north I saw a city and headed for it. We approached the city from the south, and I was frantically looking for some type of identification. Suddenly, believe it or not, my rear seat passenger came through again. He said this is Winston Salem, that's my grandfather's funeral home down there! What are the chances! This told me I had most likely overflown Statesville and had been pretty much on course but nearly 50 miles to the east. I would need to back track. Checking my front tank, it was registering below the 1/4. I knew that portions of I-40 were complete, so I followed it until it ran out still heading west. From time to time, I was being called for my location, so I calmly reported I had to go all the way to Winston Salem to find my way down. Using my map, I could see a set of power lines from Mocksville which I could follow for miles back home. I knew these power lines came near the airport yet many miles away. As I picked up the power lines, the clouds were down to the ground, I stayed on top of the power lines raising above each tower then back down not to lose the lines. Up and down. I began to have hope, but my fuel gage was hardly indicating anything. As I proceeded nearer and nearer following the lines, making occasional calls back to the airport, I suddenly came upon a farmer's silo which I recognized as the one off the end of runway 28. I made an immediate steep left bank actually below the height of the silo and found the runway dead ahead. I was so low I touched down and made the right turn off onto the ramp. I taxied up and parked the Clipper. Fuel gage 0/0. We got out and the two students got down and kissed the ground. Maybe I did too. My boss's brother Howard, the Airline Captain came up along with others and told me "I wish I could have been there with you to help you; I know you needed it." When the aircraft was fueled the next morning, the nose tank took 11.8 gallons which meant I had .2 of a gallon fuel remaining.

CHAPTER 25
Close Call

Flight to Carthage MO June 10, 1964, Senior Year in High School.

Little did I know that once again my inexperience would show in this flight filled with some adrenaline rushing events. To begin. While working at my local Statesville, NC hometown airport which began by being offered a job as line boy at age 15, I soloed at age 16, had my Private license by 17 to follow with my Commercial license by age 18. All the while I devoted my summers and afternoons from school at the airport. Exciting times for a young boy! As mentioned earlier, my career as Line Boy had begun by fueling transient aircraft, washing aircraft and most any job needed to include moving aircraft in and out of hangars and closing up in the evenings after my boss Jimmy had departed before dark for his farm some 25 miles away. We had a few other pilots as well as an aircraft maintenance shop. As years went by, I was given more and more responsibilities. One of our new money-making ventures as previously mentioned, was to take newborn chicken hatchlings to locations, some of which were quite far away. These were breeder chicks used to populate the growing needs of chicken restaurants and grocery chains. The newly hatched chirping chicks were delivered to us in perforated boxes, 80 per box. In cool weather the quantity was 100 per box. This flight on June 10th, 1964, my Senior Year of high school I was given a trip to ferry 17 boxes in our single engine Cessna 172, N7912X from Statesville to Carthage, MO. All seats were removed from the aircraft except the one I occupied. This would be a two aircraft operation, my boss, Jimmy took our twin-engine Piper Aztec, N4727P, to Carthage as well. He was much faster than I and could carry more boxes. We departed on the morning of the 10th and soon I was alone putting in many hours of flight. I would make stops in Nashville, TN, and Walnut Ridge MO before arriving in Carthage late that afternoon. In total I logged nine hours for the trip to Carthage, already a long day. To me this was an adventure so I decided to go as high as I could. Portions of this flight I flew at 16,500 feet. It would be later in ARMY flight training that we were instructed flights above 10,000 feet were not authorized without supplemental oxygen with few exceptions. Young lungs help. I saw for the first time the mighty Mississippi River and at that altitude garnered an appreciation of just how huge it was. When I arrived at Carthage, Jimmy was waiting for me. After we unloaded my boxes, he departed for home in the Aztec. I departed that evening for home as well.

Soon after departure from Carthage I flew into darkness and as before decided to go exceedingly high. This time I climbed to 17,500 feet! My first intended fuel stop was to have been Nashville, TN. It is said that "Flying is often hours of boredom mixed with seconds of stark terror". On this night it came close. During the long flight home, already tired from a day of flying, there was nothing to do but sit in the cockpit as the hours dragged by. One thing I observed when passing over Blytheville AFB, Arkansas, just west of the Mississippi River before the Tennessee border I could see way below in the darkness the silhouette of a B-52 in flight near the AFB. That was fascinating to think I was so high above a B-52! As time went by, I began to second guess my navigation instruments. My Visual Omni Range (VOR) needle seemed to be intermittent. This was most likely in my mind. I began to wonder, hey I might be off course, I had not noticed the VOR needle fluctuate before, maybe I better come down a bit to get my bearings. I began a slow descent, now over the Tennessee border heading east. The descent took some time. When I was down to six or seven thousand feet I noticed the rotating beacon of an airport ahead in the darkness, Airports rotating beacons have a white lens and a green lens identifiable by a white, green alternating blip when observed at night. I thought, just to be sure as my fuel was getting low, why not go over and check out this airport. When I got closer, I observed a lighted runway so, hey no problem in landing to get my bearings! I landed on the short lighted runway which turned out to be a grass strip and it had not been mowed lately. My propeller became a virtual lawn mower! I taxied off the runway and shut down. In the darkness, it was very quiet, not a sole in sight. I walked toward a building which happened to be across a railroad track. From what I could make out, this was an ARMY

National Guard facility somewhere in Tennessee but where? I walked farther over the tracks to an empty two-lane highway. Looking to my left, I noticed a small roadside stand. There was a large tan Indian teepee made from tin which had attached to it a sign written to say "Chief KenTuk". Looking back to my right, I observed several wood framed houses on the opposite side of the highway. Lights on one house were being turned off as I looked. Thinking there was still someone in that house not yet asleep, I headed for it in the darkness. When I approached the house, I noticed a name on the mailbox "Elvis Curtis". I walked up to the front door and gave it a few knocks. Eventually a lady opened the door. I told her my circumstances and asked how far I might be from Nashville. She pointed with her finger and said" It's about 60 miles yonder way". I thanked her and headed back to the Cessna. No problem I thought, I could take off and be in Nashville a short time for my fuel stop. I departed and before long, noticed two rotating beacons in the distance. I thought, good, the one on the left must be Nashville and the one on the right Sewart AFB (which is no longer there). I put my map away and called Nashville tower, they answered, I told them who I was and that I would be coming in from the west. They told me to continue. Now let me go back to those rotating beacon lights. Remember, each had two lenses, one green and one white. A military beacon has a vertical bar in the middle of the white beam which to the observer will be a green light, then what appears to be two blips on the white light. One does not want to land on a military base without authorization. The two beacons I observed seemed to be the proper distance of Nashville and Sewart AFB. Only there was a problem I failed to notice. In this case, the military beacon and the civilian beacon were opposites. As I got closer, not paying attention to the beacons, still in contact with Nashville tower, no other traffic but me, the tower cleared me to land but said they did not have me in sight. This was good news; I will land, get my fuel and be on my way. I lined up with the runway and began my descent but prior to touching down, I looked to my left in the darkness and thought, this looks strange, it can't be Nashville, so I gave the Cessna power and by then noticed the beacon of the airport I almost landed at was a military beacon. Plan B was now to go land at the other nearby "Civilian" airport. I landed and taxied up to the fixed base operations; being around midnight, no one in sight. I discovered this was Clarksville, Tennessee; the airport I almost landed at was Fort Campbell, Kentucky! Both airfields are close just as Sewart AFB and Nashville were and not that far from Nashville. I got to a phone and called Nashville tower to let them know I was ok at Clarksville. I slept on the floor of the aircraft until I heard a rap on the window to wake me the following morning. It was line personnel at the fixed base operation. I let them know I had come in late and requested fuel and was finally on my way. It was now June 11, 1964, and I had had quite a day; a day until now not many have heard about. Afterthought: What are the chances two airports near each other, one military, one civilian matched by another two airports near each other one military, one civilian! A few days later I graduated from High School.

CHAPTER 26
Jet Orientation Course

July 18, 1964, Charlotte Municipal Airport. Waiting for my ride in a USAF aircraft to Perrin AFB, Texas. I had been selected as the Civil Air Patrol (CAP) Candidate from the state of North Carolina to attend a Jet Orientation Course sponsored by the USAF. This was quite an honor to be the selectee. Each state, along with Puerto Rico and Washington, D.C. was awarded one candidate to attend the course. In time, my ride, a C-47 cargo plane arrived for my flight. Before being seated, I was snapped into a parachute and given instructions on how it worked should I need it. I had never worn a parachute, so this was a thrill.

Being given this honor made me somewhat of a celebrity in my hometown of Statesville. My picture and article, listing me as son of Mrs. Cordie Hardiman, were in the local newspaper, Record and Landmark. Every hour, the local radio station WDBM broadcast news of my selection to the Jet Orientation course. To have this honor, I had the CAP rank of Captain, achieving the highest cadet award, *Certificate of Proficiency* and was the only CAP cadet pilot in North Carolina. My thanks to my CAP mentors, Hassel and Dorothy Reep who worked behind the scenes to make this happen. They were a dedicated team.

Our flight to Perrin took hours with a few stops along the way to pick up other candidates.

On arrival at Perrin, I joined 51 other cadets for one of the most memorable weeks I had ever experienced at that time. We were treated to an orchestrated syllabus by the Air Force much the same as Air Force pilots.

We spent our days in Air Force uniforms and flight suits. In addition to classes, we were taught flight physiology, experiencing spatial disorientation by sitting in a spinning barany chair as well as an altitude hypobaric chamber to demonstrate effects of hypoxia (loss of oxygen).

The chamber was a sealed container holding about ten of us at a time. We donned oxygen masks and headsets monitoring directions from several masked technicians who walked among us. The exercise began with pre-breathing 100% oxygen for 30 minutes as the chamber climbed internally to 25,000 feet. When ready, we removed our masks, several at a time, to get the feel of the hazards of high-altitude flight and the physiological effects of low barometric pressure. When I removed my mask, I began writing from 1 to 4 over and over on a note pad, my chest began to tingle a little but other than that no noticeable affects. I wrote 1, 2, 3, 4 several times but within a minute or so I could only write 1, 2... could not remember what came after 2 even though I felt ok and was looking at those numbers I had just written! When I gave the signal, a technician assisted me putting my mask back on. To conclude the training, the chamber was dumped with rapid compression to the outside atmospheric pressure which produced an instant vapor cloud momentarily in the chamber. It was a learning experience. In my Military Aviation career I went through Flight Physiological training every four years or so.

Eventually each of us got flights in a T-33 jet, riding in the back seat of the trainer. In our flight suits we wore white helmets, oxygen masks and parachutes. I was fortunate, one of the cadets became ill so I requested his flight time and was granted.

My instructor pilot was Captain Van Horn, a balding 30+ aviator. On one flight we were being followed closely by another T-33 with a cadet on board. We were so high, on a cloudless day crossing from Texas to Oklahoma. I told CPT Van Horn I had seen a John Wayne movie in which he was pursued by a Russian jet and Wayne did a roll and came out behind his pursuer. I asked him if he could do that and he said, " sure, that's called the 'Scissor'". He did a right scissor maneuver, and we came out behind the other T-33. It gave me such a thrill, I literally screamed with delight! Capitan Van Horn was in radio contact with the pilot of the other T-33; I'm sure they coordinated the maneuver. After falling behind the other T-33, Captain Van Horn made a noise over the intercom, "Rat, tat, tat," making it seem he had just wasted the enemy aircraft!

We were treated to an afternoon at nearby Lake Texoma for swimming. To our surprise, we were greeted by young girls our age there to join us! I met a beautiful young girl accompanied by her twin sister. Her name was Jane Skipper. Their father was a sergeant at the Air Force base. We were also treated to a rodeo in which we were allowed to invite the girls we met. I invited Jane.

Our remaining day concluded with a formal dinner in dress uniforms, the girls were in their finest. Jane and I had pictures taken together and corresponded off and on for three years. The promises were there but at that time I had not established my future so did not pursue seeing her. She graduated from Texas Tech in Lubbock, TX a few years later.

In rear cockpit T-33 during Jet Orientation course Perrin AFB, TX 1964

Civil Air Patrol Cadet at Jet Orientation Couse, Perrin AFB, TX - 1964

<u>Landing a Cessna 172 in Field Next to Ralston Purina Farmers Mark to Drop off Baby Chicks with Allen Bost on Board.</u>

Wednesday, August 12, 1964,

Wednesday, August 12, 1964, recent high school graduate, three days after a check ride by Paul Wilke an authorized FAA examiner for my Commercial Pilots Certificate. This was my third rating starting with my first solo November 2, 1961, followed by my Private Pilot's license also by Paul Wilke on August 19, 1963 at age 17. On this day, now 18, I was given a trip to fly a few boxes of baby chicks for a local hatchery to Robersonville, N.C. The trip from Statesville, NC east to Robersonville in our Cessna 172 (N7912X) would be one hour and forty-five minutes. Along with me was a friend, Allen Bost, who was a year or two older but interested in flying. Allen and I enjoyed our 200-mile flight over to Robersonville, with not a cloud in the sky. When we arrived in the rural vicinity of Robersonville, I noticed a building down below with the name of my delivery which had large letters on the roof identifying it; as best I recall, Ralston Purina Farmers Market. The market, resembling a warehouse, provided farm implements, seeds and other accoutrements. What caught my eye was the open field next to the building. I checked it out and minutes later was on the ground. Let me say, this was not legal but at my age, hey, just another event I should have thought through better. Allen had no idea but that what I had done was routine. After landing, I taxied up to a loading ramp and shut down. Allen and I went inside to let a clerk know we had the baby chicks they had requested. She hardly raised an eyebrow, as if my landing an airplane outside her window was perfectly normal! She only told us where to put the boxes of chicks. Job completed, Allen and I got a soda and crackers from a coin operated machine and departed the building back to our Cessna. We took off from our newly designated airfield and headed back home. All in all, this, in my mind, had been a successful trip and no one was the wiser. Years later as I went over my logbook now with years of aviation experience and hindsight, I find it hard to believe I did this!

CHAPTER 27
First solo to Kennedy International

August 17, 1964, three months out of high school, late departure for Kennedy International Airport, New York; first stop for fuel was Dulles International, which serviced Washington, D.C. Arriving at Dulles I noted how empty it was, only a couple flights during my brief stay. Today hundreds of flights from around the Globe make their way to Dulles, an international hub.

My landing at Kennedy was purposely at 2:00 AM when traffic was low. After landing at an airport larger in square mileage than many small towns, I was handed off to Ground Control and then to the Port Authority. I followed a gentleman from the Port authority leading me in a Ford station wagon on the dark taxiways to a South American airline which would take my chicks. The distance was incredibly long. Once we finally arrived at my spot to drop off the 17 boxes of baby chicks, the gentleman guessed I was from North Carolina by my voice on the radio as we conversed. He told me he went through Basic Training in North Carolina in WWII and knew what us 'Tar Heels' sounded like! The chicks I dropped off were to be transported to a country in South America.

Climbing out on departure after some time, I looked down into the darkness and noted I was still over the confines of this vast airport! Mission complete, heading home, I had made my first flight to Kennedy!

Del Hardiman

Close call

Emergency Landing, Cessna 172, N7912X, OCT-NOV 1964, Trevilians, Virginia

The rural Virginia pasture drifting below me, shrinking in the haze as I strained desperately to put my aircraft on the ground at all costs. Low on fuel, there was no going back. A barbed wire fence grown over with kudzu loomed ahead, mere seconds away, to the left were three tall deciduous trees joined as one. Beyond the fence I could make out another short field with a forest just beyond. I was destined for impact to the large trees if I stayed my course. Oddly, I tasted blood and the thought that I was about to break my collar bone. On board I sat alone at the controls, the only seat in the Cessna 172, alone that is with exception of 17 stacked boxes of newly hatched chicks destined for my second trip to Kennedy International NY with an intended fuel stop at Dulles International Airport near Washington, D.C. How did I get into such a death grip situation? Dulles was a world away.

The fall day had started with a hurry to get going from my hometown airport, Statesville, North Carolina. Having just turned 19, five months out of high school, I prepared Cessna N7912X for the trip, loading 17 boxes each containing 80 freshly hatched baby chicks from Hubbard Farms Hatchery. It was already late afternoon, my boss, Jimmy had checked the weather and filed a VFR flight plan for me. I would be flying under Visual Flight Rules since I did not have an instrument rating to fly under instrument rules. Jimmy walked up to my window handing me the flight plan with forecast weather then I taxied off. In no time, I was airborne, heading north. Intent was to arrive at Kennedy in the wee hours of the morning during less traffic. Once airborne, I called the FAA flight service facility at Hickory to open my flight plan. On two occasions, the FAA inquired if I had checked my weather, I responded "yes" since I had it in my hands. In hindsight, were they trying to tell me something? They were not allowed to proactively advise me unless I requested. As my journey continued with the low murmurs of hundreds of chirping chicks, I had a nice tail wind, making good time. In time I encountered a layer of clouds and climbed above them, my first mistake. No problem I thought, I would stay up here in the clear with good visibility. As time and an hour or two passed I noticed another layer of clouds above but no worry, I had been in this situation before. By the time I made it to the Casanova Visual Omni Range (VOR) station southwest of Dulles, it became obvious I was in a pickle, Dulles was now below VFR minimums, so I decided to make that famous FAA turn which was a 180 to head back home. Going back, I was now bucking a strong head wind, making little progress, fuel was now becoming an issue. I determined that at my ground speed I could not make it back, so I called out to various small airports in the area which were telling me they were now IFR. Eventually I contacted the University of Virginia airport near Charlottesville, which was still VFR. Great! By the time I made it to the Gordonsville VOR not far from the airport, the airport reported they were now below minimums. Now I was approaching ¼ tank of fuel. I made a decision to go down 'with' fuel rather than stay in my limbo situation. Having no idea at this time exactly where I was, I began my descent into the clouds. Slowly down I went, putting out flaps to slow me as much as possible, chicks chirping ambivalent to the condition I had put them in. Suddenly, I was on top of trees!! I grabbed for the flap handle and pulled down full flaps, visibility was extremely poor since I was in the clouds. I delicately hung above the trees in slow flight hoping not to hit one. At one point I made out a pasture on my left window with a single white face bull which seemed to look up at me. Not long after, I caught the glimpse of a field off to my left before it disappeared. I made sliding left turns hoping to find the field again, I did. I was aligned with it but much too high, so I made another boxed left-hand pattern for the field and once again I was aligned with it. The third time I made the box pattern, I elected to descend to where I hoped the field would be and with much luck and the grace of God I was lined up with the field. My problem was that I was landing with a tailwind which, even though I was almost at a stall with the stall warning horn beeping, I was sailing across the field too fast to land.

Now I'm back to where my story began, looking at the kudzu covered fence with trees looming in the distance and those tall deciduous trees slightly to my left. By sheer instinct I headed for the top of those soft trees to break my glide. The trees slowed my progress substantially and I plopped into the field beyond. The nose gear collapsed but other than that I was down, safe! Some baby chicks were scattered on the floor behind the right rudder pedals. I sat in silence, as light began to fade. I turned off the switches and evaluated my situation. Once out of the aircraft, I noticed a farmhouse in the distance not far to the left of the deciduous trees I had just brushed into. I walked over to the farmhouse and knocked on the door. At first no one answered. Eventually an elderly gentleman in bib overalls opened the door,

I think he was somewhat bewildered seeing my aircraft in the field behind his house with a red rotating beacon turning round and round. He must have heard my low passes as well. I gained his confidence and asked where I was. He told me we were near Trevilians, VA. He was living in the house with his elderly mother who owned the property. I asked if he would watch over the plane, I would give him some baby chicks. From the farmhouse I took a dirt road on foot past the field of my intended landing on my left. The fog in the trees reminded me of smoke from a battle scene. In time, I came upon another house. Again, I knocked on the door and a gentleman answered. I told him I had just landed in a field nearby and asked if I might use his phone. He invited me in, so I called my boss, Jimmy to let him know what had happened. He told me to call the FAA to let them know, which I did.

The gentleman who let me use his phone told me he was a son-in-law to the elderly lady in the first house and that she had given up parcels of land to her children. As luck would have it, he was a lecturer at the University of Virginia and would be leaving soon for there. He gave me a lift to Charlottesville where I was able to secure a rental car and return to my chicks. In darkness, back in this remote area, I loaded the rental car stacked with 17 boxes of baby chicks minus a few I gave away and a couple I could not reach in the floorboard. I drove for hours to reach home and turn over the chicks next day to Hubbard Farms.

Jimmy surveyed the situation and told me to take his pickup truck which had stanchions to carry the disassembled wings. The stanchions were covered with burlap sacks for cushioning. Our mechanic's stepson William, a year older than me and with more maintenance experience than I drove back to Trevilians with me. The aircraft was sitting on its nose, tail in the air. With help of locals, we drained fuel from the wings and removed them. We had to dig a slight trench to softly roll the aircraft back to standing position. We loaded the disassembled wings and towed the aircraft from behind facing aft. We were a spectacle, I am sure.

Upon our return with the aircraft, our mechanic, C.V. Stewart told me a student, Margaret Haggerty, had landed so hard the week before that she broke the nose wheel on the Cessna. His opinion was that the nose gear strut was weakened from that landing. Did not help my situation but it was somewhat comforting that had it not been for her hard landing, I might not have incurred any damage.

I didn't know it at the time but this would be a life and career changing experience. In time I received a letter from the FAA for me to come to a hearing in Richmond, VA. Alone in my thoughts, I hitch hiked to Richmond several hundred miles away. On the day of my appointment, I was met at the FAA office by an individual in charge of my case. He informed me I had departed from Statesville enroute to Dulles with weather below VFR minimums, meaning I was in violation of FAA regulations. You no doubt have heard the expression of a Jaw dropping event. At that moment, my jaw uncontrollably dropped. How could this be? Jimmy had given me the weather which was legal for my trip. I was dumbfounded! I was told I had several options; one was to seek an attorney which was out of the question; the second to surrender my pilot's license. In a few weeks I received an official letter from the FAA for me to turn in my license by midnight, February 4th. I would lose them for a period of 90 days. My whole life was shattered but I kept this to myself. I had a plan. As it happened, I had joined the North Carolina Air National Guard, my reporting date to depart for basic training in San Antonio, Texas was February 5th. Being asked from time to time by inquisitive individuals at the airport if I had heard anything about my accident from the FAA, my reply was that I had not. As February 4th got near, I made a point of taking my license out for all to see and say, "I'm sure going to miss these". On the evening of February 4th, I mailed my license off at the post office. Next morning, I was on my way to Basic Training to be followed with Aviation Maintenance school at Sheppard AFB, Texas. While at Sheppard, my mother mailed my license to me which had been returned by the FAA. When I returned home after five months of schooling, I made a point to go right away back to the airport, took out my license to show everyone and say, "I've sure missed using these!" To this day, no one, other than my mother knew I had lost my license.

Side note: Years later, now living in Northern Virginia, I would pay a price for losing my license. After a distinguished career of 22 years ARMY Aviation service which I had transitioned to from the Air National Guard and now rated in Gulfstream jets. I applied to several airlines and had about three interviews; I had to admit I had lost my license once in my youth. This was a red flag, and I did not get a callup. I went to the local FAA Flight Standards

District Office (FSDO) near Leesburg, VA with questions about losing my license so long ago. I was told, (unofficially) hey those records are only kept five years so no one would know you lost your license; it is no longer on your record so why tell anyone? That is what I did; my next interview I did not report having my license taken. I got the job!

Instrument training

Ronald Rayle, John Gibson, Jerome Eades and I, each affiliated with Miller's Aviation in one form, or another elected to attend the Acme School of Aeronautics for instrument training at Fort Worth Texas in September 1966 for a weeklong course. Each of us aspired to get hired by Piedmont Airlines. We had an enjoyable and memorable drive out and back in John's older Cadillac. The training was conducted in WWII style Link trainers which was a wooden mounted motion device with aircraft instrumentation with feedback to an instructor who could monitor student input and give commands. The trainer was enclosed with no outside visuals. Ron, Jerome, and John eventually got hired by Piedmont; Ron and Jerome retired, after many years of service, from US AIR, which bought out Piedmont. I was not so fortunate.

CHAPTER 28
Close Call

<u>First flight using new Instrument rating – Iced up in Knoxville, TN.
Flight from Statesville to Nashville back to Statesville, Jan 18, 1967,
return Jan 19, 1967.</u>

With a brand-new instrument rating, I was all set to test the waters and file using Instrument Flight Rules (IFR). The day before I had completed my instrument check ride and recall quite vividly my check pilot, telling me, "You are not an Instrument Pilot yet, this is a license to learn". At the time, the FAA had a procedure in which you could put a code in your flight plan that would indicate you needed special handling while on an instrument flight plan. To progress into commercial aviation, the instrument rating was a necessary step. So, on the 16th of January, 1967, age 21, I filed my 'first' IFR flight plan from my home town Statesville, NC to Nashville, Tennessee, carefully checking weather prior to departure. Aircraft on this flight would be a Cherokee Six, tail number N3849W, a long, wide bodied single engine with lots of cargo space. Accompanying me would be Jerome Eades. Jerome had little aircraft time and needed to log time to progress in aviation. Our departure was in late afternoon flying west into the sunset at 6000 feet, arriving after dark. I was now one of the big boys, talking to controllers using proper protocol. I noticed the instrument controllers spoke slowly and gave me special handling which made my first instrument flight have no surprises. All went well to Nashville, and I was quite proud! We had a snack and proceeded in the Cherokee back home to Statesville at night. Again, all went well, at first. The controllers gave me special handling as we proceeded east in the dark at 7000 feet. Jerome and I conversed, enjoying the ride until I noticed our airspeed was dropping off, at least the airspeed gage indicated it was. In aviation, rule number one, keep your airspeed, without it, bad things happen. I let Jerome know of the airspeed drop off and two sets of eyes were glued on the indicator. Slowly, ever slowly, the airspeed kept dropping off until suddenly it went to zero! My heart jumped into my throat; it certainly had my total attention! We realized that we were still flying so what was happening? I took out my flashlight and shined it out on the left wing of my side to notice I had rime ice built up on the leading edge. NOT GOOD! This had not been forecast. I turned on the Pitot heat switch to hopefully deice the pitot tube through which air flowed to the airspeed indicating system. Gradually, our airspeed recovered but now we had another potential emergency, ice. Rime ice distorts the airflow over the wings which can cause loss of lift with bad outcome. I contacted the controller in the calmest voice I could muster to let them know I was icing up and requested a lower, hopefully warmer altitude. The controller acknowledged but informed me I could not descend until opposite traffic passed below me. I waited and watched the ice continue to build up. I made the election to descend without approval to 5000 feet hoping for warmer air. There was no enroute radar in those days, so my descent was not detected. Eventually, after what seemed a long time, we were cleared to 5000 feet but I was already there. I acknowledged and reported roger departing 7000 for 5000. We continued to have ice at 5000 feet, and I wanted to get on the ground ASAP. I asked for and got permission to deviate to Knoxville, Tenn. which was approved. Jerome and I made it to Knoxville and parked on the General Aviation ramp; it was near midnight. We slept in chairs in the terminal for the night. Next morning, there was still rime ice on the leading edges which we brushed off with our hands, got back in and headed home on the 19th a little late. As they say, flying is hours of boredom mixed with seconds of stark terror. This would not be my last encounter with ice which I pointed out earlier when flying in Germany.

CHAPTER 29
Close Call 1967

Flight to Keen, NH with Bob Johnson in Yellow Bonanza N180Z

Bob Johnson and I loaded the yellow 'V' tail Beechcraft Bonanza, N180Z, with boxes of baby chicks, our cargo. Destination was Keene New Hampshire, a flight of some 680 miles. Bob, in his fifties, was old school. He had been out of aviation for many years but came to work at our airport and mostly instructed students locally. He was short in stature, always dressed in a sport coat with tie. He was also the father of my high school classmate Billy. Bob was rated in the Bonanza, and I was not. The plan was to file an instrument flight using my instrument rating and Bob would fly the airplane. I filed the Instrument flight plan which would permit us to fly in clouds if encountered. We departed with me making calls to air traffic controllers. Bob sat stoically in the left seat in command of the airplane. We used my instrument charts so between the two of us collectively we took care of the tasks at hand. The flight would take us from North Carolina, north across Virginia, Maryland, Pennsylvania, New York, and Massachusetts before reaching Keene New Hampshire. I had been to Keene on two other occasions so felt confident in the trip. Neither of us thought this would be a challenging flight, but it would become a nail biter. The Bonanza was a relatively new aircraft with dual navigation King radios, KX-150s. Having dual radios gave us a backup as well as the ability to cross check our position. Trips like this were long, there was not much to do but fly the airplane and respond to air traffic control. North of Philadelphia, our KX-150 radios became unreliable, both of them, I had heard the KX-150s were subject to overheating. So, we were no longer confident we could proceed further safely. We asked to be diverted to Philadelphia International airport and received headings to do so. One problem, the airport had low cloud coverage and the approach would need to be an instrument approach. I did not have approach charts for making an instrument landing at Philadelphia. Being young, as I had often done before, I made up rules as I went along. I thought if Philadelphia approach control could put me on the final approach course and verify the heading and Instrument Landing System (ILS) frequency, we could intercept the glide slope and follow it down for the landing and no one would be the wiser. Bob was quiet and pale faced. He had no idea what I was doing. My call to Approach control: "Approach, Bonanza 180Z, could you verify the ILS frequency for the approach and give us a steer for the approach"? They did, so here we are in my naivety, shooting an approach to a runway with no charts and extremely low visibility. We intercepted the heading and glide slope descending on glide path. We broke out near minimums and landed. Whew, once again I had made up my own rules and things worked out! We parked the aircraft at the General Aviation ramp. Bob had experienced something he could not have imagined in his safe days of flying in clear skies. He told me firmly, we will wait until there is not a cloud in the sky before we head back home, and we did. Just another day of flying by seat of the pants having been influenced by others who did much the same. This was the first and only time Bob and I flew together.

CLOSE CALL

Tropical fish cargo from VERO Beach, FL in Cherokee Six.

For a while I had early Friday morning flights to Vero Beach, FL from our airport at Statesville. Miller Aviation purchased a new Cherokee Six, N3849W, single seater which had a long fuselage with six passenger seats. All seats but the front left pilot seat was removed in order to carry live tropical fish from Vero Beach to Greensboro, NC. I would depart before daylight to arrive for a 9:00AM departure. The fish were in boxes with enclosed plastic bags partially filled with water, oxygen pumped in to sustain the fish. Only a certain quantity of boxes was supposed to be loaded and each box was to weigh a certain amount to remain in weight and balance parameters. This was not happening! More boxes were delivered and heavier than authorized. On one flight the aircraft was so overloaded I had to taxi with the brakes on to keep the nose tire on the ground. Being a young kid with zero training on weight and balance I made it happen. One morning some men in dark suits observed us loading the aircraft and I figured they might be FAA so I told the distributor I would not take all the boxes. I think that saved my license. On one flight I was so heavy, the aircraft would only climb 50 feet per minute. It took me all the way to the Florida/Georgia border to get to 5000'. It was so critical, I had to delicately touch the controls, if I pulled back the slightest the aircraft would begin a buffet approaching a stall. If I pushed forward slightly on the yoke, I could not retain altitude. When I landed at Greensboro, there was a wind warning. I was still so heavy that when I landed the wind had little effect. Hard to say how overloaded I was on those flights.

PART IV

CHAPTER 30
USAPAT, Army Jets - 1986

Arrival at Davison ARMY Airfield, Fort Belvoir, Virginia

Now that you have read the 'Younger Years", I go back to departing Germany for Fort Belvoir, VA. I reported for duty in July 86' after taking the family for a week at Disney World, Orlando, Florida. I was assigned to the United States ARMY Aviation Command (USADAC) as aircraft Maintenance Officer, managing 12 fixed wing twin turbine military Beechcraft consisting of C-12C, D and L models, U-21A, and F models. Our Fixed wing section of USADAC was Command Aircraft Company – Airplanes (CAC-A). There was also the helicopter company (CAC-H) and a helicopter maintenance company (CAMCR). Main mission of the fixed wing company was in support of the Military District of Washington (MDW), transporting VIP's and staff, mostly from the Pentagon and local headquarters to various destinations of the U.S. My duties were to manage maintenance, which included mechanics and crew chiefs; perform maintenance test flights and fly missions. My first flight at Davison was check out on C-12C (23129) on August 4th, 1986. *Little did I know that two years later, August 4th, 1988, I would be flying Secretary of the ARMY on the first ever ARMY operational Jet mission!*

When the ARMY Air Force became the new U.S. Air Force on July 26, 1947, by agreement, ARMY Aviation would be restricted to smaller non-tactical aircraft. In time, the ARMY acquired heavier tactical aircraft but with the Johnson-McConnell agreement of 1966, the ARMY agreed to give up its fixed-wing tactical aircraft. Thus, ARMY fixed wing was limited to smaller gross weight aircraft. Ref-20. Through the years the ARMY fixed wing personnel transport aircraft progressed primarily through versions of twin turbine Beechcraft. Most recent versions designated as C-12's had state-of-the-art systems; with a few exceptions, limitation of 12,500 pounds max gross weight. This meant ARMY leadership was limited to a seven-passenger aircraft restricted from long overseas flights. ARMY leadership typically would request flights on U.S. Air Force aircraft for worldwide travel requirements. Hard to believe at one time, ARMY Four-star generals had been dropped from flights on USAF aircraft.

When I arrived at Davison, there were rumors of ARMY Jets, then rumors that it was not going to happen. Yet another situation where 'fate' stepped in which would forever change my aviation career. I was in the right place at the right time.

COL William F. O'Neal, USADAC Commander for the second time, was the mainstay in getting jets for the ARMY. Many would say he was the "Father of ARMY Aviation Jet Transport. Without his persistence and foresight, years in the process, there would probably not be an ARMY Jet program.

COL O'Neal, two tours in Vietnam, rated in both fixed and rotary wing aircraft, was former aid to General Bernard Rogers a former Chief of Staff, United States ARMY, and later NATO Supreme Allied Commander. COL O'Neal, law school graduate and military judge, knew the Pentagon key players both active and retired. His goal was to get jets for the ARMY. Working behind the scenes, he was turned down on several occasions for even thinking of putting jets in the ARMY, he was told by one general, "There's no requirement". Eventually, he was told if ARMY jets were to happen, it would be up to him. For this, he visited retired Generals, along with assistance from LTC Doug Crockett and CW4 Lyle Real. Language in a 1977 Congressional record said words to the effect, yes, the Army leadership deserves a mode of travel similar to their Air Force and Navy counterparts. Ref-21 Gulfstream aircraft manufacturer, Savannah, GA was holding two Gulfstream III's pending a decision. They would later be designated C-20E's.

Planning had been in progress for some time in anticipation of the ARMY getting the two new Gulfstream jets. Lyle Real approached me to ask if I might have interest in being the Aircraft Maintenance Officer for the new jet company if it happened; I gladly accepted.

January 4, 1988, prior to approval of the ARMY getting C-20's, Lyle and I were dropped off at Flight Safety training school adjacent to the Gulf Stream facility in Savannah, GA. We were the first to attend a course of instruction which included 27 hours simulator training. That Monday morning, when we sat down in our classroom, wearing ARMY class B, short sleeve uniforms, we drew the attention of 10 other students in civilian attire. Turned out, these were U.S. Air Force pilots of the 89th Air Lift Wing at Andrews AFB, Maryland. The 89th provided global Special Air Mission (SAM) airlift for senior leaders; it flew C-20B's at the time and other large jets up to and including the President's Air Force One. One individual leaned over and discreetly asked why we were there. Looking back at him, I replied, "We are here to fly ARMY jets". From what I deduced later; they (USAF) were of the opinion they would be flying the two ARMY C-20's, not us. This must have caused some anxiety since they reported back to their headquarters at first break that the ARMY was here!

The story is much too long to tell, but after COL O'Neal's persistence of several years, culminating in early 1988, he proudly sent an email February 24, 1988, to his constituents that The Vice Chief of Staff of the Army had announced the decision that the C-20 aircraft in the Army will be flown by Army Aviators! Secretary of the Army John O. Marsh gave Army Aviators the mission to fly the Army C-20E Gulfstream III aircraft. COL O'Neal would be first to say that this was a collaborative effort which would not have happened without help from many of the retired community, Alabama congressman Bill Dickinson, and Mr. Joseph Cribbins, Army Department's chief of aviation safety and logistics.

The new jet company would be designated as the United States Army Priority Air Transport Command (USAPAT). Challenges were: personnel, funding and location of operations (runway at Davison ARMY Airfield was too short and did not have load bearing capacity for the C-20). Aviators selected for standing up USAPAT would be eight CW4 Warrant Officers, LTC Doug Crockett, Commander, and MAJ Jim Haley, Executive Officer. MAJ Sam Blake USADAC Executive Officer, was instrumental in screening flight records, safety records, personnel records for non-judicial, health, physical fitness etc. School records were screened for qualifications in Maintenance, Training, Flight Instruction, and general potential. Five non-commissioned Officer (NCO) flight engineers were selected, I personally flew to Fort Riley, KS and Fort Rucker, AL to interview three. As with the Air Force and Navy C-20 aircraft, stewards would also be included. Enlisted stewards, male and female, experienced in preparing meals for General Officer functions, were interviewed and evaluated prior to selection. Flights would include prepared meals.

COL O'Neal reported an email from LTG Claude M. Kicklighter in which he said: "You better be as good as the Air Force from day one".

Original USAPAT Pilots (called Aviators in the ARMY) were: LTC Doug Crockett, MAJ Jim Haley, CW4 Lyle Real, CW4 Bob Kirksey, CW4 John Dahmer, CW4 Jack Cattilini, CW4 Bruce Barefoot, CW4 Chris Nauer, CW4 Mike McDonald and me. Soon after, CW4 Al Moros, CW4 Chuck Barr and CW4 Mike Rahm joined USAPAT.

Original Flight Engineers: W01 Mike Carrosquilla, SFC Nat Washington, SSG Gil Baez, SSG Rod Atkinson, and SSG Mark Wilson.

Original Flight Stewards: SGT Joe Castaneda, SPC Darren Connors, SPC Sherrie Vinesset, SGT Kim McCrae, SGT Pete Cokonus, SGT Polly Zuares, and SSG Dennis Sills.

Flight Operations: SFC Paul Jones, SGT Jim Ginas, and SPC Dave Hale; Suzanne Marriott, our civilian secretary, did a mammoth job of typing our founding documents.

From day one, the necessity of location became paramount. The obvious location would be Andrews Air Force Base, MD but the Air Force resisted. Eventually after an agreement at the General Officer level, USAPAT was allotted two ramp parking spaces at Andrews but no hangar space! Operations were on our own devices. The aircraft were fully maintained by Gulfstream contract maintenance operating from a mobile facility nearby. We began operations in an old wooden building on Andrews in which each of us, in our specialty, worked long hours planning a successful operation. Standard Operating procedures (SOP's) had to be written, the Air Force and

Navy both with C-20 aircraft, graciously assisted by allowing us to learn from their operations. Our stewards were taught a great deal about preparing in-flight meals by the Air Force. They would have a kitchen in our facility. I acquired our first inflight Safety briefing cards, courtesy of the Navy, with the front cover relabeled to represent USAPAT. I oversaw maintenance of our two new C-20E's, 70-139 and 70-140, as such, monitored hundreds of spare parts co-located with the Air Force Gulfstream parts inventory at Andrews.

The C-20E was a high-speed, all-weather aircraft with two Rolls-Royce Spey MK511-8 turbofan engines each producing 11,400 pounds of thrust, maximum takeoff gross weight was 69,700 pounds, max ceiling 45,000 feet with a range of 4,250 miles. Depending on configuration, it could accommodate up to twelve passengers plus two pilots, two stewards, and a flight engineer.

70139 was given the name "Yorktown", while 70140 given the name "Lexington" as a tribute to Secretary of the ARMY, John O. Marsh Jr., an American Revolution buff.

70139 "Yorktown"

Pre Mission-Training

All pilots had previous assignments in foreign country operations; each brought a wealth of experience. Flying an executive jet with crew coordination required a new level of expertise. We were trained by a commercial company in mastering the intricacies of safe international travel. The three-day course (for all crew members) included Human Factors, Accident Review, Emergency Equipment, Ditching and Water Landing, High Altitude Flight, Inflight Fire, Emergency Evacuation, International Procedures, Executive Cabin Service and CPR.

International flights required educating ourselves on foreign air traffic reporting to include dissimilar altimeter settings and getting a pre-brief on occasion of sensitive requirements. Fuel requirements were to have enough to fly to destination, to an alternate if necessary, plus 45 minutes.

Flight Training

When approval came, all pilots beginning in June 1988 went on Temporary Duty to Savannah for ground school and transition training. Prior to this, I attended the Gulfstream GIII maintenance course. Flight Engineers also attended the maintenance course. Their duties would not be major maintenance but to assist with maintenance issues that came up, keeping aircraft logs and supervising refueling. My flight training was from 5 through 27 JUL.   After instructional flights to include night operations, Mike McDonald and I made a 'solo' cross country flight at 30,000+ feet non-stop from Savannah to Lawton, Oklahoma, switched seats and flew back non-stop, all on one tank of fuel. That was impressive, something we would not have dreamed of with our former ARMY aircraft. Other pilots paired up and made similar flights to gain experience before operations began.

Our two aircraft paint schemes were dissimilar. Lower half of 70139 was light blue from nose to tail in a line up to below the cabin windows. Wings and upper fuselage were white, similar to 89th aircraft. On each side above the cabin windows "United States of America" was painted. Top of the right wing and under left wing, in bold black letters was "U.S. ARMY". The tail vertical fin on both sides had aircraft identification number 70139; above that also on the vertical fin was the American flag. Our other C-20 was a non-descript white with no decals or lettering, only the number 70140 on the vertical fin.

First operational mission

August 4, 1988, Bob Kirksey and I flew ARMY Secretary John O. Marsh from Andrews AFB to MacDill AFB, FL, with a stop at Fort Stewart, GA. Bob was pilot in command, I was at the controls for the first USAPAT operational mission. Don't know how I was selected but honored to have been. That first landing had a twist of adrenaline; on final approach, a rain shower was moving toward our landing spot from right to left. Would we beat the shower, or would we make a 'Go Around' which would undoubtedly raise concerns of our passengers on their first USAPAT mission? On the approach, Bob told me "Keep it coming" which I did. Just after touchdown we were enveloped

231

with the brief rain shower. We made it. So proud to have been the pilot making that first operational mission landing!

My Logbook entry for that first flight from Andrews (ADW to LHW Ft Stewart, GA).
August 4, 1988

Bob Kirksey and I flew SEC of ARMY, John O. Marsh on first operational mission of 1ˢᵗ Jet Company of the ARMY. Landed at Wright ARMY Airfield in rain. This is where I started 'ARMY' flying 20 years ago. We flew the "Yorktown" which pleased Mr. Marsh when he saw the name. He also like the words "U.S. ARMY" on the wing. We flew on to MacDill AFB, FL and Ron'd (Remained overnight). Other crew members were: SFC Nathaniel Washington, (Flight Engineer), Specialists Darren Connors and Sherried Vinesset, (Flight Stewards) and John Stark (Gulfstream). Token commemoratives were given to the passengers. Mrs. Marsh gave the crew gifts (a scarf each).

Dangerous Enclosures

Letter of Appreciation from Aide-de-camp, Secretary of the ARMY

DEPARTMENT OF THE ARMY
OFFICE OF THE SECRETARY OF THE ARMY
WASHINGTON, D.C. 20310-0101

9 August 1988

Chief Warrant Officer
  Delbert Hardiman
United States Army Priority
  Air Transport Detachment
  C-20
Building 1633
Stop 105
Andrews Air Force Base,
  D. C. 20331-5000

Dear Mr. Hardiman:

   I appreciate the efforts of you and your
crew in making the first flight of the C-20
"Yorktown" as comfortable as possible.

   First impressions are lasting and my first
flight has made a lasting positive impact on me.
Your professionalism, thoughtfulness and exceptional focus on mission accomplishment made my
first flight a tremendous success.

   I would like to personally thank you for your
part in making my flight such a memorable occasion.
Our Army can be truly proud of your service, and I
am again grateful.

                    Respectfully,

                    Kevin T. Hanretta
                    Kevin T. Hanretta
                    Lieutenant Colonel, GS
                    Aide-de-Camp to the
                    Secretary of the Army

233

Del Hardiman

As I was wont to do, at each prior assignment, I organized unit photos. With concurrence from LTC Crockett, I located a photographer at Fort Belvoir and with the aid of our Gulfstream contract maintenance, our two G-III's were positioned nose to nose on the Andrews ramp for various photo shoots. All members, in dress pants and garrison caps wore new black prototype windbreaker jackets of which we were first of the ARMY authorized to wear. A historical mantelpiece of the 'Originals' beginning the dawn of ARMY Jet Aviation.

USAPAT original members Group photo

USAPAT original members Group photo

In time, USAPAT acquired a Gulfstream II, an older version of our Gulfstream III's. This aircraft "Castle One" originally belonged to the ARMY Corps of Engineers, and it had hangar space at Andrews. Taking advantage of this, USAPAT rotated its C-20s in that hangar space for defrosting prior to missions of winter operations.

Side note: USAPAT eventually moved into a new operations building at Andrews near the newly acquired hangar space they were given.

As of this writing, USAPAT operates 2 Gulfstream V's, one Gulfstream 550 and three C-21 Lear Jets.

CHAPTER 31
Interesting Flights while at USAPAT

Flights to Panama

In March 1988, the U.S. government entered into negotiations with Panamanian Dictator Manuel Noriega seeking his resignation. Noriega had no intention of resigning. Ref-22 The U.S. launched its invasion of Panama on December 20, 1989. My log shows we flew Ambassador Lewis to Panama December 24th, 1989. Ref-23 My previous flight while in USAPAT to Panama was from Pamerola, Honduras June 19th, 1989.

Memorable Pacific trips

First memorable trip:

December 4, 1989, Chris Nauer and I, along with our designated flight attendants and crew chief, Picked up C-20, 70-140 at Anchorage, Alaska. We had prepositioned to wait for another crew to bring our passengers from Andrews, AFB, MD.

Our first stop was to Shemya, AK (PASY) for refuel late at night. Shemya is in the Alaskan Aleutian Islands. Remember while refueling, an arctic fox was making its way to our aircraft. The refueler told us to watch out, the fox would try to get into your aircraft!

Next stop was to Naval Air Facility, Atsugi, Japan (RJTA). Then on December 5th, we repositioned to Yokota Air Base (RJTY). From Yokota it was on to Osan Air Base, South Korea (RKSO) for a three day stay.

On December 8th, we departed Osan on a 5.4-hour flight to Henderson Field on Midway Atoll (PMDY) in the Pacific for fuel. <u>On this leg, we picked up a 200 knot Jet Steam tailwind and for an extended time were doing 780 MPH ground speed. My fastest ever!</u>

While at Midway, I was thrilled at seeing thousands of nesting Albatrosses, fondly called Gooney Birds. According to Timothey Foote, Smithsonian Magazine, September 2001, more than 400,000 pairs nest there. I had read about these birds while in elementary school. They come and go seasonally. One mate sits on the nest while the other travels hundreds of miles then return, to take over nesting duties. I was told they mate for life and come back to the same nest annually.

Being at Midway gave me a solemn feeling. It was here June 4th through 7th 1942 that the Battle of Midway occurred a mere six months after the Japanese attack on Pearl Harbor. The battle has often been called "the turning point of the Pacific". The intense battle saw four of Japan's best aircraft carriers, Soryu, Kaga, Akagi and Hiryu sunk. America lost the carrier Yorktown. Japan lost 3,057 service men and scores of aircraft. America losses were 307 plus great quantities of aircraft. Standing on the Atoll, one can imagine those ships a hundred miles out lying on the sea floor where they were thankfully sunk so many years ago. Ref-24 From Midway it was 3.0 hours to Hickam Air Force Base (PHIK), Honolulu, Hawaii.

On December 9th, we flew from Hickam to Colorado Springs. CO., a 6.1-hour flight, then back to Andrews AFB, another 3.0 hours.

Second Memorable trip:

Mike McDonald and I, with designated crew, departed Andrews AFB, MD on February 6th, 1990, to Pueblo, CO. This trip would be in our older Gulfstream II, 890266, our passengers were ARMY Corp of Engineers civilians. From Pueblo we flew to the Naval Air Station (KNGZ) in Alameda,

CA. From Alameda it was on to Hickam Air Force Base (PHNL), Hawaii to remain overnight.

Next day, now February 8th Pacific time, we flew to the small Johnston Atoll (PJON) 717 nautical miles southwest of Hawaii. We were limited to time at Johnston due to restrictions. From there we flew to Kwajalein Atoll, (PKWA) located in the Marshall Islands where we remained overnight.

Kwajalein a small but active site had seen battles between the United States and Japan during WWII. One could easily walk around the atoll in a short time. It was a special place for those with families whose children were taught in a Department of Defense public school. As I sat that evening under palm trees next to the shore with the moon lit ocean before me, I thought, this might be paradise.

Next morning, I observed an airliner with personnel off loading, walk over and get into helicopters to be flown to work sites north of our location in adjoining atolls.

On our departure, February 9th, we flew north at low altitude to give our passengers a view of the aforementioned installations. From there it was a 3.5-hour flight to Guam (PGUM) for a fuel stop.

Guam, you might recall, I visited several times in 1967 some thirty years earlier while in the N.C. Air National Guard.

Side Note: 17 years later (2007), I attended an American Eurocopter ground school course at Grand Prairie, TX. The Eurocopter was designated the UH-72 by the ARMY. This was during the initial fielding process for the UH-72 of which I was System Manager for the ARMY National Guard. At the course, I met two civilian pilots from Kwajalein, each having more than 20 years' service on the Atoll. I enjoyed meeting them and being told the status of their adopted home; their UH-1s were to be turned in for the new UH-72s.

Our next leg would be a 3.5-hour flight from Guam to Kadena Air Base in Okinawa, Japan.

February 10th, we had a 2-hour flight from Okinawa to Osan Air Base in South Korea for a four day stay.

With plenty of time, I ventured into Osan several times to see the city. One evening, February 11, I was in a small Korean shop which sold beautiful Korean blankets. While there, I noticed a small black and white television on the floor next to a wall. On second glance, I noticed something very interesting on the TV. Mike Tyson and Buster Douglas were about to have a Heavy Weight boxing title fight in Tokyo, Japan! I asked the store proprietor if I might watch the fight and he said "Yes". This turned out to be one of the most controversial Tyson fights in which he, at the time, was the undisputed, undefeated Heavy Weight Champion of the World. Sitting alone, cross-legged on the floor in front of the TV, I watched the breath-taking event unfold to which Buster Douglas was declared the winner, Mike Tyson's first loss. I was thrilled to be so fortunate, especially at no charge!

On the 14th, we flew 1.9 hours from Osan to Misawa Air Base, Japan to remain overnight.

February 15th it was a 1.5-hour flight from Misawa to Atsugi, Japan for fuel, then 4.9 hours to Midway Atoll where I had been some two months prior. I previously mentioned the nesting Gooney birds, now I was thrilled to see thousands of small hatchlings under the watchful eye of their parents! To be so fortunate was beyond words.

From Midway (now the 16th) we flew 2.7 hours to Hickam Air Force Base (PHNL), Hawaii to remain overnight.

On the 17th we departed Hickam for Oakland, CA (KOAK), a 4.5-hour flight, refueled, then 4.3 hours back home to Andrews Air Force Base, MD.

I had many great experiences in the two years at USAPAT prior to my retirement from the ARMY. Now operational, USAPAT would take passengers to every continent but one. Spanning the Pacific and Atlantic became routine. We proudly crisscrossed the U.S. on top level missions. Thousands of flight hours, hundreds of missions were to follow over ensuing years. USAPAT's motto: "Never fly the margins". It was an honor to have a small part in the initial stand-up.

May 30, 1990

Chief Warrant Officer Delbert Hardiman
United States Army Priority Air
   Transport C20 Detachment
United States Army Davison Aviation Command
Fort Belvoir, Virginia   22060

Dear Mr. Hardiman:

     As you depart from active duty, I want to personally thank you not only for your outstanding performance as one of my pilots the past two years, but also for your dedication and selfless service during your four years at Davison Army Airfield and your 22 years of active duty.

     Your accomplishments since 1968 have been many, but probably the most impressive among them has been the more than 8,200 flight hours -- 600 of them in jets -- that you have logged during your career. The resulting level of experience has been very evident to me; I've flown many miles with you over the last two years, and on every mission you performed in an outstanding manner. I always had absolute confidence in your abilities and the highest respect for your sense of duty and professionalism. Your high standards will serve you well as you leave the military and become a civilian pilot.

     With best wishes for every continued success in the future,

Sincerely,

Carl E. Vuono
General, United States Army
Chief of Staff

Letter from ARMY Chief of Staff Carl E. Vuono on my retirement.

240

USAPAT 35th Anniversary

Through the years, we had anniversary get-togethers sponsored by the current USAPAT team. A catalyst in coordinating and making this happen is CW5 (Ret) Fernando Avila, who had two tours with USAPAT as an instructor and examiner. I want to thank him for his persistence in helping make these happen. Fernando how flies for Southwest Airlines.

35th USAPAT Reunion Aug 2023; the "Original pilots" in attendance identified in blue blazers. L/R, Lyle Real, Bob Kirksey, partially seen, Del Hardiman, holding aircraft model, Chris Nauer, Jim Haley, Doug Crockett and Bruce Barefoot. (photo Paula Hardiman)

Del Hardiman

Speaker at USAPAT 35th Anniversary (photo Paula Hardiman)

Retirement from ARMY

June 1990, I retired from the ARMY, in particular ARMY Aviation, having had a tremendous 22-year career. My flying days were not over, however.

Side note: August 3, 2018, I had the honor of being keynote speaker for the naming of the COL William F. O'Neal Hangar, Davison ARMY Airfield, Fort Belvoir, VA in honor of the late COL O'Neal.

Side note: With our jet qualifications, each original pilot went on to commercial aviation ventures. Sam Blake would later become USAPAT commander. Bob Kirksey became Oprah Winfrey's chief pilot in her newly acquired Gulf Stream IV. In time, Sam joined Bob flying Oprah to later became Oprah's Director of Operations for The Oprah Winfrey Leadership Academy for Girls in South Africa from November 2006 until December 2018. Doug Crockett worked his way up to Captain of UPS 747's.

PART V

CHAPTER 32

Job Search, Temporary job with Mark Bragg, Tragedy of dredging personnel

After retiring from the ARMY, while job searching, I took a temporary job flying with Mr. Mark Bragg who owned a single engine Beechcraft Sierra, 200 HP, retractable landing gear. Mark had advertised for a pilot to ride along with him; I fit the bill. Mark, a pilot himself, lived in the Watergate hotel in D.C., keeping his Sierra at Washington National Airport. He was a businessman, entrepreneur, somewhat adventurous, engaging in many operations; his wife was involved with TV syndicated entertainment as I recall. It was a pleasure spending the summer of 1990 with him traveling a few days a week side by side at the aircraft controls, mostly in the southeast and once to Louisiana. Mark liked making calls with his large hand-held phone, some called a brick; from the aircraft he could reach long distances. Not sure this was in compliance with FCC rules. Mark, impulsively bought a small dredging company which consisted of a floating platform, dredging machinery complete with sparse living quarters for three or four men. Docking sites needed sand dredged from time to time to keep proper depth for shipping commerce, Mark's operation met the requirement. The dredging operation sucked sand from the bottom, then pumped it through large piping up to a quarter mile inland where mounds of wet soil accumulated. I visited the platform with Mark to check on the operation at two different locations, the last at a port in Louisiana. I met the crew and hung out on the dredging platform for an hour or so, long enough to make acquaintances with the stevedore crew. Upon completion of the Louisiana job, the platform, with crew, was to be towed east along the Florida coast to southwest Florida but for some reason the towing company took a short cut across the Gulf of Mexico. Over the vast expanse of the gulf, *tragedy*; the helpless crew was caught in a storm, losing all on board. So sad to have known these good men for a brief time and now they were all gone.

Complete electrical failure!

Mark offered his aircraft if I wanted, so taking advantage of the offer, decided to take my youngest son, 13-year-old Benjamin on a flight from Washington National Airport to Easton, Maryland. This would be a forty-minute flight, land, show Benjamin the airport and return. I had been to Easton with Mark who owned a lovely home near Easton overlooking a river which emptied into the Chesapeake Bay.

We departed the National Airport one afternoon using runway 36 heading north, then to pick up an easterly course making sure to remain clear of the restricted zones of Washington. Soon after liftoff, the aircraft experienced *complete electrical failure*! I could not communicate, only fly the aircraft. With no communication, it would not be prudent to return to Washington National due to disruption of commercial aircraft traffic. I had no choice but to continue the original flight plan to Easton. My immediate concern was getting the landing gear extended with no electrical power. I looked around and found an emergency landing gear crank just below my seat. I placed the gear handle down and began to make rotational cranks until I could not crank any more. There was always the chance the gear was not down, or completely down and locked, I could not tell for sure. I looked over to my right at young Benjamin and told him we might be in trouble and to prepare to brace himself on landing.

On arrival at Easton, I made several passes near the terminal building to get attention in event we had an accident on the landing; we might get help but did not see anyone. We landed on runway 04, touching down gently main gear first, holding the nose off as long as possible as we slowed down. All three gears held!

I called Mark to let him know the circumstances, he said no problem, he would have mechanics investigate the problem. The aircraft had sat in rain several days before our flight so it might have been water causing the electrical failure. Benjamin and I lucked out, so happens there was a husband and wife leaving Easton Airport in their twin Cessna 310 within the hour heading to Washington National. They were going to the Kennedy Center and happily offered us a ride.

CHAPTER 33
Job Interviews and Flying position

In the fall of 1990, I had numerous job interviews. Pan American Airlines, Continental Airlines, Northwest Airlines, Dunavant Enterprises, Memphis, TN which operated a Gulfstream III, Arabian American Oil Company (ARAMCO), Houston, TX and P.H. Glatfelter, York, PA, operating a twin turbine Beech King air 300. Did not get a call up from the airlines I suspect from my having had my license suspended for 90 days, early in my aviation career as youngster. At that time, the Airlines had just begun hiring pilots 40 and older. I was 44 at the time. Interestingly I drove to Memphis for the interview with Dunavant Enterprises and was put on a flight, of all places to Washington National airport to remain two days! Also interesting, all our passengers were Chinese businessmen. I did not get the job, which, in retrospect glad I didn't.

Paula and I flew to Houston for an interview with ARAMCO. One thing I did not like was being assigned to Saudi Arabia, we would need to send our children away once they became ninth graders; anywhere we wanted them to relocate for school in the world at ARAMCO expense. At the time, Benjamin was the only one to fit that parameter. In a year I received notice from ARAMCO for a pilot position as well as a letter from Northwest, both, after having been hired by NASA.

My friend, Johnny Johnston was flying a King Air 300 for P.H. Glatfelter of York, Pennsylvania, and got me a job as first officer. We operated out of Asheville, N.C. Our passengers largely consisted of customers of Glatfelter. I found myself isolated, living in a walkout basement apartment with days doing nothing, missing my wife and home. Chief pilot for Glatfelter, who flew their Cessna Citation jet out of York, wanted me to commit to a two-year contract which I was not willing to do. After six months, we parted ways.

PART VI

CHAPTER 34
Nasa

Call from Hugh Huleatt, Chief Pilot, NASA One Operations

I returned home and took jobs working for a 'Temp' agency at $6.00 per hour. I must say, I learned the value of a dollar. Primarily I was involved in office admin jobs. Saturday morning, May 27, 1991, while preparing to work a business convention at the Crystal City Marriott Hotel near Washington National Airport, I received a call from chief pilot of 'NASA One' flight operations which operated from Washington National Airport.

Hugh Huleatt, the Chief Pilot, introduced himself and asked if I was still interested in the job I had lobbied for these past 18 months. Yes! Yes! (I thought quietly). I tried to conceal my relief and joy. I would report Wednesday morning, May 1st for an interview.

I had written Hugh January 25, 1991, with my credentials, requesting a flying position, especially since the operation had recently moved to Washington National Airport, 16 miles from my home. I reminded Hugh in my letter that we had spoken the previous August.

I went on to my job at the Crystal City Marriott, in business attire, greeting 100+ conference attendees, handing out pamphlets and seating individuals for lunch, but my thoughts and joy was on the prospective job as a pilot for NASA and how my future and fortune had turned so dramatically, if I got the job.

Del Hardiman

The Interview

I reported to NASA One Flight Operations, second floor of Signature Aviation, General Aviation terminal at 9:00 A.M. Wednesday. I knew by researching the interview process, first impression was paramount. With a fresh haircut, dressed in the standard blue suit, white shirt, and red tie, I reported to Hugh at his desk. He offered a seat in front, and we got acquainted. Never once let down my guard. We spoke in generalities, then the business of flying. On and on I sat there for several hours, questions, and answers, each getting to know the other. Nearby sat Chuck Lane, a former NASA One pilot, now medically grounded. Chuck ran flight operations, taking missions etc. It was Chuck I had met a year and half previously at a hotel in Savannah, GA while getting service done on one of our ARMY Gulfstream jets. Chuck, H.D. Berner, chief of maintenance, and I shared breakfast. I let them know I needed a job. It was Chuck and H.D. who took my name and contact information, and it was they who recommended me for the job to Hugh.

Finally, which seemed forever, Hugh smiled, got up, reached across his desk shaking my hand saying these beautiful words: "You got the job"!

In processing

My wife, Paula and sons, Michael, Patrick, and Benjamin were thrilled about my selection to be a part of NASA, to once again fly which is all they had known me to do.

My in-processing consisted of introductions to other personnel, Jim Adkins the other pilot, Mike Richman, Eric Stalnaker both crew chiefs, Ben Kline our electrician/radio man. Ben would also fill in as Crew chief and of course there was H.D. Berner. I got my first class medical renewed at the downtown Washington, D.C. NASA medical facility. May 13 through 17 I attended Simuflight Aviation training facility near Dallas, TX for classroom and flight simulator refresher training. Still pinching myself!

My first flight in NASA ONE, May 20, 1991, was with Hugh, fellow pilot Jim Adkins and Crew Chief H.D. Berner, destination, the Shuttle Landing strip (X68) near Melbourne Florida. The Shuttle landing strip, 15,000 feet long, 300 feet wide, is one of the longest runways in the world. On arrival, Space Shuttle *Discovery* sat nestled on the top of NASA's Boeing 747 (NASA 905) under the Mate-Demate Device, used when a shuttle was transported by the Boeing Shuttle carrier. *Discovery*, 40th Space Shuttle mission (STS-39), had diverted to Edwards AFB when winds were too high at Kennedy. Exhilarated to see a shuttle situated on top of NASA's giant Boeing 747 and there I stood mere feet away! What lay ahead? Was this for real! I can relate that after years coming to the Kennedy Space Center, this was the only time seeing a Shuttle mounted on the 747.

Shuttle Landing Strip (X68) (NASA photo)

Del Hardiman

First flight to the Shuttle Landing Strip, near Melbourne, FL. Shuttle *Discovery* mounted on top NASA's 747 in background. (photo taken by Hugh Huleatt)

NASA ONE on Ramp at Kennedy Space Center airfield (X-68) (photo Del Hardiman)

I received my checkout ride with Hugh this day. We made a total of six landings at X68 and three ILS (instrument) approaches at nearby Patrick AFB. I was now mission qualified.

N1NA (NASA ONE)

Side Note: Discovery is now on display at the Steven F. Udvar-Hazy Center of the Smithsonian National Air and Space Museum adjacent to Dulles Airport, Washington, D.C., some 30 miles from my home.

NASA One operation as mentioned, was at Reagan National Airport, Washington, DC; we had an upstairs office above Signature Aviation, the Fixed Base Operator. It was at Signature that private and often political figures arrived and departed. Never surprising to see well knowns in the waiting room, former Presidential candidates, future Presidential candidates, Congressmen, Senators, actors and well-known businessmen and women. On one occasion, I noticed retired GEN Benjamin O. Davis, former

Commander of the Black Tuskegee Airmen of WWII fame. My son Patrick was with me, I wanted him to meet GEN Davis who was most cordial. We spent around twenty minutes in conversation with the General and I was so pleased! GEN Davis passed away July 4, 2002.

The following six years many adventures with NASA lay ahead. I flew two different NASA Administrators, Richard Truly, retired Vice Admiral, eighth administrator, former fighter pilot and astronaut who was soon replaced by Dan Goldin who served from April 1992 through November 2000.

Most flights were taking managers, scientists, engineers, occasional retired astronauts and politicians throughout the U.S. Prevalent destinations were the Shuttle Landing Facility at Kennedy Space Center, Johnson Space Center, Houston, TX, Marshall Space Flight Center, Huntsville, Al, Lewis Research Center, now the NASA Glenn Research Center, Cleveland, OH, Jet Propulsion Laboratory, Pasadena, CA, AMES Research Center Moffett Airfield, CA and Edwards AFB, CA, now the Armstrong Flight Research Center.

While flying NASA One, I witnessed 20+ Shuttle launches, most viewed from Cocoa Beach nearby. For each Shuttle launch, we (the crew) were presented cloth patches and pennants for the designated launch, some of which were canceled prior to launch. These were the same patches worn by the astronauts for the mission (each crew designed their own patches). I have over 35 patches in my collection. On occasion, I observed families on the beach, sometimes at night anxiously waiting for a launch to sadly learn the launch had been postponed.

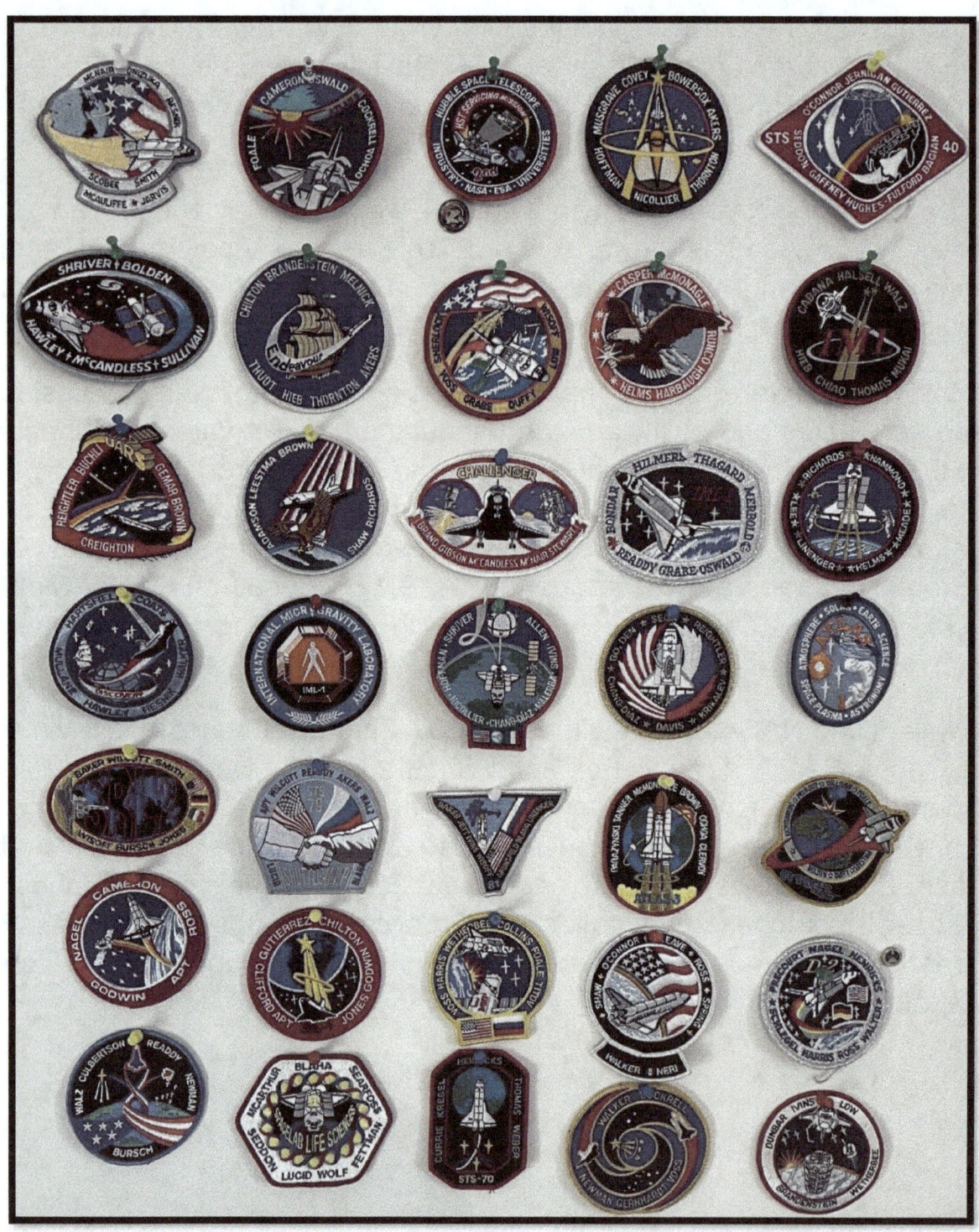

Shuttle mission patches given to me by NASA leadership enroute to that particular launch with the exception of the Challenger and Columbia which I purchased in remembrance of those two fatal Shuttle flights.

John Dahmer

John, my good friend, and fellow ARMY Aviator for many years, asked if I might get him a job with our NASA Flight Operations. This was a year or so after I had been with the operation. John and I were two of the ten ARMY Aviators previously mentioned, who stood up the first ARMY Jet Company (USAPAT). Our families were close, his daughters Stephanie and Jennifer attended school together with our sons Michael and Patrick. His wife Sue was so special to him. John had an uncanny ability for navigating his way around the world, no challenge too great. His adept sense in this regard was uncanny. I put in a word for John and Hugh, my boss brought him on board. John fit right in; we flew many missions together over the next few years enjoying each other's company.

Eddie Adams – world renowned photographer

Monday, February 3, 1992, Jim Adkins, Mike Richman, and I were on a three-day layover trip with NASA to Burbank, CA. Mike and I accompanied Jim to visit Jim's second daughter (no longer remember her name) at a residence in the Hollywood Hills. His daughter, an aspiring actress, was house sitting for a movie producer away in Europe. The house was old but historic, situated with other older homes interspersed by small streets. Joining us was Jim's son-in-law, Eddie Adams, famed photographer of many world conflicts who was married to Jim's oldest daughter Alyssa.

Eddie was one of the most recognized photographers in the world at the time; his photo of a brutal scene in the streets of Saigon, Vietnam which I will not describe was flashed instantaneously around the world, winning for Eddie, the Pulitzer Prize for spot news photography.

As we prepared to leave the residence in a Range Rover for our restaurant, Jim's daughter pointed to a walled vine covered home across the small drive, telling us actress Lily Tomlin, lived there. She then pointed uphill to a home she said was previously owned by actor/comedian W.C. Fields. It was in a pond on this property that a tragic event took place; the young son of actor Anthony Quinn and wife, actress Katherine DeMille, Cecille B. DeMille's daughter drowned.

Del Hardiman

At our restaurant, I had the opportunity to sit next to Eddie and carry on a wonderful conversation. He was quite interested in my time in Vietnam, in particular my having a Vietnamese wife.

Jim told us later that Eddie had a Wall of Honor on his New England farm with names inscribed of fallen war photographers and correspondents in which he held an annual gathering of fellow correspondents to recognize and remember their fallen comrades.

Note: Eddie's many phenomenal accomplishments are available online.

CHAPTER 35
Flights to Moscow

Tom Stafford

My time with NASA brought many interesting stories, some I will reflect on. In total I flew five trips to Moscow, this was my first. Thursday, July 9, 1992. Mr. Goldin would meet with the Russian Space Agency's General Director Yuri Koptev to work on advancing a new space agreement. Crew on this flight would be Jim Adkins, retired USAF, Chuck Doherty, retired USAF, our NASA civilian check pilot, Ben Kline (crew chief) and myself. We departed Washington National at 3:30 PM for a short stop at Andrews AFB nearby, then to Gander New Foundland (CYQX), Canada for fuel, then to Rhein-Main (EDAF) Germany arriving Rhein-Main at 3:30 AM for a day long stop. On the 11th we departed for Sheremetyevo, airport, Moscow, arriving at 7:15 AM. On this flight was former astronaut Tom Stafford an advisor for Mr. Goldin.

From Tom Stafford's bio, he flew two Gemini rendezvous missions (1965–66) and commanded the Apollo 10 mission (1969)—the final test of Apollo systems before the first crewed landing on the Moon. Apollo 10, crewed by Stafford, Gene Cernan, and John Young, was launched on May 18, 1969. Three days later the spacecraft attained lunar orbit. The flight rehearsed every phase of a Moon landing except the landing itself. Cernan and Stafford descended in the Lunar Module to within 9.5 miles (15 km) of the Moon's surface. Apollo 10 completed 31 orbits of the Moon before returning to Earth, landing in the Pacific Ocean on May 26. Stafford was on an Apollo spacecraft that docked with a Soviet Soyuz spacecraft on July 17,

Del Hardiman

1975, in which he shook hands in space with cosmonaut Aleksey Leonov. The two spacecraft were docked together for two days, and the mission was considered an important symbol of détente, the easing of Cold War tensions between the United States and the Soviet Union. Ref-25 I mention this because Tom Stafford gave me my "comeuppance". With three pilots aboard, we alternated one seated in the cabin with passengers. I was in conversation with Mr. Goldin's wife seated in front of me and the conversation led to what man-made fixture on earth could be seen from outer space. While in Vietnam, we had young girls called Doughnut Dollies who came from camp to camp to entertain us. Kind of a reminder of home. I recalled one such event when one of the girls told of the Great Wall of China being visible to the naked eye from outer space. Why of course, I thought! Just as I began telling Mrs. Goldin of what man-made structure could be seen from outer space with the naked eye, Tom, seated nearby, reading some material, supposedly not listening, stopped me in mid-sentence, looked me in the eye and said: "It's not the Great Wall of China". What could I say, he had been there, done that. Embarrassed, I quickly changed the subject. Never forget that!

Photo presented to me by Astronaut Tom Stafford, commander of Apollo 10 (written remarks no longer legible). L/R Gene Cernan, Tom Stafford and John Young, I flew both Stafford and Young in NASA ONE on separate occasions. (NASA Photo)

Cooperation agreement in 1992, origins of the International Space Station

Back to Moscow, October 3, 1992, my second trip there in three months. This flight consisted of Hugh Huleatt, John Dahmer, and Eric Stalnaker (crew chief). We had flown to Shannon, Ireland (EINN), to Kiev, Ukraine (UKBB) then to Sheremetyevo, arriving at 4:55 AM (local).

In play, which I was not aware of at the time was the signing of a cooperation agreement between Mr. Goldin and the Russian Space Agency's General Director Yuri Koptev. A few hours prior to the signing, Mr.

Goldin noticed me in the hotel lobby and asked if I would like to witness the signing. I gladly agreed!

To make the event, I was driven by a U.S. Marine from the American Embassy back to Sheremetyevo airport to retrieve dress blazers for Hugh and myself, John elected not to go.

The 'signing' took place in Mr. Koptev's office. He and Mr. Goldin sat side by side, each with respective documents in folders.

They signed together, then exchanged their documents for the other to sign. Afterwards, with big smiles, holding their folders, they stood and shook hands. A few news correspondents and cameramen were on hand to record the ceremony. Hugh and I observed from a distance.

The signed agreement was the "Implementing Agreement between the National Aeronautics and Space Administration of the United States of America and the Russian Space Agency of the Russian Federation on Human Space Flight Cooperation." This agreement further outlined details of cooperation that included: a Russian cosmonaut flying on the Shuttle mission STS-60 as a mission specialist; a U.S. astronaut launching on a Soyuz, flying more than 90 days on the Mir, and returning on a Shuttle; Russian cosmonauts on Mir being "changed out" via the Shuttle on the same flight that would return the U.S. astronaut; and evaluation of and possible contract for the Russian Androgynous Peripheral Docking Assembly developed by NPO Energia for use on the Shuttle. This program was called the Mir-Shuttle Program. Ref-26 After the signing, we were directed to a briefing room in which Messrs. Goldin and Koptev sat side by side at an elevated deas to answer questions about the significance of the agreement. In front, slightly lower in cushioned seating sat the 'Press'. Hugh and I observed from the rear.

After the briefing, we were taken (without Press) to a large room which had the longest wooden table I had ever seen. There might have been 40 or more seated, wearing coat and tie. Seating was arranged with American and Russian guests, seated alternately. Each had some investment in the program. We were served a delicious meal, with water and vodka to drink.

Dangerous Enclosures

Hugh warned me to keep my glasses full of water to prevent vodka from being poured for us. He said, "put your hand over your glass" when offered a drink. Throughout the evening, an elegant lady stepped to each individual translating in English and Russian as each person made their comments. Mr. Goldin, his wife, and Mr. Koptev sat at the far end of the table; Hugh and I way down at the opposite end of the table. Eventually, the lady came to Hugh and me. When my time came, I stood and made some comments with a toast, no longer remembering what I said.

Making toast at dinner. Lady interpreter standing to my left. Seated to my right is Hugh Huleatt. Others pictured (names unknown) are Russian guests. (photo by Bill Ingalls, official NASA photographer)

With dinner complete, I asked the NASA photographer Bill Ingalls to get a photo of me standing with Mr. Goldin and Yuri Koptev. Mr. Goldin motioned for Hugh to join us.

It took time for me to absorb the significance of the agreement but, it was the beginning of what would become the International Space Station (ISS) in which Russia and the U.S. have partnered these many years. Witnessing this part of space history was one of the highlights of my career. I often reflect on it as events unfold on the ISS.

<u>Side Note</u>: On another flight to Moscow, one of our passengers was Astronaut Bill Shepherd, later to be first Commander of the International Space Station. I met him several times afterwards as well. Bill, a former Navy Seal, and mechanical engineer is the recipient of the Congressional Space Medal of Honor. Ref-27 He presented me with an 8X10 NASA profile photo in which he wrote:

"To Del,
Thanks for the ride on NASA 1!
Shep"

Crisis in Moscow

Another most interesting and exciting trip was being in Moscow during the October 1993 constitutional crisis. Boris Yeltsin, first appointed Russian president after dissolution of the Soviet Union had an ongoing political stand-off with the Russian Parliament. He was accused of overstepping his authority; the entangled political conflict had been ongoing since 1992, culminating in a standoff by October 2nd. Supporters of Parliament erected barricades blocking traffic, storming the television premises and the White House, which served as the primary office of the government of Russia. Ref-28 Knowledge of the conflicts presented a choice for Mr. Goldin, NASA Administrator. Should he proceed with a planned meeting in Moscow or postpone the trip. Mr. Goldin elected to go. By late afternoon of October 2, 1993, Hugh Huleatt, Eric Stalnaker, crew chief and I had the NASA Gulfstream ready for departure. While traversing through the meet/greet waiting area of Signature Aviation, fixed base operations, I noticed Senator Bob Doyle. I walked over to him, extending my arm for a left-handed handshake. Senator Doyle was a WWII veteran who had sustained serious injuries in the Apennine mountains southwest of Bologna, Italy in April 1945 while serving with the 10th Mountain Division. Ref-29 His injuries, requiring many operations, left him with limited mobility in his right arm. Eric had seen the left-handed handshake and asked if this was some sort of secret greeting. Leaving Senator Doyle, I proceeded across the ramp as twilight set in; a Gulfstream IV taxied up. Observing the door open, I saw Senator Hillary Clinton descend the stairs waving to someone.

We departed DC at 6: 20 P.M. for Keflavik, Iceland (BIKF), our fuel stop. Time enroute, 5.3 hours arriving at 11:40 PM local time. We decided to take on additional fuel at Keflavik if fuel was not available at our destination in order to make it to Norway.

An hour later, now Sunday, October 3, we departed Keflavik at 12:40 AM enroute to Moscow Sheremetyevo airport (UUEE). Along the way the four and half-hour flight found passengers, some asleep others working; Hugh and myself at the controls in the dark cockpit along with crew chief Eric Stalnaker seated nearby. It was early hours of the morning, quiet, the North Star ahead strikingly seemed to be an aircraft in the distance had I not known better. Most flights are routine, but this trip would prove quite extraordinary. On board, in addition to Mr. Goldin, was John Young, Astronaut, NASA trail blazer who not only walked on the moon as Commander of Apollo 16 in 1972 but flew the first Shuttle test flight (STS-1) along with co-pilot and fellow astronaut Bob Crippen in 1981. John was said by others to be the Astronaut's Astronaut. His missions included Gemini 3, Gemini 10, Apollo 10 as well as Apollo 16. Ref-30 On our descent, now daylight, John joined us in the cockpit observing the Russian countryside, he made the comment: "Last time I passed over this area, I was 50 miles up. We arrived at Sheremetyevo at 5:15 A.M. local. Processing through customs complete, our passengers departed for the 25-mile drive to the Renaissance Moscow Hotel. Fuel was available. After refueling and putting NASA One to bed, we were driven to the hotel.

After checking in and arriving at my room, I turned on the TV to CNN. Gene Randall, CNN Moscow correspondent filled the screen covering the escalating crisis. Bob Doyle was live giving his perspective of the situation in Moscow. I had shaken his hand just 15 hours before!

This would be my 'birds-eye' view of the 1993 Russian constitutional crisis also referred to as the 1993 October Coup, Shooting of the White House or Black October. Ref-31 Throughout the day, CNN covered the crisis. From my window I observed two Russian helicopters beyond nearby buildings, circling some distance away; CNN was showing the same helicopters live.

Pro parliament supporters had taken control of the white house and attempted taking the Television Center which was badly damaged. The Television Center and TV tower was up the street, not far from our hotel.

Midday Mr. Goldin called a meeting in Hugh's room to discuss evacuation. He asked Hugh how many people could fly out? He might be thinking of American Embassy personnel. Hugh told him we could load the aircraft with (no longer remember the number he gave) but many would be without safety belts. Mr. Goldin impressed me with his command of the situation, calm and unrattled. He told us to stand by if such a need arrived.

Meantime the crisis, as I later learned, was coming to a head that afternoon of the 3rd through morning of the 4th.

Early morning darkness of October 4th, watching CNN, I observed ghostlike silhouettes moving toward the white house. What was happening? I did not know. The army, I later learned had been neutral in the conflict but now aligned with President Yeltsin. It was they who were moving toward the Supreme Soviet building (white house). By sunrise the parliament building was surrounded. Army tanks shelled the front of the building's upper levels causing extensive damage. Leaders of the resistance were arrested. Near the brink of civil war, the conflict, lasting 10 days, I learned, was the deadliest single event of street fighting in the city's history since the 1917 revolution. According to the General Prosecutor's Office, 147 people were killed and 437 wounded. Ref-32 The first morning I went for breakfast downstairs in the lush Renaissance restaurant where life seemed normal. I observed John Young who motioned for me to join him. This would be the first of three breakfasts I shared with John. I did not discuss his many NASA accomplishments, thinking it inappropriate.

When leaving my breakfast, I noticed CNN correspondent Christiane Amanpour seated, alone, eating breakfast. I had to speak to her! She told me she had just arrived to cover the crisis. I must say she was a lovely lady, gracious, more beautiful in person than on TV. I asked if I might touch her hand as I stood next to her, she said "yes".

So, here I am, witnessing a Moscow revolution, having breakfast with an Astronaut who had walked on the Moon and meeting Christiane Amanpour! Thrilling!

Next day, the 5th, crisis ended, I ventured downtown to have a look. I had the hotel receptionist write two notes (in Russian) telling my taxi where I wanted to go and another to the hotel for my return. There were no taxis, only small cars driven independently by civilians waiting across the street for fares. My tour downtown revealed near empty streets; I observed barricades on one street not yet removed. The scene was somewhat surreal but seemingly safe. No activity to indicate a day before chaos had ensued these streets.

Dangerous Enclosures

Had I known how serious and provocative the constitutional crisis had been, I would not have gone downtown. It was later I discovered the breadth of those final days.

Our flight back to D.C. on the 7th was routine. John Young came to the cockpit and presented me with an 8X10 NASA profile photo of himself which was a wonderful surprise. His inscription read:

"To Del Hardiman

With my thanks for the Great Flight on our "Mission to Moscow" 2-7 October 1993. All The Best."

John Young 7, OCT 93

Signed photo from NASA Administrator Dan Goldin which reads:
Del. Thanks for your support on the NASA NOV 94 trip to Russia.
One of his favorite photos, Mr. Goldin pointed out the thin blue line in the photo which
he said protected our environment from outer space.

Teddy Bear

On a flight in the U.S., one of our passengers asked if I might do her a favor. She had a child, can't recall if it was a girl or boy in the fifth grade as I recall which had a class project. Each child in the class was given a small brown teddy bear with a backpack. In the backpack was a log with which to sign the many destinations the bear had made by the end of the school year. The challenge was to see whose bear would have the longest journey before its return. She asked if I might take "Teddy" and pass him on. As a coincidence I had an upcoming trip to Moscow, getting the bear to Moscow would be a good start. I had met a young lady on staff at the American Embassy earlier, so I dropped Teddy off with her. Another coincidence, her father was the U.S. Navy four-star Admiral in command of the Pacific Fleet and would be coming the next week for a visit! She would give Teddy to her father who would take him to Hawaii, well on his way around the world. Never found out who won the class project but suspect our Teddy was top billing!

Laika, space dog

On another trip to Moscow, I asked one of my passengers if she might get me some information on Laika, the first dog and animal to orbit earth on the Soviet satellite 'Sputnik 2' in November 1957? As she boarded for the return flight, she handed me an autographed book (in Russian) containing many photos of Laika, signed by the author who was part of the project! I was astonished. This would be for my son Benjamin who had expressed interest in Laika.

Touring Moscow

On these many trips to Moscow, I took advantage of time there, visiting shops, museums, historic churches, touring inside the Kremlin walls, visiting Lenin's mausoleum in Red Square two times in which his embalmed body was on public display. His body, enclosed in a sealed glass enclosure, dressed in a blue suit, appeared in perfect condition just as it had been when he was laid to rest shortly after his death in 1924.

Visiting Moscow, I discovered the Moscow Metro, a tourist attraction. It was old but highly functional, the main mode of transportation in the city. It has one of the world's deepest underground stations; escalators went down, down, down! At the time, cost to ride the metro was equivalent of about five cents American.

One morning, I stood next to a busy traffic intersection observing heavy traffic. I decided to count women drivers. In about 30 minutes, I observed only one car driven by a young female and it appeared she was being coaxed/instructed by the male occupant seated beside her.

CHAPTER 36
August 92 – French Guiana

Sunday, August 9, 1992, we departed Washington National Airport at 9:10 AM enroute to Patrick Air Force Base (COF), Florida, which was our normal rendezvous site for Kennedy Space Center functions. On board were nine scientists (eight male, one female) from NASA's Goddard Space Flight Center in Greenbelt, Maryland. Our crew consisted of Jim, Adkins, Eric Stalnaker (Crew Chief) and me. Flight time, 1.8 hours.

At Patrick, we took on board Bob Crippen, former Director of the Space Shuttle program. As a former astronaut, Bob was co-pilot with John Young on the first Shuttle flight (STS-1) in April 1981. His bio reports he was Commander of STS-7 in June 1983, STS-41-C in April 1984, and STS-41-G in October 1984. Ref-33 We departed Patrick at 1205 PM, destination Cayenne airport, French Guiana (SOCA) on the northeastern tip of South America some 300 miles north of the equator. We circumnavigated west of Cuba remaining clear of its airspace. The flight time was 5 hours, arriving at 5:05 PM local.

Purpose of the trip was launching of the TOPEX/Poseidon satellite, a joint venture of NASA and the French Space Agency, the first to measure ocean surface topography with accuracy up to 4.2 centimeters. Ref-34 The launch was at the French Guiana Space Center. Enroute, I asked one of the scientists how long he had been on this project, his reply was that when he started, his daughter was in kindergarten and now she is a high school freshman.

While in Guiana, Jim, Eric and I from our hotel traveled in the direction of the spaceport by taxi just to get a feel for the land. Our 40-minute trip exposed heavy jungle on one side of our ride with intermittent views of the ocean on the other. On the roadside, one could see vendor stands sparsely located selling various native items such as fruit or handmade ornaments. Upon arrival at a small village, we walked along the coast. I was impressed that in the far distance offshore we could see the French Penal colony of Cayenne (Devil's Island) of which the movie Papillon (1973) starring Dustin Hoffman and Steve McQueen, prisoners of the Island was based.

The TOPEX/Poseidon satellite was launched August 10th; it remained operational until 2006. Ref-35 We departed Guiana on the 12th at 7:00 AM, arriving at Patrick AFB at 12:05 PM.

Bob Crippen had a photo taken next to the left side of our aircraft, NASA One; included were the nine scientists, Bob, Jim Adkins and our crew chief Eric Stalnaker. Later Bob sent me an 8X10 print on which he inscribed:

"To Del,

The Survivors!

Bob Crippen"

Arrival at Patrick AFB, FL from French Guiana; along with 9 scientists, is me with clipboard, Bob Crippen to my left in blue blazer. Far left, Eric Stalnaker, crew chief, to my immediate right, wearing tie, Jim Adkins, pilot.

Side note: I met some interesting people while flying for NASA. On one flight a heavily bearded man, trim and fit in his thirties came to the cockpit. Most unusual for our passengers. I asked him if he had done anything interesting lately; he replied, "Two weeks ago I stood on 10,000 feet of ice in Antarctica."

CHAPTER 37
Israel

We departed Washington National Airport October 5th, 1994, first stop Gander Newfoundland, Canada (CYQX) for fuel stop. On board was Mr. Goldin and associates; the crew was Jim Adkins, H.D. Berner (crew chief) and me. From Canada on to Cologne, Bonn, West Germany (EDDK) for a two-day layover. Departed Cologne, the 7th for a one-hour flight to Paris, Le Bourget Airport (LFPB). I had been to Le Bourget several times previously. It was at Le Bourget that Charles Lindberg landed at 10:24 PM, May21, 1927 after completing his 33.5 nonstop solo flight from Roosevelt Field Long Island NY. Ref-36 We departed Paris the 8th on a 4.3-hour flight to Tel Aviv/Ben Gurion International airport, Israel (LLBG).

Jim, H.D. and I took advantage of our three days stay in Israel taking an early morning all day tour from Tel Aviv by bus cross country to Jerusalem and Bethlehem. We visited the Dome of the Rock, the Church of the Holy Sepulcher, the Western Wall where I placed a prayer for my Mother in one of the cracks, walked the confined shopping sector in Jerusalem as well. Visiting the Holocaust Museum, a sacred place in remembrance of the millions of Jews who perished during WWII had a profound impact on me. Now I have visited two Holocaust museums, the other in Washington, D.C.

Our hotel in Tel Aviv was next to the Mediterranean coastline. I swam out to the breakers and back. A beautiful beach.

Rome

On the 11th we flew 3.3 hours from Tel Aviv Ben Gurion airport to Rome Ciampino International airport (LIRA). During our brief layover, Jim and I took the early morning 'crowded' metro from our hotel to Rome central. It was a short visit, but we were able to walk the confines of the Roman Colosseum, one of the New Seven Wonders of the World, which was and still is the largest amphitheater ever built. Ref-37 Completed around 79 AD, it stands in ruins but with a little imagination, one can visualize bloody Gladiator battles, public executions or man against beast.

From Rome on the 12th, we flew 2.8 hours to Shannon, Ireland (EINN) for fuel, then 5.5 hours to Bangor Maine (BGR) where we checked in with customs. The final leg of our long day, 1.5 hours, brought us home to Washington National (DCA). This had been a memorable trip!

CHAPTER 38
Oshkosh: The Spirit of Aviation

On most pilot's bucket list is attending the Experimental Aircraft Association (EAA) airshow held each year at Oshkosh, Wisconsin, the World's greatest Aviation celebration. The seven-day event is held at Wittman Regional Airport. Owners by the thousands bring aircraft of all varieties to see and be seen. Campgrounds are full of spectators; hundreds of media representatives worldwide make the trek.

Aircraft range from vintage, home builds, War birds, ultralights, seaplanes, aerobatic and rotor craft. Daily air shows included flybys of these exotic aircraft, aerobatics, and pyrotechnics. 'Over flights' of the Boeing 747, B-52, SR-71 and many others have made their presence at the show. The EAA estimated the attendance in 2021 at 608,000 people. In 2018, 2,714 international visitors registered from 87 nations. There were approximately 10,000 aircraft, 2,979 show planes, and 976 media representatives on-site from six continents, along with 867 commercial exhibitors. Ref-38 It was a wonderful experience to fly our NASA ONE Gulfstream two times to Oshkosh. The first was July 31, 1993. We flew into Appleton, Wisconsin, then drove to the airshow. My second trip was July 29, 1995. The Air Show management wanted 'NASA One' to fly into Wittman Regional but due to the density of air traffic, we elected not to unless the airfield was temporarily shut down for our arrival and departure. This they agreed to. Now we were part of the show! Hours of walking, looking at all these aircraft parked by category while on the loudspeaker system could be heard discussions with such aviation celebrities as Chuck Yeager and Bob Hoover. I had made it to the Mecca of Aviation!

Side note: During my tour in West Germany, I had the opportunity of attending the world-renowned Paris Air Show at Le Bourget airport two times.

CHAPTER 39
Bill Dana – Nasa Test Pilot

February 15, 1994, NASA Dryden Flight Research Center (DFRC), [now the NASA Neil A. Armstrong Flight Research Center (AFRC)] a section of Edwards AFB, Nevada. Hugh and I were seated in NASA ONE waiting for our passengers. We had systems powered up by use of auxiliary power, hot outside but cool inside. Behind us nearby sat NASA's eight engine B-52, a legacy. In front of us on the ramp sat several NASA F-104 chase planes. To the left front behind the F-104s sat one of NASA's SR-71 Blackbirds.

Earlier I had climbed through the B-52 which had small decals on both sides of the airframe representing test missions flown over the years, too many to count. Inside, I was astonished at the old gages on the instrument panel. This B-52 dated back to the early 50's one of the first manufactured. Its most recent mission at that time was launching the Pegasus Hypersonic launch vehicles attached next to the fuselage under the right wing.

On a previous trip I had the opportunity to view the SR-71 up close. From a maintenance stand next to the cockpit, on the left side, I viewed the cockpit interior of which very few pilots ever flew.

While seated, a gentleman with some years on him came up the stairs into the cockpit. Did not know him. As we spoke, he said he was there for the retirement of the F-104 chase planes which were being replaced by F-18's. He had flown the F-104s there at Dryden. As we spoke, I mentioned my favorite photo was the one I had of the small lifting body just landed on the Rogers dry lakebed, with the pilot, in pressure suit, bare headed, standing, facing the lifting body, his back to the camera, looking up as the B-52 from which he was previously dropped, was making a low pass over head coming toward him. Surprisingly he told me that was he in the photo, "would I like an autographed copy of the photo"? Wow I was surprised! This was none other than Bill Dana, NASA test pilot!

Research from Wikipedia, I learned Bill Dana was an internationally recognized former research test pilot. His research also included test flights on the X-15 rocket plane of which he earned his astronaut wings for going beyond 50 miles in space. A West Point graduate, his 40-year career as a test pilot earned him many prestigious honors. Ref-39 The lifting body was designed as wingless aircraft to demonstrate proof of concept of a wingless vehicle returning to earth from space and landing like an aircraft. From this evolved the Space Shuttle.

I received my coveted autographed photo from Bill by mail. On the photo he wrote:

"To Del Hardiman, with best wishes, Bill Dana".

I was permitted to look at photo archives at several NASA facilities, a wonderful opportunity. I got this photo from the NASA Dryden Flight Research Center which continues to fascinate me! On the left are several 'Lifting Bodies', on the right X-15s. Quite a contrast. These two aircraft were in competition, in some respect, for the space program. Interesting fact: Bill Dana flew both the last Lifting Body and X-15 test flights. (NASA photo)

Dangerous Enclosures

NASA Dryden Flight Research Center, Edwards, AFB. This is where we parked NASA ONE on our trips to Dryden. (NASA photo)

<u>Side Note:</u>

From Wikipedia, the free encyclopedia,

The SR-71 flew three and half times the speed of sound at 85,000 feet. On 6 March 1990, Lt. Col. Raymond E. Yeilding and Lt. Col. Joseph T. Vida piloted SR-71 S/N 61-7972 on its final Senior Crown flight and set four new speed records in the process: Los Angeles, California, to Washington, D.C., distance 2,299.7 miles, average speed 2,144.8 miles per hour, and an elapsed time of 64 minutes 20 seconds. It is now on display at the Udvar Hazy Air and Space Museum, near Dulles Airport, Washington,

Del Hardiman

D.C. NASA was the final operator of the Blackbird, who used it as a research platform, and was retired in 1999. Ref-40.

CHAPTER 40
Falling on my Sword – A Dark Day

"Falling on One's sword" is a term sometimes used to describe a voluntary sacrifice for the good of the cause. The opportunity availed itself in my fourth year with our operations. We had an upcoming flight to Beijing China. My boss Hugh Huleatt put himself on it as Pilot in Command, but Dave Dingee, our operations monitor for NASA ONE put himself on the flight. Dave, in his position, was authorized to fly as co-pilot on NASA ONE but with little experience; having him on as second pilot could be problematic, a potential safety issue. Dave had less than 100 hours total in the aircraft, some of that in training and a trip with me to Moscow. Dave, a soft-spoken friendly guy had been a POW, shot down over North Vietnam in 1973. It was an honor to know him. Added to this dilemma was that Hugh, tall, balding white hair, had recently turned 60 and was having family issues, recalling his son being concerned. Hugh wrestled with the situation, wringing his hands on what to do. He did not want Dingee on the flight but did not have the courage to buck the system. The clock was ticking. It is imperative that the second pilot be able to take command in event something should happen to the Pilot in Command, Dave clearly was not capable. Hugh had no experience in that part of the world. Situations are always in flux, flight plans quite often are altered by air traffic controllers, not to mention Chinese parameters would be different; decisions would need to be made 'on the fly' and that's without an emergency.

As the unit Safety Officer, the assigned crew chief Eric Stalnaker and fellow pilot, John Dahmer pressured me relentlessly to do something! As time went by with no action, I took it on myself to contact Fred Gregory, astronaut, and former Shuttle Commander, now head of NASA Safety to avail him of the situation. Fred knew me as one of the NASA ONE pilots, having been on a few flights with me as a passenger. When I explained the situation, his comment to me was "That's not going to happen". He intervened to take Dave off the flight. Thinking I had helped Hugh solve the issue but that was not the case. He felt I had usurped his authority; calling me on the phone, very angrily saying "You are through!" I became persona non grata, no more flights and soon let go. I was devastated! John, with excellent navigation skills, was put on the flight with Hugh.

I checked the aircraft prior to its departure to discover the navigation aids for China and the 'Far East' were not loaded. There was only international data which would not have many of the navigation aids needed for China. This would have been problematic as well. I directed Ben Kline, our electrician and nav loader to insert the Far East Nav package, he said he had not been authorized by Hugh. I directed Ben to load the data, telling him I would take responsibility. The flight taking the NASA Administrator to Beijing went as scheduled, but I had lost my job! My livelihood as pilot was taken from me, leaving me staggered at my prospects.

To say I was depressed would be an understatement. I had to move on, needing gainful employment, by now aviation was out of the question. I took a two-month Novell course at the Computer Training Center, Alexandria, VA, graduating as a Certified Novell Engineer (CNE). My skill set was installing, maintaining, and supporting Netware systems to include hardware. My first employer was Advanced Technology Systems, Inc., McLean, VA.

When my thoughts were on my NASA job, the best job I had ever had, I thought of John (Dahmer). Why had he not called me out of concern? He was one of the main reasons I had fallen on my sword. I was the reason he had his job earning a salary. Out on the streets, thrown under the bus and yet not a call.

About nine months later I received a call from Hugh asking if I wanted my job back. Jim Adkins had retired, and they needed another pilot. Fate had stepped in once again, I was thrilled! I had gone from August 11, 1995, until March 30, 1996, without flying.

Upon my return, I was treated cordially, life went on as if none of this had happened. Eric, the crew chief on the Beijing flight came up to me, smiled, and said: "Thank you for saving my life!" I'd like to think I prevented a potential life challenging situation.

Next time I saw Fred Gregory on a flight, he gave me a smile which said something. Was he aware of what I had endured?

So, there is a lesson here about "Falling on One's sword". In retrospect doubt I would do it again. I remained loyal to Hugh through the years, helped him and his wife clear the office at National Airport, when our operation shut down, no one else did. We remained friends through the years. Had it not been for Jim's retirement, I might not have had the opportunity to fly commercially again. Things have a way of working out but as you can read the bitterness is still there.

It was some ten years later that John publicly acknowledged and thanked me for getting him a job with NASA.

Del Hardiman

Del Hardiman
Great flying!
With Best Wishes and
Continuing Success
Fred Gregory
24 Jan 94

Very proud to have this autographed photo by Astronaut Fred Gregory

CHAPTER 41
Last Shuttle Arrival I Witnessed

September 26, 1996, I witnessed my last Shuttle arrival which I observed from nearby Cape Canaveral Space Force Station (XMR) also referred to as the skid strip. We had dropped passengers off at the Shuttle Landing Strip and relocated to XMR ten miles south. Watching the sky we saw the Shuttle (Atlantis) coming downwind to the Landing Strip breaking the sound barrier with a pop, pop sound; a NASA Gulfstream chase plane trailing. On board this shuttle was Astronaut Shannon Lucid who had been in space 188 days; she held the record for the most hours in orbit by a non-Russian and most hours in orbit by a woman. This was her fifth and last space flight. Altogether, she participated in five orbiter missions accumulating 223 days in space and more than three decades at NASA. Ref-41 Next day (September 27), we flew from Washington National Airport to Ellington Field, Houston, Texas. On our descent we had Air Force One with President Clinton onboard not far behind. It was interesting to hear "NASA One cleared to Flight level (FL) 230, Air Force One cleared to FL 250".

President Clinton officially welcomed Shannon, now at Houston, back to Earth. He said: "Her record-breaking six months in space is a "monument to the human spirit". Ref-42 We watched live on TV from the hangar nearby. Three months later Astronaut Shannon Lucid received the Congressional Space Medal of Honor. Ref-43

Del Hardiman

Low circle around Space Shuttle Columbia on launch pad 39B

November 18, 1996, landing at Kennedy Space Center (X68) for the next day launch of Space Shuttle Columbia (STS-80). In addition to Mr. Goldin, NASA Administrator, we had a full complement of notable people on board. As we neared Kennedy, Mr. Goldin came up to the cockpit and asked that we get permission to do a low-level circle of Columbia; the request was approved. Columbia was on launch pad 39B, all lit up, awaiting the next day's launch, an impressive site. Time was 7:00 PM, dusk was setting in when I went quite low (as by now you know I have no problem doing). We made two close circles around Columbia, before angling to land at the Kennedy Shuttle landing strip. Our passengers got a spectacular view out the cabin windows. I was surprised at the request and that we were approved for this most unusual maneuver in this strict 'NO FLY' zone, the first and only time I ever heard of. Making my request with the NASA Administrator on board was key, no doubt for the approval. Something I will always remember.

Del Hardiman, NASA ONE (photo by Bill Ingalls, official NASA photographer)

CHAPTER 42
Behind the Scenes Emergency Repair

Departed Washington National Airport February 16, 1997, in NASA One, first stop Albuquerque, NM. This was the first day of a weeklong trip carrying Mr. Goldin and nine passengers. This important trip had been planned for some time. From Albuquerque, we would proceed to Burbank, CA on the 17th, to Boeing Field, Seattle on the 18th, to Grand Rapids, ND on the 19th, to Minneapolis, MN on the 20th to return to Washington on the 21st.

Pilots were myself, Hugh Huleatt, and crew chief Eric Stalnaker. On arrival at Albuquerque, our passengers departed, Eric got the Gulfstream refueled and began his post flight inspection. Hugh and I were getting a rental car and talking to personnel at the general aviation desk. As I went back to the ramp to check with Eric; departing through the general aviation exit door, I was face to face with the actress Goldie Hawn coming in from the aircraft ramp! I looked over at the counter attendant and given a nod, that yes it was (Goldie). The attendant said Kurt Russell, Goldie's partner had his own twin engine aircraft and that they stopped from time to time for fuel.

During post flight inspection, Eric identified a short stainless steel hydraulic tube in the tail compartment leaking. <u>This automatically grounded the aircraft.</u> It would take days to get a replacement which left us with a sinking feeling.

I recalled we were on the same airfield as Kirtland Air Force Base; what are the chances they had an aircraft hydraulics shop? I had previously been a Gulfstream Maintenance Officer in the ARMY so knew my way around enough to make some calls. I confirmed, indeed there was a shop and that we could bring the damaged tube over for them to look at. The tube was only five or six inches long, but it had an unusual twisting shape. To fabricate one would not be an easy task plus, did the shop have that type tubing? The shop felt they could make the tube, but before they could proceed, I had to contact Gulfstream back in Savannah, GA for diagrams, testing requirements and approval. This took an hour or so and the clock was ticking. The two Air Force sergeants were quite adept, giving Eric and me confidence in their technical skills. I was impressed at how they, using the diagrams, drew everything in detail, presenting a three-way image before beginning the process. The tube must conform exactly. Hugh and I were getting close to our mandatory crew rest, so I went back to the civilian aviation to pick him up and head for our hotel. Eric stayed behind but eventually made it to the hotel. Once the new tube was made, it was tested to 3,000 PSI and passed! By early morning, Eric had the new tube installed, we started the engines with Eric in the tail compartment to confirm *no leaks*.

It was only minutes after the tests were completed that our passengers were scheduled to arrive. Relieved and proud (an understatement), we had pulled off this overnight repair. We departed on time and made all scheduled stops; our passengers never knew how close we came to canceling the mission. Cannot say enough about the excellent support and teamwork of the Air Force who worked into the night on our behalf and our great Crew Chief Eric!

Meeting a Mother and two sons in Cleveland DEC 18, 1996

Once in a while, one hears a story so rich with adventure, it's hard to comprehend. This was such a story. To summarize, this had been a routine flight, December 17, 1996, to Cleveland, Ohio, departing Washington National (DCA) 1115 PM local just before midnight, arriving NASA Lewis Research Center 1220 AM local. Our crew this flight was Hugh, Mike Richmond (Crew chief) and me. We were having a late hotel breakfast when Hugh struck up a conversation with a young mother with her two sons eating at a table nearby. The boys were approximately 9 and 11. It was a few days before Christmas, and they had come home from Australia for the holiday.

Dad remained behind to guard/watch their ship. Curious, we asked what ship? The story we were about to hear was incredible! The family, dad, mom and the boys had departed the US in what I believe was a Catamaran, sailing down the east coast, through the Panama Canal, across the Pacific, spending time in Tahiti eventually to Australia. The oldest son wore a small hand carved wooden pendant on a rawhide string given to him by natives in Tahiti, which had special meaning. The boys were getting a rare glimpse of the world's largest ocean, an incredible journey, months in duration, schooled along the way by their parents. They caught fish, which must have been an adventure! Mom and her sons were deeply tanned. The stories of their journey left us in awe! Do not recall what their plans were after returning to Australia to join dad. Perhaps they continued their journey to farther destinations. We were delighted to have met this brave family, which, by their telling, made our stories seem insignificant.

CHAPTER 43
Nasa Flight Operations terminated.
Walking the Shuttle Landing Strip runway

Due to budget restraints and the high cost of NASA ONE operations, we were shut down in 97'

May 15, 1997, my final nostalgic trip to Kennedy Space Center, Shuttle landing strip, I climbed the huge mate-demate structure, taking pictures. It was here, six years prior I had my photo taken with 'Discover' in background, under this structure mounted on the NASA Boeing 747.

I asked for permission and was Allowed to walk the landing strip. Carrying a handheld radio to maintain contact with the tower, I made the long walk, 15,000 feet of runway plus 3,000-foot overruns at each end equivalent to 6.8 miles. I was embellished by my surroundings, walking over tire marks made by shuttle landings over the years. I'm one of few who have walked that runway!

NASA1 Aircraft Commander Del Hardiman with Mr. Dan Goldin, NASA Administrator on Mr. Goldin's last flight in NASA ONE – MAY 1997 (photo courtesy Del Hardiman).

Last NASA One mission

May 27, 1997, John Dahmer, Eric Stalnaker and I brought NASA ONE home for the last time. We departed Ellington Field, Houston at 9:55 P.M, landing at Washington National 12:35 A.M. I was at the controls making the landing on runway 18, my final flight ever. I am proud to say, after all, I had endured, I made the last NASA ONE landing!

Bill Ingalls, NASA photographer, fortunately was on board, he took our photos, one with me wearing my blue NASA flight jacket in front of NASA ONE, I'm most proud of.

Last official flight of NASA ONE and my last flight ever. Washington National Airport, Washington, D.C. (photo by Bill Ingalls, official NASA photographer)

Side note: I call Jim Adkins each year on the anniversary of his birth, February 1, 1933. Hugh, also born in 1933, and I remain friends, corresponding regularly over the years. John passed away in October 2020.

PART VII

CHAPTER 44
Life after Nasa

Two days after that final landing, I was seated at the Pentagon Courtyard, an outdoor pavilion located in the inner center of the building. I had taken my wife Paula to work that morning at the Pentagon; my thoughts were on my last flight two days before. As I sat watching airliners pass nearby overhead for touchdown on runway 18 at National Airport, I relived my last landing on that same runway mere hours before, and now there would be *no more*.

What would a former pilot do? I had no interest in pursuing another flight position. My experience in the computer technology field might be appropriate.

My credentials included Certified Novell Engineer, COMPTIA A+ certification, Dell Certified Systems Expert, hardware and software in most systems at the time.

During the fall/winter of 1997 I took a position as a substitute teacher at local schools. Interesting times with kids of all age ages. Some of the older ones were difficult to handle. I found to my chagrin at a shop class I substituted for, certain students were not being taught anything. I listened attentively as these students who were not gifted in maintenance type functions told me they had taken the class to learn about automobiles, only to be taught how to change a tire during the whole semester. Other male students merely left the class without my permission to go to a local fast food.

Del Hardiman

Alcatel USA – September 11, 2001 (9/11)

Later I worked for Advanced Technology Systems, then for Alcatel USA, a French major international provider of Telecommunications equipment regionally located in Chantilly, VA. My son Patrick's company, Enginuiti, had a contract with Alcatel for hardware and software support. I was at Alcatel September 11, 2001 (9/11) when the World Trade Center and Pentagon were hit by three highjacked U.S. airliners. Later it was learned a fourth airliner intended for a similar attack was thwarted by passengers and crashed in a field near Shanksville, Pennsylvania killing all on board. All hijackers were Islamist terrorists. Around noon, Alcatel employees, several hundred, were told to go home; Bob Whitely who also worked for Enginuiti and myself, both Vietnam Veterans stayed and continued work as usual. We were the only two in the building I believe. Not long afterwards Alcatel moved their Chantilly operations to Texas.

Side note: Bob Whitely and I became good friends just as he was with my son Patrick. There was none like him. Born in Coeur d'Alene, Idaho, he served as a Marine in Vietnam, father of a son and daughter, slim, medium height, thinning gray hair, in jeans, always laughing and telling great stories. He studied for several years to be a monk. As a Jesuit priest, he worked with **Mother Teresa**, winner of countless awards for helping the poor. She was recipient of the Nobel Peace prize in 1979. Bob first met Mother Teresa at an Abbey in Utah. He had only been told there was a Nun coming to speak to the Monks; when he saw who it was, he wept. Bob volunteered to work for Mother Teresa in 1974 first in Phnom Penh, Cambodia, later in Vietnam and the Philippines, each of which she came to visit on occasion. He traveled to India to meet her several times. Bob said Mother Teresa, founder of the **Order of 'Missionaries of Charity'** was a tough task master! She would travel to any country regardless of their political affiliations; she only wanted to help the poor.

Bob came from a tough pioneer spirit, his granddad, also slim, had his own timber business in Idaho where his team sawed huge trees by hand, hauled them with horse drawn wagons. Bob was extremely talented in computer hardware/ software, always teaching me. Today, in retirement,

302

Bob lives in Washington State spending much of his time in prayer and meditation.

Noteworthy:

The New York Stock Exchange, a major contributor to the world financial markets, following the terrorist attacks, did not re-open until September 17th. One outlier not mentioned that I have searched for, was that Alcatel had a Source Router, used for training purposes same as that used in New York. Several Alcatel employees disassembled the Source Router, took it to New York to be reassembled and operational which helped the Exchange get up and running in short time.

Unisys

Next, I worked for ADECCO Technical Services in Sterling, VA contracted with Unisys.

Later, with Unisys, I signed on to travel within the region of approximately a hundred-mile radius, repairing computers, laptops, and printers. My duty was to arrive at a Unisys facility early in the morning along with other technicians, look over my daily job listing and along with others, sort the overnight boxes of hardware shipments on a long table needed for our day's tasks. This was a different type of challenge I had ever been part of. It was tough, tedious, typically taking care of eight or nine calls daily driving to each in my own car. The disassembly of never-before-seen laptops to replace screens and internal parts was particularly challenging. This job took me to businesses and homes, a few in remote locations. Some businesses and government agencies required I have an escort. Once I repaired a computer at the guard building of the Naval Observatory, residence of the Vice President. This job gave me an insight into how hardworking technicians, behind the scenes, kept the business and home computing field moving.

Eventually Unisys assigned me to the United States Securities and Exchange Commission in Washington, D.C. My fellow workers were Andy Ness and Steve Graves. Those two were the professionals who were more than willing to teach me how to support the systems. Andy is my friend to this day, his father was a WWII veteran, serving as a B-17 crewmember.

Andy was so proud of him. He enjoys sending me aviation trivia, pushing my knowledge of the subject.

Back in ARMY Aviation

Meantime, my dear wife Paula, searching for a job for me found a position with the Aviation and Safety Division, ARMY National Guard in Alexandria, VA. It was three months after I applied before I got the call. I started work in September 2003 to remain for 16 years. I was hired by MAJ Ed McGee, Bob Godwin (retired Colonel) was Deputy Division Chief for COL George Gluski, the Division Chief. Bob served in this capacity for years as Division Chiefs came and went; he was the catalyst for a professional Aviation and Safety program.

Thrilled to be back in ARMY Aviation!

PART VIII

CHAPTER 45
Army National Guard Aviation And Safety Division

The ARMY National Guard Aviation and Safety Division (ARNG-AV) is under the command of the Director of the ARMY National Guard, headquartered at ARMY National Guard Readiness Center, Arlington, VA. The Director, a three-star billet, reports to the Chief of the National Guard Bureau, a four-star who is a member of the Joint Chiefs of Staff.

Side note: The building in which I worked contained the brain trust of the National Guard. It is sometimes referred to as a mini-Pentagon of which management of all facets of ARMY National Guard are conducted. Near the Pentagon, shuttle buses run to and from the Pentagon daily. The property, once a girl's school in Arlington, VA, was occupied by the Signal Intelligence Service (SIS) in 1942. While temporarily at the Munitions building on Constitution Avenue, Washington, D.C., prior to its new location, the SIS made cryptic history when they solved Japan's diplomatic cipher, termed the "PURPLE" Code". Of note, it was SIS's codebreakers who discovered that Tokyo had ordered its ambassador in Washington to cease all negotiations with U.S. officials effective December 7, 1941. Ref-44 During my tenure the ARMY National Guard Aviation and Safety Division (ARNG-AV) consisted of some 65 men and women in sections: Program Integration, Systems Readiness, Training and Standardization, Safety, Occupational & Health. The mission was to provide strategic guidance, set policies, provide resources, participation, and coordination, serving as communication channel to the states. I worked in Systems and Readiness.

Dangerous Enclosures

My initial assignment was that of Program Analyst of the ARMY National Guard UH-1 fleet. These helicopters, now in their final days in inventory, took up the slack for deployed UH-60 Black Hawks until they were retired. When I took over, the Guard had 263 UH-1s throughout the U.S., down from over 700 to 800. Over time, I processed turn-in orders for each aircraft, most of which went to Fort Hood, Texas for final disposition.

Giving tour of Smithsonian Udvar Hazy Aviation museum

The Guard is unique in that its 50 states, three territories and the District of Columbia come under control of state Governors not the ARNG Directorate. Each state aviation unit has a State Aviation Officer (SAO) who coordinates with ARNG-AV but reportable to his/her Adjutant General, the senior military officer, appointed by his/her respective governor. New SAO's came to our facility annually for a weeklong training course. On one of these courses, (January 2005) I was asked if I might take the new SAOs on a tour of the Smithsonian Udvar Hazy Aviation museum near Dulles Airport since, by then, I was known as somewhat of an aviation history buff. I met the bus of Colonels (COL), Lieutenant Colonels (LTC) and Majors at the museum to give them the tour. A few weeks later I received an envelope from LTC Peter Seitz, Tustin, CA, thanking me for the tour. In his comments he stated: "Del, Thanks for the great tour of the Air and Space Museum at Dulles. You mentioned that Chuck Yeager was one of your heroes, he's one of mine too! I thought you'd enjoy this autographed picture of him." The photo is a close up of Chuck, in G-suit standing next to a jet fighter with the inscription painted on the aircraft "Glamorous Glennis" which he had on his many aircraft throughout his career. The photo was taken for the 50th anniversary of Chuck breaking the sound barrier. LTC Seitz also enclosed a great story he received from Otto Kerstner, B-29 aircraft commander returning to Guam after a bombing raid over Japan during WWII. The crew had to bail out over the ocean due to fuel exhaustion. With two engines no longer running, Commander Kerstner ordered all crewmembers to bail out, he was the last to go. As he floated down under his parachute, his B-29 was circling above; it passed directly over him coming within 50 feet! On a second circle, it came for him again before crashing into the ocean!

Side note: Two memorable events during my time at AVS:

Meeting Neil Armstrong, Apollo 11 Astronaut

December 16th and 17th, 2003, my wife Paula and sons Patrick and Ben spent two days at Kitty Hawk, NC for the commemoration of the 100th anniversary of the Wright Brothers memorable flight of 12 seconds! An attempt was made to duplicate the flight on the 17th with a replica of the Wright Flyer but due to the conditions, it was not successful. Paula and I ventured *unintentionally* into a glass enclosed display of an exact replica of the 1903 Wright Flyer at the completion of that aircraft's dedication. We had no idea we should not be there! As the few *invited guests* were departing, including Harry Combs who had donated the Flyer to the National Park Service at a cost of over one million dollars (at that time), we noticed to our astonishment Apollo 11 Astronaut Neil Armstrong standing alone in front of the left wings. Should I invade his privacy? He looked at me, as if to say, "its ok", so I went over 'stealthfully' to shake his hand! I mentioned I used to be a pilot on NASA ONE. He permitted a photo of the two of us which Paula took. He did not speak a word, just looked me in the eyes with a smile, then we departed, I was so exhilarated! Unfortunately, a lady stepped in front of Paula as she took the picture which ruined the shot of a lifetime!

I mentioned Harry Combs, a friend of Neil's I was told. He passed away 10 days after this event at age 90. I encourage you to research Harry B. Combs and be astonished at his many aviation accomplishments.

Doolittle Raider 70th Anniversary

Friday, April 20, 2012, Paula and I attended the 70th Anniversary of the Doolittle Tokyo Raid of which four of the last five remaining B-25 crewmembers who launched from the aircraft carrier USS Hornet were present. It was held at the Hope Hotel and Richard C. Holbrooke Conference room near the National Museum of the U.S. Air Force in Dayton, OH. The theme of this anniversary was "Among Friends... The Rescue of the Raiders" in which China was thanking the American flyers for their sacrifices during the war against Japan. Guest speaker was Zheng Weiyong a young Chinese gentleman who had spent 10 years researching the Doolittle Raiders. He actually found the grave of one of the Raiders. Along with him were Chinese ladies who gave each of the attending Raiders a painted board with Chinese inscriptions. Mr. Weiyong did not speak English, so his presentation had English subtitles. Such an honor to be in the presence of these 'Heros" who helped change the war.

Photos of the Doolittle Raiders in attendance: Paula encouraged me to get a photo of each which they generously accepted. I was the only one to get a photo with them. I thank Paula for her persistence in getting these:

LT COL Richard E. Cole (then LT) was LTC Jimmy Doolittle's Co-pilot on aircraft #1. LTC Cole was the last survivor of the 80 crewmembers from 16 B-25 bombers on the Raid on Tokyo, he passed at age 103. (Photo Paula Hardiman)

Staff Sergeant David J. Thatcher, Engineer/Gunner Aircraft #7. (Photo Paula Hardiman)

Major Thomas C. Griffin, Navigator, Aircraft #9, holding a hand painted board given to each crewmember by the Chinese at the event. Later assigned to North Africa, his B-26 bomber was shot down over Sicily, where he bailed out and became a Prisoner of War until 1945. (Photo Paula Hardiman)

LTC Edward J. Saylor, Engineer/Gunner Aircraft #15. (Photo Paula Hardiman)

Tenure of 16 years at ARNG-AV

In my 16 years, ARNG-AV managed all National Guard helicopter Aviation assets throughout the U.S. which included AH-64 Apache's, CH-47 Chinooks, UH-60 Blackhawks, OH-58's and UH-1's. Also included were ARNG Fixed Wing assets, the C-23, C26 and C-12. The OH-58s, C-23s and UH-1s were eventually retired. Aircraft systems were being upgraded with the latest enhancements on a seemingly constant basis.

In addition to its State responsibilities in many capacities, the ARMY National Guard also deploys to worldwide conflicts alongside the Active ARMY; its role in world conflicts increased exponentially after the terrorist attacks of September 11, 2001. Ref-45

I found myself amongst highly professionals, nearly equally divided between Active Guard Reserves and civilians as myself. Most civilians were prior military service of various branches. Of the specialized civilian personnel working at the Aviation and Safety Division (AVS), three were former West Point graduates. In time, some of us were authorized to wear the ARMY Staff Identification badge. Active Guard Reserve personnel were deployed to war in Iraq to be gone for a year then return. By 2013, 40% of the US ARMY's combat capability was that of the ARMY National Guard. Ref-46 Today the ARMY National Guard has over 47 Airfields and Heliports throughout the United States and Alaska. Ref-47

ARMY National Guard Aviation heritage – John Stanko

Eventually, I became aware of ARMY National Guard Aviation heritage, how it had advanced from tepid beginnings in the late 1940's. I was privileged to meet (Ret) COL John Stanko, who many would say is the "Father of ARMY National Guard Aviation". During his frequent visits, I conversed with John, (87 at the time, on his portable scooter) about his illustrious past. He was a Plethora of information! In September 2006, My good friend and co-worker, Tom Petrick and I, along with my wife Paula, visited John and wife Pinkie in Danville, PA to spend the day and interview him.

John, small in stature, permanent smile, loved to tell stories! He told us he was a commander in B-24's near the end of WWII. He flew 17 missions, 12 of which were combat. His last missions were dropping supplies from approximately 1000 feet to POW camps. He told us that in 1947 the ARMY Air Force became the U.S. Air Force; this left smaller, fixed-wing aircraft which would become components of ARMY National Guard Aviation. For several decades, the ARMY National Guard Aviation program was relegated to hand-down aircraft from the active ARMY and USAF. ARMY National Guard Aviation was yet to become a cohesive organization of collectively combined states in a common effort.

After the war, John took up residence in Danville, Pennsylvania, and joined the Air Force Reserve. He became a light aircraft pilot in the Pennsylvania ARNG in 1954, and since the day he volunteered, John loved serving in the Guard. In the following decade, he became a qualified armor officer, commanding the 104th Aviation Company in Lancaster, PA. In May 1966, forty-four-year-old Major Stanko reported to the National Guard Bureau (NGB) in the Pentagon for a four-year tour as an aviation staff officer. In 1972 he was recalled to serve at National Guard Bureau (NGB) as the head of the new Aviation Logistics Center with the civilian rank of GS-14 military technician. Five years later, he became Chief, ARNG Aviation Division, a position he held for sixteen years. During his tenure, he was most satisfied with his role in the creation of ARNG aviation Safety, logistics, maintenance, training organizations and infrastructure. His proudest moment came in 1990 when Guard pilots achieved a "zero" percent accident rate, an unheard-of accomplishment at the time. By the time of his retirement in 1993, ARNG Aviation was arguably the largest, separate military aviation force in the world, consisting of 2,800 helicopters, 150 fixed wing aircraft, and 6,800 aviators.

Through COL Stanko's foresightedness, ARNG Aviation progressed into a full complement of self-sustaining operations. Developments included four ARMY National Guard Aviation Training sites (AATS) and Aviation Classification Repair Activity Depots (AVCRADs), now Theater Aviation Sustainment Group (TASMGs) consisting of the following:

EAATS- (Eastern ARMY Aviation Training Site), Fort Indiantown Gap in Annville, Pennsylvania, largest Reserve Component accredited aviation training school. Primarily focused on utility and cargo helicopter training to include full motion flight simulators. Ref-48 WAATS- (Western ARMY Aviation Training Site), located in Marana, Arizona, WAATS conducts graduate level pilot training for the region. Its remote desert location lends itself perfectly to unencumbered, year-round aviation training. The Arizona Army National Guard manages WAATS. As such, it is one of the Army's premier aviation training locations for attack and scout helicopters, and it is home to a state-of-the-art flight simulator complex. Although it is primarily a training facility for the Army National Guard, WAATS trains personnel from all three components of the U.S. Army, the regular Army, the Army Reserve, and the Army National Guard as well as allied countries in Europe and Asia. Additionally, it conducts professional development and Military Occupational

Specialty (MOS) qualification courses in ARMY Aviation for Non-Commissioned Officers (NCOs). Ref-49

FWAATS- (Fixed-Wing ARMY Aviation Training Site), located in Clarksburg, WV conducts aircraft qualification courses and training in C-12 and C-26 aircraft as well as fixed wing Instrument Flight Examiner courses on those two aircraft. A Maintenance Test Pilot course is conducted for C-12's only. WAATS also conducts an Instrument Flight Examiner (IFE) prep course for the UH-72 helicopter. Ref-50

HAATS – (High-altitude ARNG Aviation Training Site), Gypsum, CO is unique in that it trains power management for high density altitude terrain operations with high gross weight aircraft in a combat scenario. The school conducts training for U.S and multinational Aviators from all over the world in rotary-wing aircraft as directed by the Department of the ARMY (DA). Ref-51

TASMG - (Theater Aviation Sustainment Group), formerly AVCRADS are in Fresno, California, Gulfport, Mississippi, Groton, Connecticut and Springfield, Missouri. Each provides Depot Level aircraft maintenance for 25% of ARMY National Guard and ARMY Aviation units. TASMGs deployed to the Iraq war effort on a rotational basis.

Aviation Safety - ARNG Aviation encompasses three separate but interconnected programs, Safety, Standardization and Maintenance (logistics). Of these Safety is the catalyst. You might say it all begins and ends with Safety guidelines built in. Each state has an Aviation Safety Officer, all trained at Fort Rucker, AL (now Fort Novosel), home of ARMY Aviation. ARNG-AV has the responsibility of monitoring and keeping states current in the latest Safety developments.

Standardization – ARNG Aviation activities often combine states in operations of national emergency or deployment. Standardized training ensures crews of different organizations interact seamlessly even though they might have never operated with each other. Instructor pilots are the impetus of standardization. Case in point, my son Ben, in the Virginia

National Guard deployed to Iraq with the Texas National Guard to fly MEDEVAC missions in UH-60 Blackhawks.

Maintenance/Logistics – Unless aircraft are in working order and supplies and parts not readily available, aircraft movement is in jeopardy. This requires school trained qualified aircraft mechanics and logistics personnel to make launches possible. Each unit has its maintenance officers (of which I was one in my ARMY career) to keep em' flying.

In my position, as with all others of the Aviation and Safety Division, I spent time telephonically with states and attended meetings, meetings, meetings to stay aware of current situations and progress. During my tenure, I visited many ARNG sites.

Through the years I kept a plaque on my desk which I procured from Alcatel during the building closeout. The plaque has sat on each of my desks over the years to remind me of what I was a small part of "Teamwork". I can't find who the quote is attributable to, but it has such meaning of which I ascribed to.

It reads:

"Teamwork is the catalyst that yields excellence from shared strengths".

A wealth of prior military experience postured itself within the Aviation and Safety Division. Photo is me with several of these highly qualified individuals. L/R Steve Mauro, BG Ray Davis, Assistant Director for Aviation and Safety, Bill Squires, Tom Petrick, Harvey Browne, Del Hardiman and Don Wellen.

Bringing on board the UH-72 'Lakota' Helicopter

In 2007, the Guard, along with the Active ARMY fielded a new helicopter, the UH-72 Lakota of which I became the Systems manager. The Lakota, built by American Eurocopter, was unique in that it was an "Off-the Shelf" civilian helicopter to be maintained under the Army National Guard's new Hybrid maintenance program. Requirements dictated aircraft maintenance be performed and administered through non-ARMY Federal Aviation Agency (FAA) regulations. Initial purchase was for 345 aircraft, 212 of which were fielded to the ARMY National Guard. The Lakota received its name from a suggestion by Ms. Andrea Rene' Gregory, Logistics Chief, Light Helicopter Product Directorate (LHPD) to honor the Lakota Indian nation. Its primary function was for Utility transport, Homeland Security, which included counter drug, and MEDEVAC. With a max gross weight of 7900 pounds, it had two twin turbine Turbomeca ARRIEL 1E2 engines, takeoff power (per engine) 738 SHP, maximum speed at sea level was 145 knots. Capacity was for two pilots and six passengers. Instrumentation was 'State of the Art' with autopilot capable of performing instrument approaches. Ref-52

UH-72 - Proof of Concept

Fielding the UH-72 was a new concept, it would be maintained, as previously mentioned, by civilian Federal Aviation Agency (FAA) parameters under a Hybrid program. This would require some ARNG maintenance personnel to be certified as FAA Aircraft and Powerplant (A&P) mechanics. Unlike the ARMY system they were familiar with, they would strictly use FAA forms and records. Could this be done efficiently with utmost safety?

The state of Mississippi was selected for blind testing as 'Proof of Concept'. In February 2008, aircraft maintenance personnel of the Mississippi National Guard attended the UH-72 Lakota maintenance school having never worked on this aircraft. Next month, March 2008, these mechanics/technicians reported to Fort Polk, Louisiana to perform tasks on an active ARMY UH-72 in the hangar facility. In a two-week exercise they would be given daily faults for troubleshooting on this 'new' aircraft. Faults were put in the system by American Eurocopter personnel such as cockpit instrumentation, electronics, avionics, navigation systems etc. When a fault was detected, the defected components were replaced using FAA forms and records. Maintenance was conducted by experts in their field of expertise.

Tasks also included engine removal and reinstallation, main rotor blade removal, tail rotor blade removal, balancing blades, hoisting aircraft off hangar floor for landing gear inspection and many more.

There were half as many observers, including myself standing off to watch. We also attended daily morning and end of day briefings conducted by Stephen Hart, Logistics System Coordinator, UH-72A Product Office (PO). Steve was highly instrumental in the successful fielding and sustainment of the Army National Guard UH-72 Light Utility Helicopter (LUH). His input to the Initial Capabilities Document (ICD) and the Logistics Demonstration Plan conducted by Mississippi ARNG to justify maintenance capability was instrumental to getting program approval. As a Systems Expert in both the Army Maintenance Management System and Federal Aviation Agency (FAA) maintenance, Stephen was influential in developing the unique ARNG Hybrid maintenance program and manning requirements as well as development and sustainment of the Mission Equipment Package (MEP), also unique to the ARNG.

After testing of maintenance personnel was complete, a Eurocopter judge commented he was very impressed with the team in all aspects.

After final inspection, two Mississippi National Guard Aviators did a thorough preflight of the aircraft and performed a maintenance flight. All systems 'GO'!

This 'proof of concept' set in motion the fielding of ARMY National Guard UH-72's to include Search and Surveillance, which incorporated a backseat operator with electronic monitor to surveil, from external camera, as was the two cockpit aviators in daylight or night operations. Pilots used night vision goggles for night operations. MEDEVAC versions were equipped with external hoists for rescue operations. Currently the UH-72 operates on a rotational basis on the U.S. southern border.

Today over a million flight hours have been logged by the UH-72 throughout the U.S. by the ARNG. Ref-53 The Lakota, has grown to nearly 500 combined ARMY and National Guard aircraft and is now the ARMY's primary helicopter trainer at Fort Rucker, AL. Ref-54

Del Hardiman

UH-1 Retirement Ceremony, 2 OCT 2009, Ft. Myer, VA

Following is an article I wrote of the UH-1 retirement ceremony published in the ARMY Aviation Association of America magazine:

On October 2, 2009, a UH-1 from Davison Army Airfield, Ft. Belvoir, VA flew to historic Summerall Field, Ft. Myer, VA for a final tribute representing a legion of Hueys which had served this country countless times through generations of contingencies most notably a conflict half a world away with pilots and crewmembers some scarcely out of high school. On this flight there would be no heavy fire team, insertions, emergency resupply, forty ship formations, heavy enemy ground fire, urgent requests for Dust-off (MEDEVAC), just a lone representative of some 15000 Bell built multi-purpose Utility helicopters which served this country well and paved the trail for today's aerial Army Assault/MEDEVAC fighting teams. More than 7,000 Hueys saw action in Vietnam. Of these, more than 3,300 were destroyed, and more than 2,700 American crewmembers and passengers lost their lives.

At the controls of aircraft 73-21776 was CW4 Mike Miles one of the few Vietnam era Aviators still flying with crew of CW5 Steve Mueck, MSG Marlin Leonard and SGT Richard Sellner of the 121st Medical Air Ambulance, D.C. National Guard. They would present this aircraft in a Departure Ceremony, honoring UH-1's retirement from the Operational Force.

A hero in its own right, this ceremony would bring the UH-1 together once again with another hero of Vietnam, Medal of Honor recipient LTC (R) Bruce Crandall, who in November 1965, then Major, along with his wingman and longtime friend, also a Medal of Honor recipient, the late Major Ed Freeman, made flight after flight over three days to deliver water, ammunition and medical supplies to a besieged Battalion. During this famed Battle of the Ia Drang Valley, they saved more than 70 wounded soldiers in support of the 1st Cavalry Division's 1st Battalion, 7th Cavalry Regiment.

LTC Crandall, graduate of the first class of advanced flight school at Camp Rucker, class of 56' and 2004 Army Aviation Hall of Fame inductee would later be guest speaker after the ceremony at a dinner at the Ft. Myer Officer's club.

CW4 Miles prepositioned 73-21776 at Summerall Field where it would be on static display 2 hours before the ARMY National Guard sponsored ceremony. Flanked on its right was a National Guard UH-60 Black Hawk from 2/224 AHB, Sandston, VA. Two fellow Vietnam veterans, CW5 Norman McIntosh, Pilot in Command (PC) and CW4 Billy Milligan, not flying, from that unit participated in the event. On its left was a UH-72 also from the 121st Medical Air Ambulance, D.C. National Guard.

The sky was overcast; a brisk breeze pressed against the faces of 200+ seated observers, some in Tuxedos and gowns, while others were in military dress and combat fatigues, to bid farewell to the representative last active UH-1 in service.

Host MG Raymond Carpenter, Acting Director, Army National Guard made his opening remarks for the 30 minutes 6 PM event. "The UH-1, more than any other helicopter or any item of equipment, became the symbol of Vietnam," said MG Carpenter. "Because of that, for many, the conflict and the aircraft will forever be linked. The UH-1, more than any other helicopter or any item of equipment, became the symbol of Vietnam. It was in Vietnam where the aircraft earned the reputation for being rugged, durable, versatile, and able to fly even after receiving damage from tremendous enemy fire and just as the Jeep became the Soldiers' best friend in World War II, for many aviators and crews there will always be something special about the Huey."

"I can attest to you that it was not just a machine, it became part of us," said Brig. Gen. Alberto Jimenez, the Assistant Adjutant General for the Maryland Army National Guard and the Army Guard's senior aviator. "It was our lives. It was our friend. It was the aircraft that took us in and out of Vietnam, and it was also the aircraft that saved countless lives as we rushed the wounded and the sick out of the battlefield."

The ceremony concluded by CW4 Miles reporting at the podium to COL Garrett Jensen, Army National Guard Aviation and Safety Division Chief, saluting with the following:

"Request permission to retire the UH-1 from the Operational Force". COL Jensen: "Roger, permission granted. Contact Fiddlers Green outbound."

With blades turning, ignition popping, 73-21776 came to life, then to a hover, making that resounding wop wop known throughout the free world. As the crowd watched in reverence to the end of a 50-year saga, some saluting, the last operational unit UH-1 made a left pedal turn and slowly accelerated through translational lift fading into the twilight toward the far horizon. The UH-1 Iroquois helicopter was officially retired by the Army National Guard, ending a service life of more than 50 years to the Army and close to 40 years in the Army Guard.

A few miles away in repose, stands the black reflective granite Vietnam War memorial inscribed with the names of over 58000 brave men and women who gave their lives in the Vietnam conflict, many of whom were delivered from their fallen places by the UH-1. May they rest in peace.

Postscript:

As mentioned earlier, I had witnessed one of the first five UH-1s in ARMY inventory as a 15-year-old at my hometown airport, I grew up to fly the UH-1 (not in Vietnam), now I was witness to the retirement of the last operational unit UH-1.

COL Paul Kelly

I had the honor of serving under COL Paul Kelly while he was the Aviation and Safety Division Chief. Paul, veteran pilot with over 1500 flying hours, was nicknamed 'the Senator' since he was always shaking hands with soldiers of all ranks. He and his wife Maria were proud parents of two sons, Paul and John. April 13th, 2006, I accompanied Paul to Arlington Cemetery to attend the burial of Medal of Honor recipient, Mike Novosel (Fort Rucker now named Fort Novosel in his honor). Little did I know the next funeral I would attend at Arlington would be Paul's. COL Kelly deployed to Iraq later that year, January 20th, 2007, not as a pilot but as a member of a liaison team from the National Guard Bureau. The Blackhawk helicopter he was a passenger in was downed in Iraq, killing Paul (age 45) along with 11 other Guardsmen. Paul was thought to be the highest-ranking Guardsman killed in a combat zone since the Korean War. A man loved and respected by all was gone, his mourners were countless. He made a difference.

Dangerous Enclosures

ARMY Ten Mile Run

My first ARMY Ten Mile Run was at age 61; it was something I challenged myself to do. Once I completed that first run, it was contagious. Next year I felt guilty for not making the historic trek again and so I did, continuing with a total of eight, finishing my last at age 73 in October 2018. Making the run took months of preparation, running evenings under lights of the Fort Belvoir quarter mile track or miles of paved trails on weekends.

The ARMY Ten Miler race, is an annual event, drawing thousands from all over the U.S. and other countries. The race starts at the Pentagon in Arlington, Virginia, north on highway 110, crossing the Key Bridge into the District of Columbia proceeding circuitously around the Lincoln Memorial, Kennedy Center down Independence Avenue toward the Capitol Building, return up Independence to the 14th Street, west across the Memorial Bridge to I-395 HOV, a brief course through Crystal City to finish back at the Pentagon. A real sense of accomplishment at the finish line!

One of my eight Ten Mile Runs

My son Michael and I after completing one of my first ARMY Ten Milers. He finished and was well rested by the time I finished!

Unmanned Aerial Vehicles (UAV)

Unmanned Aerial Vehicles (UAV) became a burgeoning new program for the ARMY to be followed by the ARNG. The program allowed ground maneuver forces to have tactical reconnaissance capability. Bob Godwin, Deputy Division Chief of AVS, directed Harvey Browne in mid-2000's to develop a program for the ARNG. Harvey organized the UAV program to include seminars attended by states having UAVs.

ARNG UAV's consisted of the RQ-7B Shadow and RQ-11 Ravens. The Shadow had a wingspan of 14 feet and 11 feet airframe, with inverted "V" tail boom and a rear mounted propeller driven Wankel pusher engine. Launched from a pneumatic catapult, it was remotely controlled and recovered by a ground station using a Tactical Automated Landing System.

A platoon set consisted of 2 officers and 22 enlisted personnel. The system was deployable with 6 High Mobility Multipurpose wheeled vehicles for transporting a ground control station, troop transport and maintenance shelter. Its primary role is to serve as a day-night, target, acquisition, surveillance and battlefield assessment platform for commanders on the ground. Built by AAI (Textron), the Shadow UAV saw extensive operational service with American forces in the wars covering Afghanistan and Iraq. Ref-55

The RQ-11B RAVEN SMALL UNMANNED AIRCRAFT SYSTEM (SUAS) is a small hand launched surveillance drone with a pusher propeller mounted in its rear, used at Company level do low level surveillance of ground maneuvering areas in proximity of operations. The Raven is rucksack portable and can be hand-launched for day or night observation. It has an optional stabilized gimbaled payload and delivers real-time color and/or infrared imagery to the ground control and remote viewing stations. Due to its advanced avionics, Raven can be operated manually or programmed for autonomous navigation. It weighs 4.4 lbs. with a 4.5-foot wingspan and 3-foot length. It operates at low level with a range of 10 KM and 75+ minutes endurance.Ref-56

In time, I attended seminars with Harvey and Frank Blough, the Raven systems program manager. I had the opportunity of touring the RQ-7B factory on two occasions and on Harvey's retirement in 2015 became the UAS logistics manager. On my retirement, I was replaced by Christina Engh.

Summer, 2016, receiving Vietnam 50-year commemorative pin, along with other Vietnam Veterans from COL Andrew Shoffner, Garrison Commander, Fort Leavenworth, KS. (photo Paula Hardiman)

PART IX

CHAPTER 46
Retirement

My retirement was held at Building 2 Auditorium, ARMY National Guard Readiness Center Tuesday, May 14th, 2019, hosted by BG Ray Davis, Aviation and Safety Division Chief. BG (retired) Tom Bordner and his wife June drove down from Connecticut. Gen Bordner was one of the presenters. In attendance were my wife Paula, sons Patrick and Ben, sister Brenda, brother-in-law John, Tom Paul and wife Thanh, friends for over 50 years, drove up from Florida, Chris Nauer, friend of many years and fellow USAPAT aviator, many friends and acquaintances from the Guard. LTC Wade Johnson flew in from WV at my request to sing the National Anthem. LTC (retired) Mike Ford, gave the Invocation and Benediction for which I am most grateful. I was presented numerous certificates, plaques, a painting, models and appreciations from the UH-72 Airbus Group and the Shadow Logistics Team. I made comments to the audience about my career. Food was provided outside the auditorium to include congratulatory handshakes. Thus concluded my career of 38 years federal service starting in the Air National Guard, then Active Army and 16 years with the ARMY National Guard as a civilian.

Final days in ARMY National Guard Aviation and Safety

Dangerous Enclosures

Friends

Friends, we all have them, at work, from past life experiences, church, school, military, socially; in time, they become a part of you. Accumulated over the years, your friend might not necessarily be thought of as a friend by others. Friends grow on you, become a part of you. They most often have your interests at heart, your concerns, when shared, become their concerns. When they have misfortune or loss of family members, you empathize sincerely with them. They are your sounding board, you theirs. Losing a friend is next to losing a loved one. I met and lost many over the years which is part of life. You recall the last time you saw them; unaware at the time you would never see them again.

I developed a trend; when meeting someone for the first time, if he/she left me with a less than favorable impression, I would say to myself as I shook their hand, looking them in the eye, "Someday he/she and I will be friends." That turned out to be true most always. Leave an 'open' door for a prospective friend.

As you have read in this book, I frequently mention friends and interesting people I met over the years; without them, my story would be incomplete.

My 16 years at AVS brought me friendships, too many to count. Hardly a week went by in which I was not shaking hands with a friend. With a changing workforce, new friends came and went while others were with me for years. In my dealings with so many states, acquaintances would stop by to say "hello" when visiting.

Several friendships, in particular, remain with me from my years at AVS, Michael Randall, Jim Schwecke and Jay Jackson.

Michael (Mike) Randall, a CW5, was the AH-64 Apache and OH-58 systems manager when we met but his hands were in so many additional things. His Dad was a B-17 aircraft commander in WWII with the 8th Air Force, aircraft named the Argonaut, similar to his father's original family name. His Dad flew many missions against the Germans and on one occasion, having his B-17 blown to pieces, returning from a mission in which his aircraft was attacked by German fighters. Ordering his crew to bail out he managed to parachute to safety just across the English Channel on English soil. One story Michael liked to tell is that of 40-year-old actor Clark Gable, assigned to his Dad's crew as a door gunner. Michael told of his Dad returning to his room one day and there stood Rhett Butler! That was the role Cable portrayed in the movie 'Gone With the Wind'. Not a day went by that Michael would not call his parents on his way home from work.

In addition to flying Apache's, and numerous other ARMY helicopters, Michael was a Black Belt in martial arts, competing in events for many years. The love of his life is his wife, Teresa. He was not only my friend but friends to hundreds from across the country.

Jim Schwecke, who sat adjacent to me was retired Commander, U.S. Navy. Jim and I were of the same age, each morning we chatted, telling stories of our youth, our commonalities and his vast experiences running maintenance and launches of jet aircraft from the aircraft carriers. I found his stories intriguing. Jim, along with his twin brother and other siblings grew up on a farm in Minnesota. Many stories of taking care of farm animals in the deep winter snows and of course his beloved Mom and Dad. Jim was the ARNG UH-60 helicopter Materials Manager of which his expertise was superb.

Jay Jackson, to whom I owe so much, going to him through the years seeking advice on projects. Jay worked in Training and Operations; his handiwork could be seen in all aspects of the Aviation programs. Charts and speeches given by leadership had his input. Quiet and unassuming Jay would gladly offer his time to anyone. I enjoyed his friendship and the time spent on many seminars across the country.

The list of those I would like to mention is too long, many are included in the Appendix.

CONCLUSION

In the 'Winter' of my years, I look back at my experiences, some as a survivor. These stories reflect me at times in an inauspicious light, or the fortune of sheer fate. Some are funny, some outrageous, painful, hard to comprehend; they needed to be told. As Nick Nolte said: The more you get hit, the more fun it's going to be.

Life is not complete until it's completed.

Opportunities are there if you seek them.

-Del Hardiman

Del Hardiman

POSTSCRIPT
MY WIFE PAULA
Sons, Michael, Patrick, Benjamin

Paula, my Dear wife followed me throughout my ARMY career of some 22 years from Vietnam, the states and two tours in Germany. She has always worked except for time off to have our three sons.

She began her career in her late teens, during the war, as Commander's secretary, of the Command Aircraft Company (CAC), Long Thanh Army Airfield, in her native Vietnam (1968-1971). Additionally, she maintained flight records of hundreds of aviation personnel over those years. It was here that she and I met and later married. I was an Army pilot assigned to the same airfield.

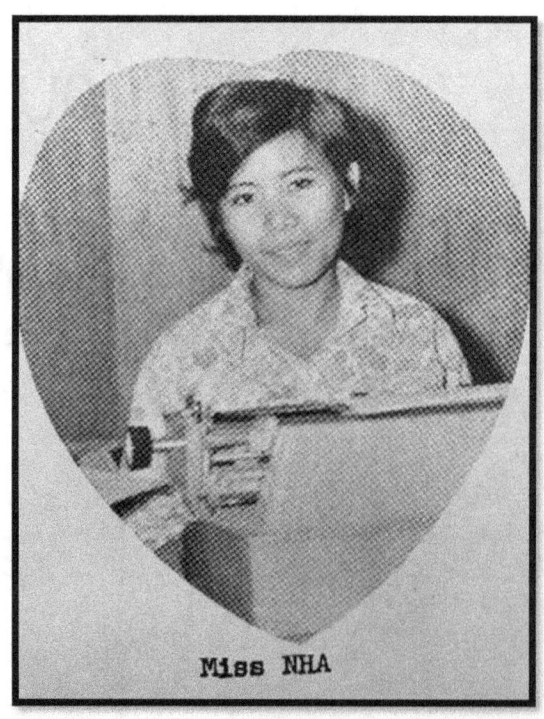

Miss NHA

From Vietnam, after six months in the States, for my military schooling, we were assigned four years, during the Cold War, to Berlin, West Germany (1972-1976). During these six months, Paula took Citizenship classes and obtained her U.S. Citizenship. In Berlin, she took a position as an office employee of a government agency providing troop support in perishable subsistence which provided perishable food for the U.S. Commissary in Berlin as well as transporting food items to the U.S. Embassy in Moscow.

From Berlin, the family transferred to Fort Rucker, AL for 18 months of additional schooling followed with a three-year tour in San Antonio, TX at Randolph AFB.

From San Antonio, we were back Germany, this time, Mannheim, for six years (1980-1986). At Mannheim, Paula was employed with Combat Equipment Groupe Europe (CEGE) as Equipment Manager which included maintaining combat equipment for US Army troops deployment to Europe for annual 'Return of Forces' to Germany' (REFORGER) exercises. CEGE, recognizing her skills, sent her back to the States to attend, as one of few civilians, Logistics training at the United States Army Logistics University, Fort Lee, VA. She was the honor graduate of her class.

Paula, seated, with associates at CEGE, Mannheim, West Germany.

After Mannheim, the family returned to the U.S. assigned to Fort Belvoir, VA. Paula's government career resumed as Medical Equipment Program Manager, Dewitt Army Hospital, (1986-1990). Her duties included managing all spectrums of medical equipment for the hospital, with approval of the Surgeon General, to include ordering and supervising the hospital's first computer system. She was awarded 'Employee of the Quarter' while at Dewitt.

From Dewitt Army Community Hospital, Paula transferred to the Pentagon as Supervisor for Self Service Supply for the Defense Supply Service Washington, for the National Capital region from 1990-2002. At the Pentagon, she received the 'Commander's 'Award for Civilian Service', with a medal, from the Secretary of the Army.

Due to renovation, Paula moved out of the Pentagon three months prior to the terrorist attack of September 11,2001. During this time her office was relocated to Camron Station. It was here that Paula was assigned to receive and list calls from Pentagon personnel to report they were safely out of the Pentagon.

From 2002 until retirement March 2024, Paula was with the General Services Administration (GSA) as Foreign Gifts Program Manager.

As Program Manager, the only one in this position, she received and processed foreign gifts obtained by Federal agency personnel and dignitaries. Items gifted were purchased by recipients at the appraised or fair market value. Gifts not purchased were opened for screening by Federal agencies with disbursement priority offered to Presidential Libraries, subsequently to federal and state agencies. On occasion, Federal judges obtain gifts on loan for their chambers. Items not selected by the aforementioned, with State Department approval, were put up for sale on GSA auction for sale to the public. Sales revenue is retained by the GSA Treasurer.

Through the years, Paula processed thousands of foreign gifts but two in particular stand out. One was a gift of a Bulgarian Shepherd puppy from the President of Bulgaria to President George W. Bush. This puppy, a

Karakachan breed, when grown, can weigh over 100 pounds able to herd sheep and fend off predators. The story, as Paula recalls, is that the prior Communist Bulgarian government tried to rid the sheep farmers from all the Karakachans and at the time of the gift only a few were known to exist throughout the world. Since the American Kennel Club did not have this breed registered, the question was how to value the puppy? A price was obtained from the American Embassy in Bulgaria. President Bush paid the fair market value for the puppy.

The second unusual gift was a WWII motorcycle with side car given to General Tommy Franks from the King of Jordan. Gen Franks paid the appraised fair market value.

Paula attended night schools while working full time to obtain her bachelor's degree in business administration, graduating class of 2010 Magnum Cum Laude from Strayer University.

Paula is an achiever, always doing something. Though small in stature, she decorated and painted walls and ceilings in our home once on a fifteen-foot scaffolding. She will not hesitate to volunteer to help paint the properties owned by our sons. At Christmas, Paula has the house fully decorated with her handmade wreaths and ornaments. We have knitted tablecloths and beautiful floral crocheted vase mats hand made by Paula! She loves baking and decorating cakes. For years she baked and decorated birthday cakes monthly to celebrate coworkers born that month. Also, she is seen frequently next to her sewing machine. She loves sewing.

Additionally, Paula runs our finances, she schedules bill payments and has been quite successful in stocks.

While I was working on my computer certifications, she obtained her CompTIA A+ certification which encompasses basics of computer hardware, networks, and computer systems. Knowing she would not use the certification, she studied for, and completed the required course tests anyway.

Paula is in constant contact with brothers and sisters stateside and relatives in Vietnam via FaceTime. She loves her Vietnamese heritage.

When she graduated from Strayer University, I had a small marble plaque made in her honor which reads:

Paula,
Forever setting goals
Forever achieving
Reaching for the impossible
Restless for more

Michael

Michael, the oldest of our three sons, has many accomplishments to be proud of. Born in Saigon Vietnam he excelled in so many ways, lettering in high school Track and Field to include cross country running, and obtaining Boy Scouting's highest award, the distinguished Eagle Scout. During his scouting days in Mannheim, Germany his troop rode bicycles all the way from Mannheim to Paris, no small feat! Additionally, his troop scaled a glacier in Switzerland and visited the French Maginot Line, a fortress built to deter border assaults after WWI. This and other ventures, some of which I drove the troop in an ARMY loaned bus accompanied with family members.

Obtaining two bachelor's degrees at George Mason University, Virginia then receiving his Doctor of Jurisprudence from the University of Akron in Ohio, Michael was a Virginia State prosecutor for 22 years and now a GS-15 with the Drug Enforcement Administration.

On June 13th, 2011, he was sworn in as a member of the U.S. Supreme Court Bar by Chief Justice John Roberts. This permitted him to literally take cases to the Court. Due to limit of attendees, it was an honor in which I and his brother Ben were able to witness the ceremony in the presence of the whole court. After Michael's swearing in, we were pleased to speak with Justice Ruth Bader Ginsberg who visited guests briefly in her black robe.

In 2014, Michael was selected and bestowed by 750 Virginia Commonwealth Attorneys and their deputies the 'Virginia S. Duvall

Distinguished Juvenile and Domestic Relations District Court Prosecutor Award' as Deputy Commonwealth Attorney for Stafford County. The summary of the Duvall Award is for outstanding and dedicated service to Virginia's citizens.

Michael and wife Katie are the proud parents of five children. Hannah Grace and Liam from their previous marriages, Kaiden, Lilika and Liberty theirs jointly.

Patrick

Patrick, our second of three sons, was born in Berlin, West Germany. He attended schools in Mannheim, West Germany, graduating from Robert E. Lee High School in Fairfax County, Virginia where he was on wrestling and Football teams. He attended Radford University, in Virginia where he studied Music and Communications. He Initiated his first business, Enginuiti, Inc. at age 25.

Patrick is Founder & President of BrightStar Communications, Inc. which has evolved into a multimillion-dollar business, providing cutting-edge solutions worldwide. The company has achieved the following:

- At the forefront of telecommunications, offering internet, data centers, and wide area network solutions globally.

- Empowered hundreds of clients across diverse industries, including manufacturing, retail, legal, non-profit organizations, and government entities.

- Spearheaded the design of a wide area network for globally recognized pharmaceutical companies, enhancing communication and data exchange across multiple offices.

- Designed and implemented robust telecommunications networks for thousands of government entities and Business to Business (B2B) clients nationwide.

- Significant contributions to critical government infrastructure projects for agencies like US Marshals, ATF, and ICE under the "HP Stars" Contract

- Retail and wholesale provider of fiber optics and voice services with diverse supplier networks

- Supply agreements with major carriers like Verizon, Comcast, Spectrum, AT&T, Crown Castle, among others

- Delivery of dedicated internet, EVPL, EPL, PRI, and more.

- Unique approach to reach underserved rural areas, eliminating constraints on high- bandwidth services.

- Significant impact on communities seeking reliable telecommunications solutions. • Pride in partnerships with industry giants such as Verizon, Cisco, AT&T, Zayo, Lightower, Comcast, RingCentral, among others

- Alliances enable staying at the forefront of innovation, offering state-of-the-art solutions to valued clients.

November 2003, Patrick had my name inscribed on the National Aviation and Space Exploration Wall of Honor at the Udvar-Hazy Center, Chantilly, VA. For this I am eternally grateful.

In February 2011, Patrick flew around the world in seven days! Departing from New Jersey, he made stops in Toronto, Canada, Paris, France, Munich, Germany Cairo, Egypt, Bangkok, Thailand, Soul, South Korea then completing his trek in New York. Of interest, he arrived in Cairo days after country wide protests resulting in the fall of then President Hosni Mubarak. Tahir Square, just days before had been the scene of tens of thousands protesting with many killed. When Patrick arrived, he told us all was quiet. He had a taxi drive him to five pyramids which were devoid of life with the exception of himself and his driver! He ventured inside one of the pyramids alone, no one present! He took self-portraits while there and had his taxi driver shoot photos outside of him with the pyramids in the background. It was only after his return we learned of his travels!

Patrick visiting the Sphinx and Pyramids – alone 2011. (photo courtesy of Patrick Hardiman

Patrick and his most talented wonderful Girl Friend, Sarah Von Pollaro have two residences, Arlington, VA and Playa Del Carmen, Mexico. Sarah's son Theo, was accepted to the Thomas Jeffersonn High School for Science and Technology, ranked 5th in the U.S. Thousands of applicants but only 500 accepted!

Ben

Ben, our youngest, was born at Fort Bragg, N.C., living in Germany with family, from ages 3 through 8 while I (his father) was assigned to an ARMY unit in Mannheim, West Germany, later attending schools in Fairfax County, VA. He is an ROTC graduate of George Mason University earning a degree in Bachelor of Science in Decision Sciences and Management Information Systems.

At the time of 9/11 2001, Ben was working for his brother Patrick in Patrick's newly formed company *Enginuiti*. He and Patrick together observed the World Trade Center and Pentagon attacks by terrorists. Ben's mother had worked at the Pentagon for some 10 years, departing there three months prior to the attack. It was these events that prompted Ben to seek a career of service to his country. In ARMY Basic training he found others who had joined because of 9/11.

Prior to George Mason, Benjamin was in the ARMY Reserves trained as an enlisted soldier in Psychological Operations (PSYOP) at the JFK Special Warfare Center, Fort Bragg, N.C. Afterwards he was assigned to the 312th Psyop Company, Upper Marlboro, MD.

Ben was Commissioned through ROTC as a 2nd Lieutenant in January 2006 then transferred to the Virginia National Guard, assigned to the 2/224th Aviation Battalion Richmond, VA. He was selected to Attend ARMY Aviation Flight School at Fort Rucker, AL, Graduating June 2007.

During flight school he attended the demanding Survive, Evade, Resist and Escape (SERE) level 'C' course which included surviving off the land, foraging for food, learning primitive medicines, and POW resistance training in which he was subjected to extreme conditions under intense situations.

Ben attended the Medical Evacuation (MEDEVAC) Doctrine Course at Fort Rucker in May 2008. He volunteered to deploy to Iraq as a 1st Lieutenant with, C 2/149th Air Ambulance Company Texas ARNG in which he flew MEDEVAC missions in the UH-60 Black Hawk. In this capacity he was involved in Life Saving missions. He presented me (his father) with an American Flag, with certificate, indicating the flag had been carried on board one of his UH-60 flights over Iraq. The certificate reads:

OPERATION IRAQI FREEDOM

This certifies that the American Flag presented was personally flown over Iraq on 21 October 2008 while conducting a lifesaving MEDEVAC mission in support of combat operations in a UH-60A Blackhawk MEDEVAC Helicopter

#88-26055, call sign "Alamo 15" especially for Delbert Hardiman, OPERATION IRAQI FREEDOM 0810. Included were crewmember signatures to include 1st Lieutenant Benjamin Hardiman and commander C Company 2/149th.

Ben with UH-60 MEDEVAC Black Hawk, Iraq 2008.

After Iraq, Ben attended the Captain's Career Course, Fort Rucker, AL In 2010, he was assigned to South Carolina National Guard Security and Support (S&S) Detachment in which he transitioned to the UH-72A Lakota Helicopter. In the UH-72A Ben was deployed to the Southwest Border in support of the U.S. Border Patrol.

Del Hardiman

With 10 years combined ARMY Reserve and ARMY National Guard service, Ben elected to separate as a Captain from the military September 2012.

His Awards include:

Air Medal, ARMY Achievement Medal, ARMY Commendation Medal, National Defense Service Medal. Global War on Terrorism Service Medal, Iraq Campaign Medal with campaign star, ARMY Service Ribbon, Armed Forces Reserve Medal with 'M' device, U.S. ARMY Aviation Badge and Texas National Guard Federal Service Medal.

Currently Ben is Systems Administrator for Brightstar Communications and Enginuiti, companies his brother Patrick founded.

AWARDS AND CERTIFICATES

Accident-Free Combat Flying Hours

HEADQUARTERS
11TH AVIATION BATTALION
(COMBAT)

FLIGHT SAFETY CERTIFICATE

PRESENTED TO

CW2 HARDIMAN, DELBERT M.

FOR ACHIEVING 1626 ACCIDENT FREE

COMBAT FLYING HOURS
IN THE REPUBLIC OF VIETNAM

8 JAN 72
DATE

COMMANDING

Awards - Decorations:

- Legion of Merit
- Bronze Star Medal –V
- Bronze Star Medal
- Meritorious Service Medal

Del Hardiman

- Air Medal (24)
- ARMY Commendation Medal (2 OLC)
- ARMY Achievement Medal
- ARMY Good Conduct Medal
- ARMY of Occupation Medal
- National Defense Service Medal
- Vietnam Service Medal (4)
- Armed Forces Reserve Medal
- ARMY Service Ribbon
- Overseas Service Ribbon
- Vietnam Cross of Gallantry Medal
- Master ARMY Aviator Badge
- Recipient of AAAA Bronze Order of St. Michael

Awarded by ARMY National Guard

- Department of the ARMY Civilian Service Award
- Department of the ARMY Achievement Medal For Civilian Service
- Army Staff Identification Badge

Civilian FAA ratings:

- Airline Transport Pilot
- Type rated in Gulfstream G-1159
- Airplane multi-engine Land
- Commercial Privileges
- Airplane single engine land & Sea
- Instrument-Helicopter
- Rotorcraft-Helicopter
- Flight Instructor

Civil Air Patrol

Cadet Pilot Wings
Certificate of proficiency

ACKNOWLEDGEMENTS

Rick Harris.

While assigned to the 74th Reconnaissance Airplane Company, Phu Loi, Vietnam, Rick, and I flew O-1 Bird Dogs performing dangerous mission support for Special Forces, Quan Loi. I was glad to rejoin Rick from flight school and thank him for his contributions to this book, especially his stories, and the many photos of the time we were there. Most of all I thank him for being a great friend these many years.

Joseph G. Wright.

Joe, Rick, and I transitioned out of ARMY Fixed Wing Class 70-1 into the U-1A DeHavilland Otter at Fort Ord California prior to Vietnam. Joe and I flew Otters in the 54th Aviation Company, Long Thanh, Vietnam prior to that company shutdown. I thank Joe for his friendship over the years and his many stories, some of which I used for this book.

Chris Nauer

My thanks to Chris for his friendship and advice, especially his research on the USAF RF-4C shot down by Anti-Aircraft Artillery of which I recovered the pilot's body.

Jim and Jenny Murdock

My thanks to Jim and Jenny for the gift *Hangar Sweepings, reflections of an airport Bum*, by Harold Mills which excited me and gave me the impetus to write this book.

APPENDIX

ARMY National Guard Aviation and Safety friends and Associates over my 16-year career

Gary Adkins	Bob Godwin, Dep Div Chief	Jon Parsons
Dale Aldredge	Mary Ellen Gonyea	Al Pendergrass
Tildon (Kye) Allen	Antonio Gonzalez	Tom Petrick
Joe Back	Keith Graham	Kirby Pierce
Dennis Balitski	Mark Grapin	Clinton Porter
Ken Barrett	Rene Gregory	Dane Powell
Clifford Bauman	David Hall	Michael Quinones
Mark Beckler	Harry Hall	Michael Randall
Maureen Bellamy	John Hamilton	COLJackie Reaves, Div Chief
COL Joseph Bishop, Div Chief	Troy Harrison	Howard Reeves
Terry Blackmore	Steve Hart	BG James Ring
James Bledsoe	Mary Haskew	Jose Rodriguez
Frank Blough	Mark Hensel	Ricardo Rodriguez
COL Mike Bobeck, Div Chief	Sean Higgins	Tony Romano
Tom Bordner	Lynette Hill	Larry Rood
Brent Bracewell	Timothy Hilty	Heather Ross
Bill Breeze	John Howe	Scott Sauer
Dave Bristol	Pete Huble	Jim Schwecke
Bobby Brown	James (Pat) Hudson	Bruce Scott
Harvey Browne	Tim Huggins	Will Sessoms

Dangerous Enclosures

Jarod Burns

Stephen Burns, Dep Div Chief

Bob Butler

Jhonda Campbell

Dudley Capps

Lou Carmona

Guy Charlton

Donna Chilson

Jeff Christy

Eddie Clendenning

Dan Cloutier

Benny Collins

Richard Comer

Joseph Conigliaro

Dave Cooper

Brent Criqui

Gary Davis

BG Ray Davis, Asst Dir for AVS

Tim Davis

Bud Delucien

Peter Derouin

Tiffany Dillard

Richard Dimarco

Lisa Dodd

Perter Doerr

MG Todd Hunt, North Carolina

Marvin Iavechia

Jay Jackson

COL Garrett Jensen, Div Chief

Mike Jewett

BG Alberto Jimenez, Asst AG, MD

Latoria Johnson

Tanesha Johnson

Wade Johnson

Jay Johnston

Walt Jordan

Vondie Judd

John Karmire

Jarred Kassel

John Kennedy

Bill Knisley

Eric Ladd

Gene Lambrecht

Major LaRowe

Rohn Legore

Todd Levendoski

Orest Luciw

Al Marshall

Steve Mauro

Charles (Chuck) McAllister

Clarence Shockley

Charles Shulze

Dennis Sparks

Bill Squires

Dean Stoops

BG Matthew Strub, USAACE

TJ Suraci

Matt Sweet

Craig Talarico

Bob Tamplet

Jamie Tardif

Lonnie Thompson

Tim Tompkins

Charles Torkelson

James Tucker

Nero Tucker

Jeanne Ulrich

Manny Vengua

Mark Ward

Jeff Warfield

Ken Washington

Sonny Watkins

Charles Weaver

Patrick Weber

Aaron Weddle

Del Hardiman

Agnes Eisenhart	Tim McCovery	COL Mark Weiss, Div Chief
Christina Engh	Matt McDermott	Don Wellen
Ray Engstrand	Mark McLemore	Kendrick West
Doug Finstad	Art Medellin	Dustin Williams
Chris Fleming	John (Dennis) Mehaffey	Guy Wills
Robert Fleming	Kevin Michaels	Larie Wilson
Wilbert Floyd	James Moore	Denny Winningham
Mike Ford	Max Moore	Gilbert Wright
Scott Franklin	Charles Morris	Paula Wynn
Patricia Gaura	Kevin Mudd	Mark Young
David Gereski	Gary Nisker	Mike Young
Steve Gladish	Mike Ober	Tim Zerbe
COL George Gluski, Div Chief	David Paolucci	Kevin Scherer

REFERENCES

1. The Travel. Underground Tunnels Vietnam Tours. Retrieved from www.thetravel.com/underground-tunnels-vietnam-tours

2. Willbanks, J. H. (2022, April 11). How US Airstrikes defeated North Vietnam in the 1972 Battle of An Loc. HISTORYNET.

3. Schleicher, A. (2019, April 4). Revealing the Unknown: The Mystery of Michael Blassie. Missouri Historical Society.

4. History.com Editors. (2024, April 25).

5. Roman, S. (2022, February 24). Stars and Stripes.

6. Military Liaison Missions. (n.d.). Retrieved from Wikipedia.

7. Walther Hewel. (n.d.). Retrieved from Wikipedia.

8. Sikorsky, S. (2020, July). Interview with Sergei Sikorsky by Art Linden.

9. Peter Lorenz. (n.d.). Retrieved from Wikipedia.

Del Hardiman

10. Associated Press. (1993, May 19). Heinrich Albertz, 78, Anti-Nazi Clergyman.

11. Achille Lauro Hijacking. (n.d.). Retrieved from Britannica.

12. The Landmark Statesville. (1891, August 27).

13. American Airborne Landings in Normandy. Retrieved from Wikipedia.

14. Klimek, C. (2012, February). More Than Just a Helicopter, the "Huey" Became a Symbol of the Vietnam War. Air & Space Magazine.

15. Sport Aerobatics. (1989, December 8).

16. Bennett, V. (1996, April 18). Charlie Hillard Biography.

17. Sears, S. (2005, March). Corrigan's Way: Right or Wrong, He Made His Mark on History. Airport Journals.

18. Edmondson, W., & "Little Butch's" Shared History. (2015, January 22). Lynchburg Museum Research Files, Virginia Aeronautical Historical Society, Smithsonian National Air & Space Museum.

19.   Monocoupe 110 Special. Retrieved from airandspace.si.edu.

20.   Johnson-McConnell Agreement of 1966. Retrieved from Wikipedia.

21.   O'Neal, W. F. (2008, August 1). Notes from COL (r) William F. O'Neal Speech Commemorating USAPAT 20th Anniversary.

22.   Dinges, J. (1990). Noreiga. Retrieved from Wikipedia.

23.   Galvan, J. (2012). Noreiga. p. 190.

24.   Battle of Midway. (n.d.). Retrieved from Wikipedia.

25.   Official Biography, Lt. General Thomas P. Stafford, USAF (RET.) NASA Astronaut (Former). (2017, February 5).

26.   Nield, G. C., & Vorobiev, P. M. (Eds.). (1999, January). NASA SP-1999-6108 Phase 1 Program Joint Report. Retrieved from https://historycollection.jsc.nasa.gov/documents.

27.   Shepherd, W. (2023). NavySeals.com.

28.   Rosenberg, S. (2003, October 3). Remembering Russia's Civil Siege. BBC Moscow Correspondent.

29.   American Heritage Magazine. (2022). Volume 67, Issue 3. Bob Dole and the Nazis' Brutal Last Stand in Italy.

30.   Neal, V. (2018, January 19). John W. Young, An Astronaut's Astronaut (1930-2018). National Air and Space Museum.

31.   Russian Constitutional Crisis of 1993. Retrieved from https://www.cs.mcgill.ca/~rwest/wikispeedia/wpcd/wp/r/Russian_constitutional_crisis_of_1993.htm.

32.   Russian Constitutional Crisis of 1993. Retrieved from https://www.cs.mcgill.ca/~rwest/wikispeedia/wpcd/wp/r/Russian_constitutional_crisis_of_1993.htm.

33.   Biographical Data, Lyndon B. Johnson Space Center, Houston, Texas. (2001, July). Robert L. Crippen (Captain, USN, RET) NASA Astronaut (Former).

34.   Jet Propulsion Laboratory, California Institute of Technology. Missions > TOPEX/Poseidon.

35.   Fu, L. (2006, January 1). TOPEX/Poseidon: Sails off into the Sunset. Jet Propulsion Laboratory, California Institute of Technology.

36.   This Day in History. (1927, May 21). Charles Lindbergh Completes the First Solo, Nonstop Transatlantic Flight. Historytm.

37.   Enjoy Rome. (2021, February 22). Best Places in Rome, Holiday, Things to Do in Rome.

38.   Experimental Aircraft Association. Overview. Retrieved from www.eaa.org.

39.   Bill Dana. (1999, September 29; updated 2019, June 14). AVweb, World's Premier Independent Aviation News Resource. By Editorial Staff.

40.   The SR-71 Blackbird, Aircraft Records. (2023). Copyright © 2023 The SR-71 Blackbird.

41.   Shannon Lucid. Retrieved from Wikipedia.

42.   The Spokesman-Review. (1996, September 28). Clinton Greets Shannon Lucid in Houston. Spokane, Washington.

43.   Shannon Lucid. (1996, December). Retrieved from Wikipedia.

44.   WWII History Magazine. (2023, April). pp. 22.

45.   Siripurapu, A., & Berman, N. (2023, May 26). What Does the U.S. National Guard Do? Council on Foreign Relations.

46.   Soucy, J. (2016, March 22). National Guard Remains a Vital Component of the War Fight. Retrieved from https://www.army.mil/article/164663/National_Guard_remains_a_vital_component_of_the_war_fight/.

47.   Alexander, G. (2023). Supporting More Than Just Army National Guard [ARNG] Training. ARMYAVIATION Magazine.

48.   Citizen-Soldier. (2019, June 24). The Eastern Army National Guard Aviation Training Site (EAATS).

49.   Arizona Army National Guard. (2016). Western Army Aviation Training Site.

50.   FWAATS. (n.d.). Our Mission, Our Vision. West Virginia National Guard Official DOD Website.

51.   HAATS. (n.d.). Colorado National Guard Official DOD Website.

52.   Airbus Helicopters UH-72 Lakota. (2021, September 9). Aviation/Aerospace. Authored by Staff Writer. Retrieved from www.MilitaryFactory.com.

53.   Johnson, K. (2021, October 12). Military's UH-72 Lakota Fleet Surpasses 1M Flight Hours. Flying Magazine.

54.   Belcher, K. (2022, March 24). AMCOM's Aviation Center Logistics Command Has Vital Role in Training Army Aviators. U.S. ARMY.

55.   AAI (Textron) RQ-7 Shadow, Multirole Unmanned Aerial Vehicle (UAV) [2002]. Retrieved from www.MilitaryFactory.com.

56.   AeroVironment RQ-11 Raven. Retrieved from Wikipedia.

THE END